D1520491

Contemporary Management of Innovation

Contemporary Management of Innovation

Are We Asking the Right Questions?

Edited by

Jon Sundbo, Andrea Gallina,
Göran Serin and Jerome Davis

First published in 2006 by
PALGRAVE MACMILLAN
Houndmills, Basingstoke, Hampshire RG21 6XS and
175 Fifth Avenue, New York, N.Y. 10010
Companies and representatives throughout the world.

PALGRAVE MACMILLAN is the global academic imprint of the Palgrave
Macmillan division of St. Martin's Press, LLC and of Palgrave Macmillan Ltd.
Macmillan® is a registered trademark in the United States, United Kingdom
and other countries. Palgrave is a registered trademark in the European
Union and other countries.

ISBN-13: 978–1–4039–9672–5 hardback
ISBN-10: 1–4039–9672–5 hardback

This book is printed on paper suitable for recycling and made from fully
managed and sustained forest sources.

A catalogue record for this book is available from the British Library.

Library of Congress Cataloging-in-Publication Data
Contemporary management of innovation : are we asking the right
questions? / edited by Jon Sundbo ... [et al.].
p. cm.
Includes bibliographical references and index.
ISBN 1–4039–9672–5 (cloth)
1. Technological innovations—Management. 2. Industrial management.
I. Sundbo, Jon.

HD45.C677 2005
658.4'062—dc22   2005049328

10 9 8 7 6 5 4 3 2 1
15 14 13 12 11 10 09 08 07 06

Transferred to digital printing in 2006

Contents

MAY 0 5 2008

List of Tables

List of Figures

Notes on Contributors

Jon Sundbo is Professor in Business Administration with speciality in innovation and technology management at the Department of Social Sciences, Roskilde University, Denmark. Director of Center for Service Studies, coordinator of the department's research area Innovation and Change Processes in Service and Manufacturing. He has been doing research within the fields of innovation, service management and the development of the service sector, tourism and organization. He has published articles in several journals on innovation, entrepreneurship, service and management and has published several books, among these *The Theory of Innovation* and *The Strategic Management of Innovation.*

Göran Serin is Dr in Economic History and Associat Professor at the Department of Social Sciences at Roskilde University in Denmark. He has long experience within the fields of technology, innovation and regional development. He has particular interest in industrial analysis, especially within low technology where he has published many books and articles. In later years his research has primarily been focused on the relation between changes in the industrial structure and policies for regional development. Together with local networking organizations he has also been active in developing regional policies within the ICT and the environmental sectors in the Öresund region.

Andrea Gallina, PhD in Economics, is Assistant Professor at the Department of Social Sciences of Roskilde University, Denmark, where he coordinates the Latin American-European Network on Technology Innovation Studies and Co-development, and the Federico Caffé Center of Studies on Globalization. He has published internationally several articles and books on the socio-economic dimension of the Euro-Mediterranean Partnership; the socio-economic impact of free trade on small- and medium-sized enterprises, innovation in small- and medium-sized enterprises in industrial and developing countries.

Jerome Davis is a Professor of Business Economics, Roskilde University He has previously been consecutively Professor of Public Economics and Policy (1984–1998) at Roskilde University, Denmark, and Visiting Professor International Business Economics (Copenhagen Business School, 1998–2001). An energy specialist (oil and natural gas), he has published extensively on the oil and natural gas industries. A parallel interest has been the economic theory of industrial organization and the function of markets as instruments for innovative activities. He was Visiting Scholar at the Oxford Institute for Energy Studies (1988) and has served as the outside board member of the Petro and Petropol research initiatives, the Norwegian Research Council, 1992–2000. He holds an MA and PhD both from the Johns Hopkins University SAIS.

Staffan Laestadius is Professor of Industrial Dynamics at the School of Industrial Engineering and Management, Royal Institute of Technology, Stockholm. His main research interest is knowledge formation processes in industry and he is currently engaged in analyzing the potential for reforming/widening the dominant innovation concept.

Marius T.H. Meeus is Professor of Innovation and Organization at the Department of Innovation and Environmental Studies at the Faculty of Geography of Utrecht University. He graduated at Tilburg University with a degree (cum laude), and also his PhD was rewarded with a degree (cum laude). His research focuses on the development and empirical exploration of organization theory applied to the innovative behaviour of firms. His most recent work includes articles and book chapters on patterns of interaction in regional innovation systems, theory forma-tion in innovation studies (Porter, Network Theory, Resource Based Theory, Structuration Theory, Transaction Cost Theory, Institutional Theory, Evolutionary Theory, Behavioural Theory of the Firm, Innovation Systems Approach), the selection-adaptation debate and innovative per-formance, interactive learning, innovation and proximity, intervention and implementation. He was a member of the editorial board of Organization Studies, and is acting organizer of the EGOS standing working group on Business Networks. He has published in journals such as: *Research Policy, Technology Analysis and Strategic Management, Journal of Social and Economic Geography*, papers in *Regional Science, Review of Industrial Organization* and *Organization Studies, Industry and Innovation*, and *Regional Studies*.

Philip Cooke is University Research Professor in Regional Economic Development, and Founding Director (1993) of the Centre for Advanced Studies, University of Wales, Cardiff. In 2002 the UK Economic & Social Research Council awarded core-funded UK Research Centre status to CESAGen, a partnership initiative on the Social and Economic Analysis of Genomics in which Professor Cooke's Centre has 'flagship project' status. His research interests lie in studies of Biotechnology, Regional

Innovation Systems, Knowledge Economies, Clusters and Networks. He co-edited the first and recent second edition of *Regional Innovation Systems* (Routledge) in 1998 and 2004, co-authored *The Associational Economy* published in 1998 by OUP, and *The Governance of Innovation in Europe* in 2000. In 2002 he released *Knowledge Economies*, also published by Routledge. Professor Cooke is a UK government advisor on innovation since 1999, and advises EU, OECD and UNIDO similarly. He is also Editor of *European Planning Studies* a bi-monthly-plus journal devoted to European urban and regional governance, innovation and development issues.

Povl A. Hansen is Dr in Economic History and Associated Professor at the Department of Geography and International Development Studies at Roskilde University in Denmark. He has long experience within the fields of technology, innovation and regional development. He has a particular interest in industrial analysis, especially within low technology where he has published many books and articles. In later years his research has primarily been focused on the relation between changes in the industrial structure and policies for regional development. Together with local networking organizations he has also been active in developing regional policies within the ICT and the environmental sector in the Öresund region.

Jeremy Howells, Professor, BSc, PhD is Executive Director of the ESRC Centre for Research in Innovation and Competition (CRIC) and Policy Research for Engineering, Science and Technology (PREST) within the Institute of Innovation Research (IoIR), at the University of Manchester. He has written, co-authored and edited several books and papers on research and innovation, R&D and technology transfer. In addition to the UK Economic and Social Research Council (ESRC), the Engineering and Physical Sciences Research Council (EPSRC; together with the LINK programme), he has conducted research projects for the OECD, the European Science Foundation (ESF), the European Commission and UNCTAD. He has also worked on more specific management and development studies funded by national and international ministries and agencies.

Søren M. Pedersen (MSc, PhD) is a Senior Researcher at The Food and Resource Economics Institute at KVL. He has 10 years' experience in production economics, agro-industrial system analysis and technology assessment. He has participated as a researcher and with project management in several national and European research projects.

Jørgen L. Pedersen (MA Economics) is an Associate Professor at the Department of Manufacturing Engineering and Management at Technical University of Denmark (DTU). He has worked with technology assessment, innovation policy, product configuration and modularity in R&D. He has taken part in Danish, Nordic and European research projects.

Jan Faber is Associate Professor of Methodology of Innovation Research at the Department of Innovation and Environmental Sciences at the Faculty of GeoSciences of Utrecht University. He holds degrees in economics (MSc) and political geography (PhD). His research focuses on decision making within management in policy contexts regarding innovation and on related topics concerning mathematical and statistical methods, methodology, system dynamics and philosophy of science. He has published in, for example, *Research Policy, Statistica Neerlandica* and *Quality & Quantity*.

Leon A.G. Oerlemans is Associate Professor of Organization Studies at Tilburg University, Faculty of Social and Behavioural Sciences and Extraordinary Professor of Economics of Innovation in the Department of Engineering and Technology Management, University of Pretoria, South Africa. Research topics include systems of innovation, interactive learning and inter-organizational networks. He has published in, for example, *Research Policy, Technology Analysis and Strategic Management, Journal of Social and Economic Geography*, papers in *Regional Science, Review of Industrial Organization* and *Organization Studies, Industry and Innovation*, and *Regional Studies*.

Lars Fuglsang is Associate Professor at Roskilde University, Denmark. He has been doing research within the field of innovation and technology development. He has published several articles in international journals, among others on innovation in services. He has been director of international study programmes on innovation.

Jaume Guia is Associate Professor at the Department of Business Organization and Management at the University of Girona. His research interests include organizational network dynamics, social capital and their implications on innovation processes. Currently he is Director of the Tourism Industries Innovation and Research Center (CRIIT).

Lluís Prats is Assistant Professor at the Department of Business Organization and Management at the Universtity of Girona. He has just completed his PhD dissertation on local systems of innovation in tourism districts. Other research areas of interest include organizational networks and relationship dynamics. He is also a member of the Tourism Industries Innovation and Research Center (CRIIT).

Jordi Comas is Associate Professor at the Department of Business Organization and Management at the Universtity of Girona. He has just completed his PhD dissertation on organizational networks, innovation, and seasonality of demand in the hotel sector. He is also a member of the Tourism Industries Innovation and Research Center (CRIIT).

Pim den Hertog graduated as an economic geographer. In 1990 he joined TNO Strategy, Technology and Policy Studies. In 1998 he co-founded Dialogic Innovation & Interaction, a research based consultancy in Utrecht in the field of innovation studies and innovation policy-making where he is a Senior Researcher/Co-Director. His research interests include management of national innovation systems, service innovation and innovation policy-making.

Tom Poot is Assistant Professor of Economics of Innovation at University Utrecht, Faculty of Geosciences, Department of Innovation and Environmental Sciences. From autumn 2000 until 2004 he completed his PhD thesis on R&D-cooperation at Delft University of Technology. Before that he was a Senior Researcher at the Foundation of Economic Research at the University of Amsterdam (SEO) from 1989–2000. He received his MA in Human Geography at the University of Amsterdam.

Gerhard Meinen graduated as an applied mathematician. After four years of research at Twente University, he started working for Statistics Netherlands (CBS) in 1996, first as a Statistical Researcher, and then from 2001 onwards as Project Manager on R&D and innovation statistics. In this capacity he also has final responsibility for the annual CBS publication (in Dutch) on the knowledge-based economy.

Cristiano Antonelli is Professor of Economics at Department of Economics, University of Torino, Italy. He has published books and many articles on the economics of technology development and innovation.

Lee Davis is Associate Professor at the Department of Industrial Economics and Strategy, and Research Associate at the Centre on Law, Economics and Financial Institutions, both at the Copenhagen Business School in Denmark. She has conducted research on economic incentives to research and development and the role of intellectual property rights for the past two decades, and published widely in this field. She teaches courses on the management of innovation, and intellectual property rights strategy and policy, in the MSc and Law and Economics programmes at the Copenhagen Business School, and in executive MBA programmes. Her main research interests include: what motivates inventors to invent (including the role of alternative incentive systems such as prizes), how firms capture the profits from their investments in R&D, the appropriability aspects of university-business relationships in biotechnology, and the new perspectives on appropriability raised by advances in digital technologies.

Part I: Management of Innovation – Are We Looking at the Right Things?

Introduction

New Tendencies in Society.
The Management of Innovation and Innovation Research

Jon Sundbo

Are we looking at the right things when we undertake innovation research?

As a point of departure for editing this book, we asked the following question: Why should we not look at the right things and why is it that we might not be looking at the right things? Our answer was that both society and the market have changed, and with them the art of innovation management has changed. In June 2004, we organized a workshop involving researchers from several countries to discuss this question. The book is a result of that workshop. Part I provides an introduction and outlines the societal changes and the resultant changes in the nature of innovation activities and their consequences for innovation management. All of these changes can be characterized in one phrase – increased complexity. This means that the factors (innovation research, basic research in natural sciences and classic entrepreneurship) that classically have been thought to ensure innovation, firm development and economic growth are too limited for the present situation. In the next two chapters of the introduction, Staffan Laestadius and Marius Meeus discuss in greater depth the development of innovation research and the challenges it faces today.

Society has changed – appearance of the problematization society

We are looking for societal changes that can explain the introduction of new factors of innovation. New aspects have appeared in society during the past decades. The economic surplus has increased, markets have been satisfied, the service or experience society (cf. Pine & Gilmore, 1999) has arisen. The firm has gained a new relationship to society. Its exposure in society has become important for sales and for the success of its innovations, and the public has become much more interested in firms' internal affairs. The existence of the knowledge society means that firms can procure much of the knowledge needed for innovation activities from outside, and they involve external actors in innovation processes to a greater extent. Employees have more education, independence and initiative. Customers want individual solutions to problems (not goods or simple services) or entertainment. Meanwhile, because prices are still an important competition parameter, firms need to cooperate with external actors and even competitors (the network society, cf. Castells, 2000). Communication channels have become a thousand times more efficient (e.g., via the Internet), which for example has promoted e-business (a new part of the innovation task). The protection of innovations has become a greater problem.

These changes have led to what could be called the complex or problematization society, in which innovations solve complex problems and become complex themselves, as do the processes of solving them. The more knowledge, engagement and conscious customer behaviour, the higher and more varied the expectations to goods and services. As a result, a more advanced society means that everything has become problematized (not simplified). Everything in this society becomes a complex problem (which follows from the advanced knowledge, engagement of employees, customers and citizens – that all lead to many expectations and many problems in relation to each innovation). The complexity arises when social factors are added to technical-practical and economic factors.

To sum up, complexity in innovation can be many things. If we talk about the conditions for innovation, we could sum up complexity into the six most important new developments in society:

Market

- Product packetation: the combination of goods, services and experiences.

- Individualization of the product.
- Extras to the product (environmental protection, ethics, experience, meeting the customer's customers and so on).

Organization

- External networking-cooperation with many actors.
- Employees engaged and involved.
- Renewed importance of the price mechanism and productivity (back to basics in a complex world).

Innovations become complex

Innovations themselves have become more complex. The development of firms has become broader than innovation that is understood as technology-based development of new technological products. Many innovations are non-technological or a mix of technological and social aspects. Innovation within services becomes important since services comprise 80 per cent of economic activity. There has been greater focus on market behaviour as part of goods, service or experience (and of the innovation). Generally, innovations have been more integrated in that they are a renewal of already existing products, processes, organization and market behaviour all at the same time. Often goods and services (and maybe even experiences) are renewed and marketed as a complex product packet. This is done because the problem that the innovation is to solve has become complex and involves more side activities (such as services and experiences). All must be marketed in a special way that emphasizes this particular combined product/image packet to differentiate this product and firm from others, to demonstrate that the product meets ethical and other requirements, and to protect the innovation (since patents are not longer as efficient as they once were in the industrial society). Each customer expects an individual innovation made just for him – but at the price of a mass product. Flexible specialization (cf. Volberda, 1998), mass customization (cf. Pine, 1993) and modulization (cf. Sundbo, 1994) have become part of the innovation task – each new product or service must have a high-productive basis, but be delivered individually.

Change of firms' innovation activities – the management of innovation becomes complicated

The innovation process in firms has become complex, while innovation activities have become broader. Innovations are less dependent on in-house specialized research and development (R&D) activities. The environment is more involved. Customers play a central role. If they are business customers, there is more focus on innovations' importance to their production and their customers – the innovation process must be seen from the customers' side. Market reputation is part of innovation. Political considerations concerning both the public and governments must be taken into account. The employees are more involved and play entrepreneurship roles. Small, but many, improvements become increasingly important (e.g. quality improvement). Innovation activities increasingly are based within the firm's strategy. Innovation activities in networks – some regional, others structured otherwise – become important.

New common characteristics across industries can be observed. Certain types of firms have similar innovation behaviour (e.g. depending on size) and there is regional coherence. These characteristics are often more important than industrial traits. This makes the management of innovation more complicated. Managers become dependent on the efforts of other people and must continuously reflect on the innovation route in relation to the firm's strategy and unpredictable changes in the environment. Innovation management has become the art of balancing different factors of development and development against stability.

New factors in innovation research

The situation outlined above has led to new innovation factors being introduced in the firms. They should be studied in innovation research. These factors become a supplement to the old factors and thus there is a development of innovation research and theory. The new factors that should be included in innovation research are, for example, increased dependence on market structure, collaboration in networks, active placement in the market structure as a result of strategic behaviour, and better exploitation and exploration of internal and external resources – involvement of employees, involvement in customers' innovation and production. More efficient research and development (R&D); R&D of social factors (such as a new market behaviour, a service as an addition to goods, new organizational or management forms) should be included. There should be more efficient use of external knowledge channels and new decision mechanisms – prices as a direct development parameter of innovations, non-patent protection mechanisms, which must be decided.

The book

The book both investigates and discusses some of the new factors behind innovation, and provides an insight into the new empirical and theoretical research that is taking place in this area. The work is far from complete and thus this book is more a state-of-the-art report.

The book is structured as follows: Part I discusses the various perspectives there are within innovation research; Part II deals with the environment and complexity of the market. In Part III, the internal, organizational aspects of innovation will be analyzed and discussed. Part IV looks at information and knowledge and their importance to the appropriability of the innovations. Each part has an introduction that explains the ideas and contents in greater detail.

Bibliography

Castells, E. (2000), *The Network Society* (Oxford: Blackwell).

Pine, J. (1993), *Mass Customization* (Boston: Harvard Business School Press).

Pine, J. & Gilmore, J.H. (1999), *The Experience Economy* (Boston: Harvard Business School Press).

Sundbo, J. (1994), 'Modulization of Service Production', *Scandinavian Journal of Management*, 10 (3), pp. 245–66.

Volberda, H. (1998), *Building the Flexible Firm* (Oxford: Oxford University Press).

1
The Rise and Fall of Management of Innovation. *The Transformation of a Concept and of Management Practice in the Knowledge Economy*

Staffan Laestadius

1.1. The management of innovation concept

Management of innovation (as a concept) was invented by Burns and Stalker (1961). Managing innovations, of course, was the natural outcome of a process, which, among innovation theorists, has been called the Schumpeter Mk II mode, that is, the transformation of innovations to corporate research and development (R&D) departments. This phenomenon, discussed in Schumpeter (1943 [1981]), was one of the consequences of the development of corporate capitalism, observed by Berle and Means (1932) and Burnham (1941) already but was a process with origins (also) in the German chemical industry in the late 19th century (cf. Schmookler, 1957; Freeman, 1974; Mowery & Rosenberg, 1998). This chapter argues that the management of innovation concept has become increasingly irrelevant for the understanding of management problems – and thus as a basis for management decisions – related to industrial change. The conditions for this loss of relevance were present in the 1980s already, that is, during the phase when management of innovation theory developed as a research field in academia. This loss of relevance is also, it is argued, related to the emerging problem of isolating 'innovations' from activities in general in the knowledge-based economy.

The transformation and diffusion processes of the innovation concept during the almost century-long period elapsing since the publication of *Theorie der Wirtschaftlichen Entwicklung* (Schumpeter, 1911 [1968]), is probably not finally analyzed. It has been argued (cf. Sundbo, 1998) that there have been three paradigms of innovation, closely related to the

Kondratieffs of the last century. Thus the original Schumpeterian entrepreneurial theory may have had its intellectual roots in the capitalist spirit of the upswing in the third Kondratieff. The organized innovation processes, the management of which was analyzed by Burns and Stalker (1961), thus have their origin in the fourth Kondratieff dominated by Fordism and by corporate capitalism. The innovation paradigm of that period was, following Sundbo, heavily based on technology, engineering and science; it was, as is well known, not the case with the original Schumpeterian (1911) texts. In the fifth Kondratieff, finally, there may be a formation of a strategic paradigm of innovation less focused on technology but more on organization, on services and on markets (cf. Sundbo, 1998, chs 4–5).

Such a contextualization is important and may contribute to the discussion on whether our understanding of innovations remains relevant as industrial activities transform. It may be argued, however, if the shifts in the understanding of innovations during the last century qualify for being labelled paradigmatic. The argument in favour of continuity is that the material/industrial as well as the intellectual foundations for the development of the corporate understanding of innovations' and their management, were laid already at the time of Schumpeter's book. In addition, the heritage from the fourth Kondratieff seems to have survived long into the fifth without significant and clear revolutionary change – which is what paradigm shifts are supposed to be.

1.2. Historical development of the concept

Let us, first of all, focus on the industrial foundation. The origin of modern mass production dates back to the 18th century; at the eve of the industrial revolution and at the time of the attempts to organize human labour efficiently (Giedion, 1948; Laestadius, 1992).

The spirit of the time when Schumpeter was working with his text was – at least from an industrial perspective – dominated by systematic industrial management in general and Taylorist principles in particular. Although the continuous assembly line at the Ford factory may be dated as late as 1913, mass production systems based on advanced division of labour had a rapid development in the United States during the whole period after 1850 (Hounshell, 1984) but in fact started much earlier in Europe. Fordism was the crown of the process rather than it's beginning! We can in this development (in theory as well as in industrial practice) identify not only a division of labour between different tasks in the direct manufacturing of artefacts, but also – and more important – a clear division between manual and intellectual labour (Laestadius, 1992). This is obvious in the practical and theoretical works of Taylor (1911) but also in subsequent theories of industrial organization as well as in industrial practice on the eve of the century (cf. Kimball, 1913 [1919]). The industrial context – in theory as well as in practice – was a world dominated by repetitive industrial mass production of homoge-nous products intended for mass consumption.

The shop floors of this industrial world, where an increasing number of workers became employed, were certainly not the places where inno-vations occurred or were supposed to occur. In the Taylorist and Fordist dominated industries this is totally clear: some people work with their hands only; others – and only a few – with their brains. There is – in such systems – a clear division of labour between production and knowledge formation, between those who produce and those who innovate (cf. Koebke, 1941). The heritage from the 18th century – strengthened in the Taylorist/Fordist heydays in the beginning of the 20th century – has been carried forward as an implicit foundation in subsequent develop-ment of innovation (and management) theory: we search for innovative activities (and thus innovators) assuming both that they are separated from industrial production (and thus producers) in general and – not the least – that they are separated for ever.

Integrated with the development of large-scale industry was *the for-mation of the modern engineering profession.* To a significant extent this professionalization process also included discussions on how to identify or socially construct the relations between science and technology, between scientists and engineers, and between natural science and 'engineering science'. The importance of this process of creating a profession and instituting an engineering science is revealed in the many studies available within the discourse of what is sometimes called 'engineering studies' (cf., e.g., Downey & Lucena, 1995; cf. also Lenoir, 1997). It may be argued that this scientification of engineering has had its impact on two levels: first, on a cultural level it may have contributed to a scientification of the understanding of knowledge formation and thus also contributed to a shift of focus or perspective among those who analyze knowledge formation in industry and technology as well as among those who take part in, or run/manage, creative and cognitive processes. Second, it may have contributed to the transformation (that is scientification) of engineering in itself.

Although Schumpeter in his (early) writings had a very distant view on the role of science – in fact he explicitly wrote about new combina-tions of what was already known, not about science – it is clear that the role of science and its relation to engineering, has been a core question in later discourses on industrial development.

The relation between science and technology has been analyzed over a long period (cf., e.g., Whitehead, 1925; Merton, 1938; Schmookler, 1950; Musson & Robinson, 1969 and Landes, 1969 for different approaches). Many of these writers were also clear in their view that the links between scientific discoveries and the world of artefacts are far from simple. There is also a well-known modern discourse with roots in engineering studies, as well as in science studies, which reveal a relative independence as well as two directed influences between science on the one hand and engineering/technology on the other hand (cf., e.g., Gibbons & Johnston, 1974; Price, 1982; Gibbons & Johnson, 1982; Vincenti, 1990; Brooks, 1994; Faulkner, 1994). One of the frontiers in this discourse, opened in the 19th century, is to sequentially order the activities of scientists and engineers; giving the later the role of applying the knowledge achieved by the former. Despite of all stylized facts and academic reports falsifying such a linear model of science and technology – intellectually strengthened by the Bush Report (1945), which makes a clear distinction between 'basic research' and 'applied research' – such a view maintains a strong position in policy circles and also in significant segments of academia, although its attractiveness to managers is far from clear (cf. also Stokes, 1997).

Let us return to Burns and Stalker (1961). As we have seen, although pioneering in formulating a coherent view of management of innovation they were analyzing processes, which had been developing for decades. Their point of departure was sociological, although related to industrial organization and management. Their understanding of innovations had no connection to Schumpeter – he was not even referred to in their book – and they analyzed a domain that was dominated by a management discourse with origins in engineering and industrial organization strongly influenced by Fordism and Taylorism. In addition they were alone for a long time in this field of research. In short, it may be argued that, on the one hand, there is very little research explicitly related to innovations, that is following the Schumpeterian track, until the mid or late 1970s. Christopher Freeman's *The Economics of Industrial Innovation* (1974) is a watershed in this area. The management literature, on the other hand, had very few, if any, connections with innovation theory, not even with the concept of innovation or a notion of Schumpeter. Even in this case, the late 1970s seem to be the period of formation of the management of innovation discourse with publications such as those from Abernathy and Utterback (1978); Granstrand (1979).

So, the management of innovation discourse basically emerged in the late 1970s and the early 1980s, integrating a neo-Schumpeterian perspective – by that time developed into a Mk II mode – with the long tradition from industrial organization and engineering management. Far from original Schumpeterian thinking from 1911, this emerging discourse easily became integrated to a science and technology perspective: first, because the Schumpeterian Mk II mode was strongly related to corporate R&D. Second, because the strong scientific ambitions within the professional culture of engineering management. And, finally, because this was fully in line with the linear model with origin in the Bush Report (Stokes, 1997). The late 1980s and the 1990s may be looked upon the heydays of the management of innovation theory. Paraphrasing Utterback (1994) and Vernon (1966), we may label this period the fluid phase of the development of management of innovation/technology literature followed by a maturing period in the late 1990s and early 2000. This is supported by looking into well-known readers like Tushman and Moore (1988) and Tushman & Anderson (1997), as well as standard textbooks such as Tidd, Bessant and Pavitt (1997) and Dodgson (2000).

1.3. Biometric analysis

This classification is also supported by a simple bibliometric test (cf. Table 1.1) based on the frequencies of registered literature and journals in Swedish university libraries with 'management of innovation' in the title sorted according to year of publication. There is, of course, a risk that recent publications have not hitherto found their way to the university libraries. To compensate for that, data for the last six years are shown in Table 1.2, indicating that the decline in the publication of management of innovation literature is not only a recent phenomenon.

This period – the 1980s and 1990s – was also a period of convergence between various aspects of management thinking and innovation

Table 1.1. Frequencies of 'Management of Innovation' publications in the LIBRIS system (Swedish university library database) sorted for year of publication

Year	71/75	76/80	81/85	86/90	91/95	96/00	01/04
Frequency	1.6	2.8	4	17.8	19.4	29.6	20

Note: Five/four year averages. Dates of search: 17 may 2004 and 12 September 2004 (2001–04).

Table 1.2. Management of innovation publications in Swedish university libraries published during the past six years

Year	1999	2000	2001	2002	2003	2004
Frequency	35	30	28	18	18	16

Note: date for search: see Table 1.1.

theory. The roots in industrial economics/engineering management are integrated with organizational theory, with general (strategic) management and – during the 1990s – with the management approaches related to network theory and the new theory of the firm. The Weberian-inspired organizational ideal types mechanistic – organic, developed by Burns and Stalker (1961), have – in slightly modified varieties – survived into later innovation management literature although they became moulded into product cycle approaches (cf. Utterback, 1994).

The 1980s and the 1990s – well in line with what Sundbo identifies as the fifth Kondratieff – was also a period of transformation within several areas of importance for the discourses on innovations as well as on its management. We may – depending on how we cut them out – identify for example six areas of transformation. They are linked to each other in several ways; here we discuss them separately to make the argument more clear:

- The decline of Fordism/Taylorism.
- The return of the entrepreneur in new technologies.
- The relative decline of manufacturing in favour of services.
- The growing importance of design and logistics.
- The network character of the economy.
- The rise of the new professionalism.

All of these could justify a chapter of their own for a deeper overview. Here there is just space enough to indicate the character of the phenomena.

1.4. Recent developments

With regard to the *decline of Fordism/Taylorism*, the forecasts by Braverman (1974 [1977]) have not realized. Even allowing for the phenomenon of global sourcing of simplistic tasks, it may be argued that the most simple and unqualified tasks have been automated. And although the routine work following automation should not be neglected, long traditions of research show that automation is far from having an obvious connection to downgrading (cf. Bright, 1958; Zuboff, 1988). As Kern and Schumann (1987) showed, fewer jobs are left in manufacturing, and those left, on average, need more skills, and new skills, than was the case before. The decline of Fordism has taken place through significant organizational innovations that have transformed production processes in several directions. Although the impact of these organizational innovations should not be overestimated – there are indications that they do not keep up to the demands from the increasingly highly educated employees – the relative decline of traditional 'raw labour' – not supposed to be creative or innovative – is significant. The mirror image of this decline is, of course, that the innovative potential is spreading throughout the organization. The R&D departments are becoming less exclusive as creative centres within the firms.

The return of the entrepreneur in the 1980s was a process with its origins in the Californian ICT industry but eventually it had an impact on the whole industrialized world. Even in countries such as Sweden, which was supposed to lack any entrepreneurial spirit due to the historical dominance by large corporations and social democratic policy, there were flowering ICT firms and a rapidly growing venture capital market. In short, there has been a shift of focus towards entrepreneurial creativity related to new business ideas and creative combinations – and in research on these phenomena.

The relative growth of service activities is of importance from an innovation perspective as the theories on innovation and its management to a large extent have developed in relation to manufacturing. The growing role of services has many aspects of which only a few can be dealt with in this context. What it is about, basically, is that indirect production activities are substituted for direct production activities; a growing amount of tasks consist of planning, coordinating, supporting, changing, buying, selling, drawing, designing, transforming, logistics, financing and so on. Some of these tasks are performed within manufacturing plants/firms, others at a geographical or organizational distance. Part of this process is visible through the transformation from manufacturing to service sectors and firms. Parts are visible through the relative shift from blue-collar workers to white-collar workers within the manufacturing sectors. And parts are less visible but consist of the transformation of traditional blue-collar tasks; making them more 'white-collar like'. In short, our old understanding of how to identify and classify innovative activities in this area has become blurred (cf., e.g., Andersen, 2000; Dankbaar, 2003, part II). Besides the fact that service firms may innovate as regards their own products and organizations significant parts of 'knowledge intensive services (KIBS) consist of innovating for their clients. So, to some extent at least, managing services is also managing innovations! In particular this relates to professional activities to which we will return below.

Design is one of these knowledge intensive service activities. Relating ourselves to the Faulkner (1994) typology, we may conclude that it is design, not R&D, which is one of the pillars of success stories such as those at H&M and IKEA. Neither of these firms reports any significant R&D on their web pages. Although their value chains as a whole are far from our image of the knowledge-based economy, important sections are extremely innovative and thus indicate corporate capabilities to a large extent out of reach for those innovation analysts equipped with the *Oslo Manual* only (cf. OECD, 1997). In fact, several of the most successful industries worldwide (global as well as local) allocate a surprisingly small share of their turnover to what may be labelled (R&D-based) innovations in a Schumpeter Mk II sense. Like many other globalized firms, the organizational and/or technical competence for IKEA and H&M is based on *a combination of design and logistics capabilities* related to a strong interactivity with the market. Firms such as these continuously create new combinations in the original Schumpeterian sense but they are, of course, very far from science. The complex interplay between design and other forms of knowledge – newly created (flow) as well as 'available' (stock) – was outlined by Kline and Rosenberg (1986).

The growing importance of *networking in the economy* has received significant attention in recent years, not the least through the publications by Castells (2000). Industrial networks – informal and formal as well as the cooperation/collaboration within them – have been in focus for analysts for decades. Of importance for our purpose is the fact that an increasingly networking character of the economy blurs the understanding on how innovative processes occur as well as how capabilities are created. It may, for example, be difficult to isolate which actor, if any, is the innovative actor within a value chain. Networks of formally independent actors, in addition, are difficult to manage.

To a large extent highly skilled *professionals* work with the 'service' activities mentioned above as well as within finance and technical consulting and coordinating activities. This segment of the labour market and the economy has increased. All professions naturally have moments and tasks, which are more routine based than others. However, what characterizes professional activities is, on the one hand, skilfully performing advanced tasks which in their details are not identical and which in their variations much be mastered by experience (such as surgery). On the other hand, professional activity is often related to explicit transformation of existing systems, that is, creating new solutions (such as design activities). In both cases it may be argued whether these professional activities are innovative or not. The growth of sophisticated routine work necessitates creative management but this is not managing of innovation. And the management of qualified services provided on a large scale in the 'new economy' may create more incremental innovations than the providers themselves identify. In short, we face a transformation away from 'innovations' to qualified and creative problem solving, although to a various degree combined with routines.

In summary, what we have presented above is a multidimensional way of describing the knowledge-based economy, sometimes also labelled post-industrial (cf., e.g., Neef, 1998; Bell, 1973 [1976]). What we see is a complex picture of knowledge formation, of symbolic activities such as creating images, as well as scientific results and of organization of these activities on micro as well as on macro level. Science is just a small part of all this and even the concept of innovation – as it is traditionally understood – captures only a fraction of this domain. The mirror image of the decline of manual labour (and the decline of manufacturing employment) is that the cognitive, learning and creative capacities of humans are increasingly engaged in industry as well as in the rapidly growing professional services that in addition organize themselves totally differently compared to the Fordist/Taylorist tradition. The old division of labour between innovative and non-innovative activities disappears.

The combined effect of, on the one hand, reducing the borders between thinking and non-thinking units in industry and, on the other hand, a general upgrading of the tasks of employees, will increase the problem for innovation analysts to identify what activities to classify as innovative and thus supposed to contribute more to the explanation of growth (or industrial transformation) than the rest. It is, of course, attractive to broaden the innovation concept to include more of those hitherto neglected innovative/creative activities discussed above. Leaving the narrowness of the R&D focus is also the intention both of the *Oslo Manual* (OECD, 1997) and the CIS questionnaires related to it.

However, rediscovering that ingenuity/creativity takes place also outside of R&D departments, we will face an insoluble problem of discriminating between non-innovative and innovative creativity. And that problem will increase as industries are reorganized towards mobilizing the creativity potential of a majority of the employees, that is, leaving the old division of labour between units (and individuals) supposed to think and those supposed to produce. The problems with classifying the design of tools (innovation?), clothes (non-innovation?) and cars (partly innovation?) are obvious. For management of innovation theory, the problem becomes somewhat different; the dissolution of the innovation concept creates new opportunities. Leaving the innovation concept behind – or expanding it into creativity in general – opens for a broader analysis of the formation of knowledge and capabilities in firms, the whole firms and not only the R&D departments. This is also where the bridge spans over to the new theories of the firm.

Firms, that stay profitable have acquired at least some kind of competence or *capability*, which their competitors have not. The persistence and continuous rebirth of markets characterized by monopolistic competition reveal that these capabilities – or whatever they are called – are in many cases far from easy to buy, imitate or for which to compensate.

This is not the place for a detailed review of the discourses related to the resource or capability based theories of the firm or the related knowledge management and organizational learning theories. As the role of learning and knowledge formation within economics and management theory is reviewed elsewhere (cf. Boerner *et al.*, 2001), we can in this section limit our analysis to problems of importance for this article: the essential discourses on knowledge creation within firms/organizations are to a large extent independent from references to R&D activities and R&D departments. Although individual research projects within these traditions may focus on R&D units and R&D processes, this is normally not the case. The analyses and their results are instead applicable to, or even explicitly focused on, firms and organizations as a whole. We may thus conclude that while significant parts of innovation theory are based on the assumption of a division of labour between innovative and non-innovative activities, that polarization is absent or not necessary in those discourses.

Although the interest for *learning* among economists is old, it became an important part of innovation economics in the 1990s (Lundvall & Johnson, 1994). Learning processes and learning competence (capabilities) is a core theme also within the resource-based theory of the firm. Although innovation theory during the past decade has focused on learning, it may be argued that learning grasps a much wider area than the innovation concept of the *Oslo Manual*.

Also, for the family of *new theories of the firm* – inspired by Penrose (1959 [1995]) among others, is knowledge creation, although embedded in a complicated and not fully standardized conceptual world – of core concern (cf. Foss, 1997). Explicit connections of knowledge to R&D activities are, however, not frequent in the core texts usually referred to. Nowhere in this discourse is knowledge creation primarily, or exclusively, supposed to occur in R&D-units or identified as 'innovations'. Capabilities are created all over the organization – also in the R&D department!

Teece and Pisano (1994) add the concept 'dynamic capabilities' to the analytical framework. With dynamic capabilities they understand the ability of a firm to organize and mobilize its resources/assets in a way that creates competitiveness. This may be regarded as a meta level of competence and knowledge (competence to create capability) but may as well be looked upon as the locus of the tacit dimensions of industrial creativity, innovativeness and management. What is in focus here is the creation of capabilities on corporate, firm or plant level rather than mobilizing the R&D department.

The *knowledge management literature* in this area is dominated by Ikujiru Nonaka and colleagues who published a series of papers and books during the 1990s on the knowledge creation problem for firms and organizations (cf., e.g., Nonaka, 1996; Nonaka & Takeuchi, 1998; Nonaka, Toyama & Nagata, 2000; Nonaka, Toyama & Byosiere, 2001). Beneath the progress in their theories and models there is continuity in their basic concepts and approaches. Firms are *knowledge creating entities* and significant parts of organizational *knowledge and knowledge processes are tacit*. Creating knowledge is not just learning and definitely not restricted to the R&D department (Nonaka, Toyama & Boysiere, 2001).

In summary, a thorough analysis of the RBT and capabilities literature (not presented here) may reveal that there are conceptual problems within these approaches still left to solve. Of importance in our case, however, is that they start by analyzing the revealed capabilities of firms and how all knowledge resources have become transformed into capabilities instead of starting on the level of poorly defined innovations. As the old division of labour between innovative and non-innovative units (persons) disappears, this family of theories may be one means – at least to start with – to catch an industrial creativity that otherwise threatens to fall out of sight of our analytical or management tools.

1.5. Concluding discussion

The distinction between innovative and non-innovative work was easy in a period of strong divisions of labour between the hand and the brain.

This also fitted well within the linear model for science and technology as well as for development of corporate capitalism transforming innovativity to managed processes sacrificing creativity for R&D. To a large extent, management of innovation theory for a long time mirrored this model. The decline of manual labour, the rise of the service sector, and the rise of new professionalism, challenge, however, the established view on innovative activities. This is a process occurring within professions, firms, and industries as well as between them. If organizations increase their mobilization of the creativity of the staff, all employees – in the extension – become innovators and the traditional taxonomy between innovative and non-innovative work becomes obsolete. Although the taxonomy problem may be less important by itself, it may have significance if the terminology limits our vision on where to find – and where to locate – industrial creativity. In the economy of today, management of innovation thus turns into the more general problem of how to orchestrate knowledge intensive organizations.

The creativity mobilized in the modern knowledge-based economies is far from focused on R&D in the traditional sense. On the contrary, the main difference between Tom Kelley's *The Art of Innovation* (2002) and the bulk of literature in management of innovation theory is not only that the former book is a bestseller at the airport book shelves and the latter books not, but it is also the fact that the R&D departments play a minor role in the former and a dominant role in the latter. What Kelley introduces – while promoting the hitherto successful concepts from his Silicon Valley-based innovation and design consultant firm IDEO – is a concept of combinatorial creativity in close relations with, and observations of, presumed customers. We here face innovative processes which are creative, artistic, borderless and which might mix new and old technologies in designing the mouse as well as a new medical instrument. In reading the book we learn that the staff of the firm seems to be highly academic and from several disciplines – thus synthesizing/integrating knowledge fully in line with the ideas from Gibbons (1994).

Phenomena such as these contribute to the background for management analysts such as Dankbaar (2003, ch. 15), who argues that the old paradigm of innovation management becomes difficult to maintain as industrial activities increasingly develop into what often are labeled knowledge intensive business services. Innovations are there transformed from exceptions from daily business to the normal state of activity (every service produced is unique, that is, innovative). Likewise von Stamm (2003), fully integrates innovativity, creativity and design in her recent management handbook.

Important, from our point of view, in both these management texts are that they focus on the creative combinatorial aspects of innovativeness rather than the science based or invention oriented aspects. In doing so, they not only reintroduce a neglected leg in management of innovation theory (the creativity aspect) but also one of the core arguments in the original Schumpeterian (1911) contribution. And while management of creativity and knowledge formation may still be needed, the innovation concept will become more vague in its contours.

Bibliography

Abernathy, W.J. & Utterback, J.M. (1978), 'Patterns of Industrial Innovation', *Technology Review* (2), pp. 40–47.

Andersen, B. (ed.) (2000), *Knowledge and Innovation in the New Service Economy* (Cheltenham: Edward Elgar).

Barnes, B. & Edge, D. (eds) (1982), *Science in Context* (Cambridge, MA: MIT Press).

Bell, D. (1973 [1976]) *The Coming of Post-Industrial Society* (New York: Basic Books/Harper).

Berle, A.A. & Means, G.C. (1932) *The Modern Corporation and Private Property* (New York: Macmillan).

Boerner, C., Macher, J. & Teece, D. (2001), 'A Review and Assessment of Organizational Learning in Economic Theories' (in Dierkes *et al.*).

Braverman, H. (1974 [1977]) *Arbete och monopolkapital* (Stockholm: Raben & Sjögren).

Bright, J.R. (1958), *Automation and Management* (Boston: Harvard University Press).

Brooks, H. (1994), 'The relationship between science and technology', *Research Policy*, 23, pp. 477–86.

Burnham, J. (1941), *The Managerial Revolution* (New York: John Day).

Burns, T. & Stalker, G.M. (1961), *The Management of Innovation* (London: Tavistock).

Bush, V. (1945), *Science, the Endless Frontier* (Washington, DC: Government Printing Office).

Castells, M. (2000), *The Information Age: ... Vol. 1: The Rise of the Network Society* (Malden, MA: Blackwell, 2nd edn).

Chandler, A., Hagström, P. & Sölvell, Ö. (eds) (1998), *The Dynamic Firm* (Oxford: Oxford University Press).

Dankbaar, B. (ed.) (2003), *Innovation Management in the Knowledge Economy* (London: Imperial College Press).

Dierkes, M. *et al.* (eds) (2001), *Handbook of Organizational Learning & Knowledge* (Oxford: Oxford University Press).

Dodgson, M. (2000), *The Management of Technological Innovation* (Oxford: Oxford University Press).

Dosi, G, Teece, D.J. & Chytry, J. (1998), *Technology, Organization and Competitiveness* (Oxford: Oxford University Press).

Downey, G.L. & Lucena, J.C. (1995), 'Engineering Studies' in Jasanoff *et al.* (eds), *Handbook of Science and Technology Studies* (Thousand Oaks, CA: Sage).

Faulkner, W. (1994), 'Conceptualizing Knowledge Used in Innovation: A Second look at the Science-Technology Distinction and Industrial Innovation', *Science, Technology and Human Values*, 19(4), pp. 425–58.

Foss, N. (1997), *Resources, Firms and Strategies: A Reader in the Resource-based Perspective* (Oxford: Oxford University Press).

Freeman, C. (1974), *The Economics of Industrial Innovation* (Harmondsworth, Penguin).

Gibbons, M. (1994), *The New Production of Knowledge* (London: Sage).

Gibbons, M. & Johnston, R. (1974), 'The Roles of Science in Technological Innovation', *Research Policy*, 3(3), pp. 220–42.

Gibbons, M. & Johnson, R. (1982), *Science, technology and the development of the transistor* (in Barnes & Edge, pp. 177–85).

Giedion, S. (1948), *Mechanization Takes Command* (Oxford: Oxford University Press).

Granstrand, O. (1979), *Technology Management and Markets* (Göteborg: Kulturkompaniet).

Hounshell, D.A. (1984), *From the American System to Mass Production 1800–1932* (Baltimore: Johns Hopkins University Press).

Kelley, T. (2002), *The Art of Innovation* (London: Harper Collins Business).

Kern, H. & Schumann, M. (1987), 'Limits of the Division of Labour', *Economic and Industrial Democracy*, 8, pp. 151–70.

Kimball, D. (1913 [1919]) *Principles of Industrial Organization* (New York: McGraw-Hill).

Kline, S. & Rosenberg, N. (1986), 'An Overview of Innovation' (in Landau & Rosenberg, pp. 275–305).

Koebke, C. (1941), *Plant Production Control* (New York: John Wiley).

Laestadius, S. (1992), *Arbetsdelningens dynamik* (Lund: Arkiv Förlag).

Landau, R. & Rosenberg, N. (eds) (1986), *The Positive Sum Strategy* (Washington, DC: National Academy Press).

Landes, D. (1969), *The Unbound Prometheus* (Cambridge: Cambridge University Press).

Lenoir, T. (1997), *Instituting Science* (Stanford: Stanford University Press).

Lundvall, B. & Johnson, B. (1994), 'The Learning Economy', *Journal of Industry Studies*, 2, pp. 23–42.

Merton, R.K. (1938), *Science, Technology and Society in Seventeenth Century England* (Bruges: Osiris).

Mowery, D.C. & Rosenberg, N. (1998), *Paths of Innovation* (Cambridge).

Musson, A. & Robinson, E. (1969), *Science and Technology in the Industrial Revolution* (Toronto: University of Toronto Press).

Neef, D. (1998), *The Knowledge Economy* (Woburn, MA: Butterworth-Heinemann).

Nelson, R. & Winther, S. (1982), *An Evolutionary Theory of Economic Change* (Cambridge, MA: Belknap Press).

Nonaka, I. (1996), 'The Knowledge Creating Company' (in Starkey).

Nonaka, I. & Takeuchi, H. (1998), 'A Theory of the Firm's Knowledge-Creation Dynamics' (in Chandler, Hagström & Sölvell).

Nonaka, I., Toyama, R. & Nagata, A. (2000), 'A Firm as a Knowledge-creating Entity: A New Perspective on the Theory of the Firm', *Industrial and Corporate Change*, 9(1), March.

Nonaka, I., Toyama, R. & Byosiere, P. (2001), 'A Theory of Organizational Knowledge Creation: Understanding the Dynamic Process of Creating Knowledge' (in Dierkes *et al.*).

Nonaka, I. & Teece, D. (eds) (2001), *Managing Industrial Knowledge* (London: Sage).

OECD (1997), *Oslo Manual* (Paris: OECD).

Penrose, E. (1959 [1995]), *The Theory of the Growth of the Firm* (Oxford: Oxford University Press, 3rd edn).

Petroski, H. (1994), *Design Paradigms: Case Histories of Error and Judgment in Engineering* (New York: Cambridge University Press).

Price, D.J. de Sola (1982), 'The Parallel Structures of Science and Technology' (in Barnes & Edge).

Schmookler, J. (1950), 'The interpretation of patent statistics', *Journal of the Patent Office Society*, Feb., pp. 123–46.

Schmookler, J. (1957), *Invention and Economic Growth* (Cambridge, MA: Harvard University Press).

Schumpeter, J. (1911 [1968]), *The Theory of Economic Development* (Cambridge, MA: Harvard University Press).

Schumpeter, J. (1943 [1981]), *Capitalism, Socialism and Democracy* (London: Allen & Unwin).

Starkey, K. (ed.) (1996), *How Organizations Learn* (London: International Thomson Business Press).

Stokes, D.E. (1997), *Pasteurs Quadrant – Basic Science and Technological Innovation* (Washington, DC: Brookings Institute).

Sundbo, J. (1998), *The Theory of Innovation* (Cheltenham: Edward Elgar).

Taylor, F.W. (1911), *The Principles of Scientific Management* (Westport, CT: Greenwood Press).

Teece, D. & Pisano, G. (1994), 'The Dynamic Capabilities of Firms: an Introduction', *Industrial and Corporate Change*, 3(3), pp. 537–56 (reproduced in Dosi, Teece & Chytry, 1998).

Tidd, J., Bessant, J. & Pavitt, K. (1997), *Managing Innovation – Integrating Technological, Market and Organizational Change* (Chichester: John Wiley).

Tushman, M. & Anderson, P. (eds) (1997), *Managing Strategic Innovation and Change* (New York and Oxford: Oxford University Press).

Tushman, M. & Moore, W. (eds) (1988), *Readings in Management of Innovation* (Cambridge, MA: Ballinger, 1988).

Utterback, J.M. (1994), *Mastering the Dynamics of Innovation* (Boston: Harvard Business School Press).

Vernon, R. (1966), 'International Investment and International Trade in the Product Cycle', *Quarterly Journal of Economics*, May, pp. 190–207.

Vincenti, W.G. (1990), *What Engineers Know and How They Know It: Historical Studies in the Nature and Sources of Engineering Knowledge* (Baltimore: Johns Hopkins University Press).

von Stamm, B. (2003), *Managing Innovation, Design and Creativity* (Chichester: John Wiley).

Whitehead, A.N. (1925), *Science and the Modern World* (New York: Macmillan).

Zuboff, S. (1988), *In the Age of the Smart Machine: The future of work and power* (New York: Basic Books).

2

From R&D Management to Management of Innovation. *Research on the Organizational Factor, Trends, Mainstream and Hidden Treasures*

Marius T.H. Meeus

2.1. Introduction

Answering the question 'Management of innovation: are we looking at the right things?' is an important but difficult task. The 'we' in the phrase 'are we looking at the right things?' is at minimum twofold in this chapter: the community of practitioners in innovation management, and the innovation researcher community. The 'things' I look at in this chapter are the organizational aspects of research and development (R&D) management. One short conceptual remark is relevant here to understand the purpose of my contribution. I consider R&D management as part of the management of innovation, with the distinction that commercialization and implementation issues are in general more important in innovation management than in R&D management. Yet, the main trends in R&D management show that the importance of commercialization and implementation issues has grown considerably over time, which justifies my contention that R&D and innovation management have become synonyms. Or, to put it differently, the evolution of thinking and conceptualization of R&D management over time has made R&D management a misnomer because it has been integrated in the innovation function.

Of course, what is right or wrong depends heavily on roles and perspectives of the actors involved. The aim of this chapter is to discover whether innovation management practice and innovation research converge or diverge with respect to emerging themes and challenges over several generations of innovation management, the actual strategic and organizational issues of innovation managers, and the schools of thought as to innovation management adhered to by researchers and practitioners. The extent into which there is divergence would imply that innovation researchers should either elaborate, or expand their research agenda, *if possible*. The question is whether the research agenda follows trends in R&D management, or not?

In this review we ask three kinds of people whether we are looking at the right things in innovation management. First, there are the R&D trend watchers, then there are the publishing R&D practitioners and innovation researchers, next we switch to the non-authoring R&D practitioners, and finally we ask the innovation research community how their work evolves and what are their main challenges. Of course a very straightforward and preferable answer is that the big issues of innovation managers and those of the research community would be about the same. But this is not so, because other issues and problems guide the world of innovation managers other than the universe of research. I think that the main issue is to which extent there is a co-evolution or whether there is a big gap between main trends in innovation management and the work of the innovation research community.

The chapter has the following structure. In section 2.2, I review the main trends in R&D management, and the big issues, and I also try to find out to what extent they are related or detached. In section 2.3, I switch to empirical research on the kind of schools of thought to which R&D practitioners and R&D researchers adhere, and to what extent their views converge. In section 2.4, the thinking of the innovation managers on the one hand, and of the innovation researchers on the other hand, are considered. The main splits are identified and linked to a review of reviews of innovation research, which reveals the theoretical and methodological problems pervading our work. This will give a basic idea of the state-of-the-art and the main theoretical and methodological challenges. In section 2.5, I draw some inferences from the analyses and findings described.

2.2. The evolution of R&D management over the past 40 years?

This overview of the main characteristics of the development of R&D management from the first to the fifth generation (Amidon, 2001) illustrates that the world of R&D has expanded significantly beyond the laboratory settings that Cicourel's and Knorr Cetina's laboratory life's described.

Looking at the main trends in R&D management, one can see that the R&D world indeed evolves into a more elaborate and complex interactive networked structure in which business activities of focal firms are aligned with vertical – upstream and downstream – business partners, and innovation systems partners. I think that the trends indicated in Table 2.1 justify a relabelling of R&D management into innovation management. The whole process of discovery, invention, to product development and market introduction is pulled together under the umbrella of R&D management, whereas, in general, R&D is not associated with implementation or commercialization processes.

The first trend is that the core asset is broadening over time. A second trend is that whereas first generation R&D managers' competencies were defined in terms of science and specialization in science and technology, the second and third generation R&D managers cannot do without a broader competence profile. The later generations of R&D managers preferably are multidisciplinary, and are much more specialized in organizational and managerial issues.

A third trend reflects a change in criteria for successful innovation. Whereas the first generation evaluated R&D output in terms of technological superiority, its successors extended the criteria set significantly and this resulted in a dominancy of commercial over technological success. Inventions, discoveries, and patents are not enough today, they are no more than a logical starting point for, on the one hand, the real innovation process transforming patented knowledge into new marketable products and services and new production and delivery systems, and, on the other hand, they are the basis for future intellectual capacity and impact.

A fourth significant trend is that the organizational context of R&D and innovation gradually evolves from the world of the R&D labs to alignment with business strategy, to the value chain, and to the whole collaborative innovation system. This implies that project structures became more complex and evolve from cross-functional teams consisting of colleagues internal to the company, into teams with customers, and eventually almost every player in the innovation system. Larger organizational contexts also multiply the number of interactions in innovation trajectories, which develops management of innovation into internal and external management of innovation. Besides the extension of organizational structures toward elaborate collaborative structures, communicative efforts grow significantly together with the potential for non-alignment and misunderstanding. This tendency also impacts on leadership, which seems to dissolve into self-managing knowledge workers with substantial autonomy.

Table 2.1. Five generations of R&D management

R&D Generation →	1st	2nd	3rd	4th	5th
Core asset→	Technology as the asset	Project as the asset	Enterprise as the asset	Customer as the asset	Knowledge as the asset
Other features					
Core strategy	R&D in isolation	Link to business	Technology/business integration	Integration with customer R&D	Collaborative innovation system
Change Factors	Unpredictable serendipity	Interdependence	Systematic R&D management	Accelerated discontinuous global change	Kaleidoscopic dynamics
Performance	R&D as overhead	Cost-sharing	Balancing Risk/reward	'Productivity paradox'	Intellectual capacity/impact
Structure	Hierarchical; functionally driven	Matrix	Distributed coordination	'Multidimensional communities of practice'	Symbiotic networks
People	We/they competition	Proactive cooperation	Structured collaboration	Focus on values and capacity	Self managing knowledge workers
Process	Minimal communication	Project-to-project basis	Purposeful R&D/portfolio	Feedback loops and information 'persistence'	Cross-boundary learning and knowledge flow
Technology	Embryonic	Data-based	Information-based	IT as competitive weapon	Intelligent knowledge processors

Source: Amidon (1996).

Now we have seen how R&D management generations evolve, it is interesting to know whether those trends translate in innovation management challenges in the 21st century.

Table 2.2 shows that R&D performance, speed, the R&D performance measurement, in tandem with leadership, direction (alignment with business strategy), and R&D focus, are the persistent challenges confronting US innovation managers. Although the key asset in the fifth generation of R&D management is 'knowledge', knowledge management has not been considered the biggest problem over the past years as Table 2.2 indicates. These findings do not differ very much from European findings reported by Thurlings and Debackere (1996). Based on interviews with 25 CTOs (chief technology officers), they identify five major foci of attention in managing innovation. They classified them as (1) scope, (2) organization, (3) control, (4) strategy, and (5) people. The CTOs pointed out that the scope of innovation is changing from 'getting a product out' towards taking into consideration the full context of a potential new product, meaning that it will develop as a part of a system of interrelated products and services. Concerning the organization of the innovation process, CTOs stressed the integration of various knowledge areas, implying that innovation management is

Table 2.2. Percentages of 'biggest problems' facing technology leaders in 2000

R&D managers and their problems	2000	1999	1998	1997	1996	1995	6-year average
Managing R&D for business growth	19.9	16.1	13.8	17.0	10.0	5.9	13.78
Accelerating innovation	17.28	12.2	16.1	10.3	9.5	7.8	12.19
Integration technology planning with business strategy	13.09	13.0	12.1	13.0	11.2	7.4	11.63
Balancing long-term/short-term R&D objectives/focus	11.52	13.5	12.6	14.7	12.1	11.0	12.57
Measuring and improving R&D productivity/effectiveness	5.24	5.7	6.3	4.0	11.8	11.5	7.42
Cycle-time reduction in R&D	5.24	4.8	5.7	3.1	8.5	8.4	5.96
Leadership of R&D within the corporation	4.19	6.5	5.7	4.0	4.2	2.3	4.48
Management of global R&D	4.19	3.9	3.4	5.8	4.5	3.5	4.22
Knowledge management	3.66	na	na	na	na	na	3.66
Selling R&D internally or externally	3.66	6.5	2.3	4.0	4.2	2.6	3.88
R&D portfolio management	2.62	5.7	5.7	4.0	4.5	4.5	4.50
Total company responses	191	230	174	223	242	258	–

Source: Industrial Research Institute (2000).

evolving toward a coaching role with an emphasis on information sharing to enable the accrual of distinct competencies instead of control over results. Also, the broadened organizational innovation context is found in this work. Engagement of competitors and key players along the value chain will grow in the coming years in innovation strategy and innovation management.

Gupta and Wilemon (1996) collected data among 120 R&D directors of technology-based companies. Their results indicate a significant increase of cross-functional teams, and a stronger focus on business impact of R&D. Organizations increasingly make R&D accountable for improved business performance and the alignment of business and technology strategy, and therefore R&D departments should improve their technology commercialization capabilities, understanding of customers as well as changing market development. Managers of R&D departments expect that in the near future the importance of technology strategy for business strategy will increase, together with a growing sense of urgency for meeting business needs and a quicker response to market opportunities. The formation of partnerships is also increasing in order to reduce R&D costs and to share risks in product development.

Scott (1997) reports on a Delphi study among entrepreneurs, the purpose of which was to identify and rank the major unresolved issues faced by companies in their development of technology intensive products. The 63 participants in the study were from 17 European countries and included technology educators, general managers, project managers, technology managers, consultants and technology experts form government agencies.

It is remarkable to see the distance between the development in core assets and features of several generations of R&D management (see Table 2.1) on the one hand and the main big R&D issues on the other hand (see tables 2.2 and 2.3). The latter issues obviously fit more the features of third generation R&D management than the features of fourth and fifth generation R&D management. The focus on alignment of business strategy and R&D, its output and speed, and measurement are typically third generation R&D features. Knowledge and customers were not such a big issue for R&D managers in the late 1990s and early 2000s as one would have expected. Another remarkable contrast is that stretching of R&D over company boundaries is not at all an issue for R&D managers, whereas the alliance option had already made a great leap forward at that time as a good alternative for avoiding large and risky R&D investments (Meeus & Faber, 2005). Yet this finding clearly reflects the idea that the distinction of internal and external innovation

Table 2.3.   Ranking of issues for innovation management

Issue	Importance of issue (10-point scale)
1. Strategic planning for technology products	8.18
2. New product project selection	7.30
3. Organizational learning about technology	7.29
4. Technology core competence	7.22
5. Cycle-time reduction	7.08
6. Creating a conducive culture	7.06
7. Coordination and management of new product development teams	7.06
8. Technology trends and paradigm shifts	7.03
9. Involvement of marketing groups	7.01
10. Customer/supplier involvement	6.97

Source: Scott (1997).

management (Tidd, Bessant & Pavitt, 2001), which is implied in the fourth and fifth R&D management generation is not reflected in the big R&D issues. The fact that large companies such as DuPont and AKZO Nobel swapped from technologically driven R&D to R&D that is driven by market opportunities of business units also reflects more third generation issues than 4th–5th generation issues and are probably exceptions that confirm the third generation patterns. An important conclusion derived from this remarkable misfit between the big R&D issues and general trends in R&D management reveals that thinking about R&D management and the day-to-day R&D business are not all closely linked.

2.3. Does the (re-)search behaviour of the innovation research community guide management of innovation?

Researchers in the field of innovation management acknowledge the importance of systematic, cumulative theorizing on innovation. Effective innovation management requires a broad conceptual toolkit derived from a range of different disciplines, and based on sound empirical research covering the many different aspects and stages of innovation. Brady et al. (1997) distinguish two ways in which academic research could make a distinctive contribution to technology management: (1) through analytical and theoretical advances, and (2) through the development of practical tools for complex problem solving. At the analytical level, academics are able to scrutinize and evaluate existing tools impartially. Evaluation of existing tools simultaneously enhances their capabilities in developing new tools of technology management.

The question is, however, whether schools of thought about R&D derived from publications of the innovation research community and R&D management issues match the main directions of innovation research? Falkingham and Reeves (2001) report some insights about R&D managers and their thoughts about their core business. Their inspiration was a series of illogical decisions of a company CTO. 'Small decisions concerned project approvals and terminations, whereas a typical large decision was to purchase a technology from outside while it already existed within the company.' Because they were certain that the R&D people had the same information, they continued to prefer distinct ways of how to proceed after in-depth discussions. A possible explanation for this is that these people simply have different perceptions of the R&D situation.

In order to classify these different modes of thought on R&D management, Falkingham and Reeves went through some 650 papers relevant to the topic of R&D management concerns. Initially, after reading some fifty papers they identified four *schools of thought*: biological, chaotic, deterministic and empirical.

The *Biological School* stresses the change over time in situations and consequently a management approach that can evolve. Building an organization capable of adapting is more important than the tactics for a particular project. The main concern is how to create an organization that is robust and sufficiently adaptable to cope with change as it occurs.

With regard to the *Chaotic School*, the notion of chaos is used in a mathematical sense of referring to situations that are acknowledged to be ultimately susceptible to logic, but which are too unstable or complex for logic to be used in practice. Patterns of chaos can be described, but a given case cannot be meaningfully worked out. Managers in R&D do not plan detail, because things will change. Each case is individual, and it is a waste to put a lot of effort into trying to manage it.

The *deterministic school* stresses measurement as the main basis for management. This approach concentrates on methods of measuring R&D outputs, for example by counting patent productivity or calculating return on R&D expenditure. It derives from traditional production management.

The *empirical approach* consists of a series of rules or guidelines based on empirical analysis of a large number of R&D projects. This 'cookbook' approach assumes that universally applicable success factors can be derived from past experience without needing any theoretical justification for their importance. Project SAPPHO is a classic example.

After reading some 600 additional papers, this classification turned out to cover pretty much the range of approaches. The next step was a cross check with the authors of the 650 papers, asking them how they would label their conceptual framework. It turned out that the classification of Falkingham and Reeves fitted the labelling of the author for more than 95 per cent, implying that the inter-rater reliability was appropriate. An interesting part of Falkingham and Reeves' paper is that the research community is defined in distinct categories of people publishing theses about R&D management. Most categories speak for themselves, the categories 'corporate' and 'practitioner' is explained in the legenda in Table 2.4. The practitioners* are people directly involved in R&D that publish about their work, and do research on R&D management, whereas the data on P** are based on a survey of practitioners that attend courses and conferences on R&D management, which asked for peoples' background and the school of thought they believed most closely described the process of managing R&D. Most attendees were R&D practioners and managers, and only few had published.

When comparing the totals in the last column in Table 2.4, it can be seen that the proportions present for each school are reversed in the two cases of researcher and non-authors. Members of the research community adhere to the deterministic and empirical school, whereas the non-authors seem to believe that the chaotic and biological school describes best day-to-day R&D management. Using the date in the fifth column it can be determined that the publishing practitioners as well as the non-publishing practitioners see the biological and chaotic school as closest

Table 2.4. Schools of thought on R&D management

School of thought	Journalist RT	Journalist P**	Academic RT	Academic P**	Consultant RT	Consultant P**	Corporate RT	Corporate P**	Practitioners* RT	Practitioners* P**	Total RT	Total P**
Biological	5	0	10	1	3	2	7	15	21	8	46	26
Chaotic	7	0	26	4	8	2	2	11	13	5	56	22
Deterministic	9	0	89	4	11	1	93	3	12	2	214	10
Empirical	30	0	189	0	55	0	46	1	11	2	331	3
None	1	na	6	na	0	na	1	na	0	na	8	na
Total	52	0	320	9	77	5	149	30	57	17	655	61

Note: RT = Researcher type (Corporate = hands-off corporate level manager), P = Practitioner. We discern two categories: Practitioners* = people with hands-on involvement in R&D or its management, P** = people attending courses and conferences on R&D management; na = not applicable.

Source: Falkingham and Reeves (2001).

to R&D management practice. These findings point at a distinct gap between the research community's work and the world of the R&D managers. The deterministic and the empirical school in general dominate the research community, whereas the practitioners favour the biological and chaotic school.

2.4. Confrontations: generations of R&D management, big issues, and intellectual upper bounds of the innovation science community

Confronting the findings of Falkingham and Reeves (2001) with the findings of Gupta and Wilemon (1996), Thurlings and Debackere (1996), Scott (1997), and the findings of IRI displayed in Table 2.3, one can see several important intellectual cleavages. On the basis of some further innovation and organization literature reviews, I will elaborate these cleavages in terms of intellectual challenges for the innovation research community.

2.4.1. Cleavage 1

Over time the notion of innovation management becomes more complicated in terms of competences needed to perform the task, in organizational scope, and cumulated factors to work with and to account for. The research community sticks largely to the deterministic and empirical approach, whereas R&D practitioners seem to favour the biological and chaos schools of thought.

2.4.2. Cleavage 2

Although the evolution from the first to the fifth generation of R&D management fits with a preference for the biological and chaos approach of R&D management, the big issues do not at all fit the biological and chaos school. On the contrary, the big innovation management issues fit very much the empirical and deterministic approach of measuring and optimizing in a rational planning approach – the dominant research approach of innovation scientists. The non-linear notions of the chain-linked model of innovation, network collaboration are prominently absent in the issues Table 2.3, whereas these issues define the main intellectual challenges in innovation sciences.

2.4.3. Cleavage 3

The developments in the notion of R&D management has strong theoretical and methodological implications because the core assets that are taken into account over time multiply, and this would require more complex theoretical models to integrate them in well-specified models. This defines basically the third cleavage and that is a lack of empirical findings that confirm these complex theoretical models. In fact there is more research pointing toward a sort of a drawback to the deterministic model when R&D managers are coping with environmental pressures.

Empirical research shows that most preferences and priorities of innovation managers are more to do with ideals than to reality. Several researchers have pointed out that strategy and innovation are often at odds with each other (Hitt *et al.*, 1996, p. 1068). Institutional and environmental dynamics are internalized through the adaptation of corporate strategies, which can have major implications for innovation. However, executives facing selection pressures are likely to increase financial controls, to decrease strategic controls and to reduce the time that they devote to innovation-related activities (ibid., p. 1071). Dougherty and Hardy (1996) claim that senior managers preoccupied with downsizing and other cost-cutting efforts tend to pay little attention to innovation as a result.

Van de Ven *et al.* (1999) claim that the composition of innovation project teams varies too much in general, because if daily operations

Table 2.5. Major differences between the context approach and the industry dynamics approach to innovation

Dimensions	Context approach	Industry dynamics approach
Major research question	What multilevel organizational factors predict the generation or adoption of an innovation?	What are the population effects on the production of innovations?
Types of sample	Large, multi-industry; focus on generalizability Example: Fortune 500 firms	Small, typically comprising all or most firms in an industry Example: Semiconductor firms
Conceptualization of organizations	Complex systems	Black boxes
Conceptualization of innovations	Number of innovations produced	Innovations are events differing in success and diffusion rates
General approach of innovations	Variance theory	Process theory
Research methods	Cross-sectional designs; factors that predict innovativeness	Longitudinal, event-histories; population-level factors

Source: Drazin and Schoonhoven (1996).

require more people team members are withdrawn from innovation teams. This makes innovation the stepchild in almost any business.

The need for more complex and elaborate theoretical models is strongly at odds with the parsimony rule in model specification, implying that one should not include too much variables in a model. This has led to a strong bifurcation in innovation science between the study of innovation at different levels of analysis of: (a) organizations (micro level), and (b) industry-level dynamics (meso level), and (c) the study of diffusion/adoption rates of innovation (macro level).

Drazin and Schoonhoven (1996) discussed the bifurcation between the context and the industry dynamics approach to innovation (see Table 2.5). They see the two approaches as 'almost antithetical'.

Fiol (1996, p. 1014) identifies another cleavage in innovation research. In her opinion, research on innovation diffusion and absorption has remained largely separate from studies of organizational determinants of innovation (*the context approach*). In order to understand the determinants of organizational innovation, Fiol recommends innovation researchers:

- to be sensitive to the effects of the broader institutional and market context that is the source of knowledge that accumulates *in organizations*;
- to pay attention to the ability of organizations to continuously build stores of knowledge and recombine them in novel ways.

Thus both the review by Drazin and Schoonhoven, and the review by Fiol, point to the importance of taking different levels into account in innovation research (multilevel research).

The barriers separating research within the different approaches impede the development of models that integrate innovation activities at the micro (organizational) level with meso-level processes in sectors and markets and macro processes that operate at a societal level.

2.4.4. Cleavage 4

The emergence of elaborate notions of innovation management also pushes the innovation research frontier towards its intellectual upper boundaries. This defines the fourth cleavage between innovation management and innovation science. The big issues really demand sound measures and models, but are they available? I briefly review some reviews on measurement issue here, one from the late 1980s (Cohen & Levin, 1989), one from the 1990s (Patel & Pavitt, 1995) and one from 2005 (Damanpour & Aravind, 2005). Their message is not very encouraging.

Cohen and Levin (1989, pp. 1061–2) characterized the empirical literature on Schumpeterian hypotheses as 'pervaded by methodological difficulties':

- equations have been loosely specified;
- the data have often been inadequate to analyze the questions at hand;
- satisfactory measures of new knowledge and its contribution to technological progress are absent;
- the construction of indicators for innovative input, especially of stocks of knowledge, is problematic, in particular with regard to depreciation rates, the specification of the time lags with which current R&D efforts are added to the stock, and the extent to which knowledge spillover generated by other firms, industries, government agencies or universities supplement the knowledge created by a firm's or a sector's own R&D;
- there are no measures of innovation that permit interpretable cross-industry comparisons;
- moreover the value of an innovation is difficult to assess, for example in the case of patents and particularly when the innovation is embodied in consumer products;
- direct measures of innovation output are the most scarce;
- data on significant/radical innovation have only been assembled for particular industries.

Patel and Pavitt (1995) review some 30 years of techno-metric research and describe three challenges in the field of techno-metrics:

- the development of information technology (IT) is measured inadequately because of a bias in survey samples toward large firms;
- the measurement of technology accumulation in developing countries is unsatisfactory;
- although improved measurement and a wider range of indicators offers more opportunities to construct theories and test them against a rich range of empirical evidence, there is still too much 'theory without numbers' and 'numbers without theory'.

Damanpour and Aravind (2005) reviewed explanatory factors for levels of process and product innovation – the organizational factor, the environmental factor. The organizational factors included by Damanpour and Aravind are: firm size, profit, capital intensity, diversification, exports, ownership, and technical knowledge resources. The environmental variables examined are competition, concentration, technological opportunity, appropriability conditions, and growth of demand. Organizational factors turned out to have a differential affect on process and product innovation. Size influences both innovation types positively, profit does not significantly affect process innovation, capital intensity, diversification and exports more consistently affect levels of product more than levels of process innovations and the effects of ownership and technical knowledge resources are mixed and inconclusive. With the exception of firm size, which impacts on process innovations more positively than upon product innovations in several studies, the review suggests that other determinants do not clearly differentiate between these innovation types.

As to the environmental factor, findings are mixed and inconclusive still. Concentration and competition were expected to have opposite associations with innovation, but do not seem to distinguish between innovation types as both have similar effects on product and process innovations in the majority of the studies. Technological opportunity, however, influences product and process innovations differently, but the studies do not conform on the direction of influence. The results across studies for appropriability conditions and growth of demand are mixed and inconclusive. In general, most environmental determinants do not differentiate between product and process innovations. Lack of differences in the impact of various determinants on product and process innovations and lack of consistent findings for many of the factors suggest that: (1) there may be contextual conditions under which the effects of the determinants on the innovation types vary; or (2) product and process innovations may be complementary and not distinct.

2.5. To be forewarned is to be forearmed: some inferences

To what degree does the world of innovation science and innovation management differ as to intellectual and practical interests in the near future?

A critical issue is that the knowledge used by the innovation manager and the knowledge of innovation scientists differs strongly despite their common object: the innovation process. IM knowledge is context-specific, embedded in regional, sectoral, and company settings, and is always both operational and strategic at the same time. Innovation managers are accountable for the project investments and are rewarded by means of performance evaluations. Therefore their world view is holistic, and they must be able to explain every day what they do, why they do it, and what will come out, although they can predict this only with high uncertainty. IS knowledge is very specific and focused – more than some ten variables in one statistical estimation is too much for a sound theoretical argument – and hopefully less context specific than IM knowledge. Otherwise it will be less valuable in the eyes of reviewers and editors of innovation science journals. Reliability, validity, and authenticity of the research models is what counts in this context, which implies in general that one chooses to model 'small problems' instead of the whole system in which innovation processes take place. These differences in knowledge base lead to a very strong divergence in focal object between the IS and IM community. Yet, this does not necessarily imply that there is no commonality in the intellectual agenda of both communities.

When one describes the evolution of R&D management into innovation management, taking the complexity approach *à la* Dooley (2004) as the starting point, the innovation process is evolving into a more complex system. Both the dimensionality of the system and the nature of interdependences in the innovation process grow. Dimensionality refers to the number of variables driving the system behaviour. For instance, the number of assets involved in innovation grows considerably over time from technology, to projects, to the whole enterprise, than with its customers, and finally to knowledge. These variables may work independently, in which case the aggregate effect is the sum of the individual effects, or there may be significant interactions between them. In innovation processes the latter situation applies: performance effects of projects, of enterprise, and value chain and are strongly related, which means that numerous contingencies must be analyzed to understand how these interdependencies affect innovative performance. The number of variables driving the systems behaviour grows with the number of actors involved, and also because an innovation process is an interest-driven process the interdependence of actors grows (Dooley, 2004, pp. 365–6).

On the basis of these two dimensions, one can infer that the innovation process is embedded in a so-called high-dimensional system with strong interdependence, which makes the performance of such a system unpredictable, and difficult to explain. This implies that, theoretically, the complexity approach, which is intellectually related to the biological and chaos school of thought, fits both the agendas of innovation researchers and innovation managers. Yet, the main implication of my review of measurement and modelling issues is that if researchers or practitioners want to move on to the more complex models and measures, they are facing a rugged landscape that cannot be cultivated without an enormous research effort. Simply leapfrogging this landscape by means of simulation and computational models is insufficient to substantiate theoretical claims implicit in the evolutionary and complexity approach.

Instead of introducing the next meta-theory, I prefer middle-range theoretical schemes that allow for the conceptualization of the big problems for innovation managers. Nevertheless, the complexity approach allows for a substantial approach of multifaceted problems facing the innovation community. For instance, a very inspiring middle-range theoretical programme can be defined in terms of search processes and learning processes. Research on the topics is still dominated by conceptual work lacking an empirical basis. The complexity definition of the innovation process implies a stronger reliance on specific types of decision making, networking, search, and learning processes that guide switching behaviour, simply because one cannot reduce complexity in a straightforward manner. In terms of learning, high-dimensional, and highly interdependent systems are managed by means of trial-and-error learning and interactive learning respectively (Lundvall, 1992; Meeus et al., 2001, 2004; Meeus & Faber, 2005). Thus, learning by failure becomes very important and this defines a 'new' empirical research agenda in innovation theory that has been ignored in management literature, by and large, except for the works in the Carnegie School of, for instance, Olsen, March, Cyert and Simon. The point is that learning by failure does inform the participants that their approach of a problem does not work, but does not give guidance how to proceed (van de Ven et al., 1999). This happens very often in the context of collaborative efforts, which is causing tensions between participants, and which another thing one would like to avoid. Innovation science could try to come up with new insights on unproductive, conflicting interactions that evolve throughout innovation processes. This is an important hidden treasure that can be studied by looking at drug innovation processes, in which interaction between researchers, physician, and patients are prescribed in regulations.

A final remark on the way the innovation community interacts. The fact that the IM community and the IS community are both internally divided with regard to the main topics and challenges they have, makes them myopic and internally oriented. New notions on innovation management advanced by the IM community are merely sensitizing, even for their own audience. At the same time, the research findings of innovation scientists are too general and detached from technological content to really guide innovation managers. Although this is a trivial observation, I think that it is an important threat to the IS community to close the doors of the university and go it alone. In the same vein, a real option would be missed if the world of innovation managers does not jump on the innovation science bandwagon. In closing this gap, management of innovation research programmes should aim at setting up creative interactions between theory driven and management research. Such an interaction would enable impartial research on management of innovation, while learning from the application and implementation of theoretical ideas concerning innovation in firms.

Bibliography

Amidon, D.M. (1996), 'The Challenge of Fifth Generation R&D', *Research-Technology Management*, 39(4), July–Aug., pp. 33–41.

Archibugi, D. & Pianta, M. (1996), 'Measuring technological change through patents and innovation surveys', *Technovation*, 16(9), pp. 451–68.

Brady, T., Rush, H., Hobday, M., Davies, A., Probert, D. & Banerjee, S. (1997), 'Tools for technology management: an academic perspective', *Technovation*, 17(8), pp. 417–26.

Cohen, W.M. & Levin, R.C. (1989), 'Empirical studies of innovation and market structure' (in Schmalensee & Willig).

Damanpour, F. (1991), 'Organizational innovation: a meta-analysis of the effects of determinant and moderators', *Academy of Management Journal*, 34, pp. 555–90.

Damanpour, F. & Aravind, D. (2005), 'Product and Process Innovations: a review of organizational and environmental determinants' (in Hage & Meeus).

Dooley, K.J. (2004), 'Complexity science models of organizational change and innovation' (in Poole & van de Ven).

Dougherty, D. & Hardy, C. (1996), 'Sustained product innovation in large, mature organizations: overcoming innovation-to-organization problems', *Academy of Management Journal*, 39(5), pp. 1120–53.

Drazin, R. & Schoonhoven, C.B. (1996),'Community, population, and organization effects on innovation: a multilevel perspective', *Academy of Management Journal*, 39, pp. 1065–83.

Falkingham, L.T. & Reeves, R. (2001), 'Four Ways of Thinking About R&D Management', *Research-Technology Management*, 44(4), July–Aug., pp. 11–14.

Fiol, M. (1996), 'Squeezing harder doesn't always work: continuing the search for consistency in innovation research', *Academy of Management Review*, 21, pp. 1012–21.

Gupta, A.K. & Wilemon, D. (1996), 'Changing Patterns in Industrial R&D management', *Journal of Product Innovation Management*, 13, pp. 497–511.

Hage, J. & Meeus, M.T.H. (eds) (2005), *Institutions, knowledge, dynamics and institutional change* (Oxford: Oxford University Press).

Hitt, M.A., Hoskisson, R.E., Johnson, R.A. & Moesel, D.D. (1996), 'The market for corporate control and firm innovation', *Academy of Management Journal*, 39, pp. 1084–119.

Industrial Research Institute (2000), ' "Biggest Problems" Facing Technology Leaders', *Research-Technology Management*, 43(5) Sept.–Oct. pp. 15–16.

Lundvall, B. (ed.) (1992), *National systems of innovation. Towards a theory of innovation and interactive learning* (London: Pinter).

Meeus, M.T.H., Oerlemans, L.A.G. & Hage, J. (2001), 'Patterns of Interactive Learning in a High Tech Region. An empirical exploration of an extended resource-based model', *Organization Studies*, 22, pp. 145–72.

Meeus, M.T.H., Oerlemans, L.A.G. & Hage, J. (2004), 'Industry – Public Knowledge Infrastructure Interaction: intra and inter-organizational explanations of interactive learning', *Industry and Innovation*, 11(4), pp. 327–52.

Meeus, M.T.H. & Faber, J. (2005), 'Interorganizational relations and innovation. A review and some speculation' (in Hage & Meeus).

Patel, P. & Pavitt, K. (1995), 'Patterns of technological activity' (in Stoneman 1995).

Poole, M.S. & van de Ven, A.H. (2004), *Handbook of Organizational Change and Innovation* (New York: Oxford University Press).

Schmalensee, R. & Willig, R.D. (1989), *Handbook of industrial organization*, Vol. II (Amsterdam: Elsevier Science).

Scott, G. (1997), 'Management of technology DELPHI study: a summary', *Technology Studies*, 4(1), pp. 164–6.

Stoneman, P. (ed.) (1995), *Handbook of the Economics of Innovation and Technological Change* (Oxford: Blackwell).

Thurlings, B. & Debackere, K. (1996), 'Trends in Managing Industrial Innovation – First Insights From a Field Survey', *Research-Technology Management*, 39(4), pp. 13–14.

Tidd, J., Bessant, J. & Pavitt, K. (2001), *Managing Innovation, Integrating Technological, Market and Organizational Change* (Chichester: Wiley, 2nd edn).

van de Ven, A.H., Polley, D., Garud, R. & Venkataraman, S. (1999), *The Innovation Journey* (Oxford: Oxford University Press).

Part II: The Dynamics of Innovation and the Role of Companies, Institutions and Territories

Introduction
Diffusion Processes in the Firms and in the Territory

Andrea Gallina and Göran Serin

The external environment and innovation

The chapters in this section stress the importance of the external environment for the company's innovation capabilities. With increasing global competition, it has become increasingly evident that, on the one hand, firms no longer can rely on their own resources for development of innovation, and on the other hand, that social and market acceptance of innovation plays an increasing role in the diffusion of new profitable ideas. This section considers these problems from two somehow complementary perspectives: the first looks at the role of proximity as a spur to industrial innovation, while the other focuses on the complexity of market and social forces in fostering innovation within and among firms. However, common to both is the role of linkages between firms, their complexity and their relationship with the actors external to the networks.

Networks, clusters and diffusion

This section of the book concerns two of the oldest and still scrutinized issues in innovation studies: clustering and diffusion. On the problem of diffusion, since the pioneering works of Griliches (1960), Mansfield (1961) and Rogers (1962) on the introduction of new hybrid corn varieties in the United States and by David (1985) on typewriting systems, researches have been focused on and confined to the confirmation and explanation of certain empirical regularity. The S-shaped sigmoid curve, which explains the lapse of time between the process of adoption and imitation, has since then been tested on different industries, sectors, countries or regions showing different speeds, but confirming some stylized facts – the relationship between the average firm size and the rate of adoption profitability (see Lissoni & Metcalfe, 1994, p. 107). This view has recently been supplemented with a large body of literature whose empirical foundations are based on the analysis of diffusion of innovation within clusters of small and medium-sized enterprises (see the chapter by Hansen and Serin). Furthermore, only recently, studies on diffusion processes have been more concerned with the dynamic of innovations and have enlarged their scope to include diffusion of knowledge not only in a geographical space, but also within companies and organizations, while including the social acceptability aspects of innovation (see Howells, Chapter 5). These trends reflect the complexity of the relationship between innovation dynamics and an increasingly problematized society.

External network organization is not a new phenomenon but has a long tradition. The literature on different forms of network organization is also substantial. These discussions have often been restricted to different forms of cooperation between firms for example alliances, partnerships and joint ventures. There is also much literature that discusses the advantages and disadvantages of networks that are compared to other forms of organizations, such as vertical integration and market organization. As a result, increasingly, studies in industrial dynamics have been cross-fertilized with theories and perspectives evolving from innovation management studies.

Managing external resources

A central aspect of innovation strategy and innovation management is therefore the question of how to integrate and manage these external resources and making them a part of the firm's own innovation base.

One expression of this increasing interest in the firm's external resources has been the growing interest in cluster theory. In this theory, it can be seen that innovation and productivity growth is not only dependent on the firm's external resources but also more precisely on a very complex interplay between different actors in the firm's environment.

The central element of cluster theory and also the most controversial, is the idea that proximity matters. According to the theory, it can be no coincidence that the most advanced companies are agglomerated in certain localities. This implies that localization matters and must be a central part of the company's overall strategy as well as its innovation strategy. The importance of proximity and agglomeration for innovation has been coupled to factors such as economies of scale, while at the same time retaining keeping flexibility, technological spillover and local rivalry between firms.

The interest in clusters is not new. For many years it has been an important part of location theory in geography where, for example, Marshall (1890 [1960]), with his 'industrial districts', stressed the importance of agglomeration for competitiveness. In economics, the cluster concept brought together a series of earlier debates and traditions that related to 'industrial districts, regional innovation systems and the learning region' (Brusco, 1982; Piore & Sabel, 1986; Raines, 2002; Cooke & Morgan, 1998). This in turn has resulted in a somewhat fuzzy cluster concept. However, this has often implied a fruitful discussion between the different traditions. Besides the classical geographical discussion, the resource and competence perspectives have also been important contributors to the cluster discussion, where these perspectives have been extended from the firm to include studying of geographical productive systems (Penrose, 1959 [1972]; Prahalad & Hamel, 1990; Lawson, 1999).

When proximity is a central part of the theory, an important issue has been to define the borders of a cluster. This has often been defined as the theory's weak point, at least in the more market-oriented form presented by Porter (see Martin & Sunley, 2003) One answer to the problem of understanding these links has been, instead, to take the point of departure in the concept of the learning region (see Cooke & Morgan, 1998). There has also been an empirical criticism that points out that the firm's innovate linkages, especially those of large firms, go beyond the region (Malmberg, 2002; MacKinnon *et al.*, 2004; Fuelhart, 1999), but there are also studies that support the view that proximity stimulates innovation (Glaeser *et al.*, 1992; Audretsch & Feldman, 1996). Studies also show that there are great differences between different industries as to how they can use the potential advantages of a cluster (see Swann & Prevezer, 1996). The different empirical results point to the need for further empirical research, to test the theory and to further develop it. One way of analyzing the importance of the cluster can be to analyze the linkages of the firms on different geographical levels, where different levels can contribute to the innovative capability of the firm in different ways depending on the type of firm (see Malmberg, 2002).

The chapters

This section includes four chapters. The first, by Cooke, addresses a central issue in cluster theory, namely the importance of proximity for research collaboration and the importance of outsourcing of research for innovation development where regional innovation systems play a central role. He stresses that there is no Schumpeterian 'one-size- fits-all' in innovation. Innovation is not a generic, universally similar process, nor does it occur in similar places. In this way analysis of innovation processes is a complex process where a Penrosian (Penrose, 1959) 'regional knowledge capabilities' approach must be applied to different industries. The article takes its point of departure in biotechnology and especially pharmaceuticals. With the point of departure in co-publishing of scientific articles between firms and universities in the United Kingdom, the article shows that geography plays a strong part in who collaborates with whom and how they rank among all of the university's co-industrial research partners. Characteristic for this industry is a larger dependence on external R&D, and especially university research, than is the case in other industries. This is manifested in a strong dominance of co-publications between academics and company researchers within pharmaceuticals. One of the author's conclusions is therefore that the search for the origins of pharmaceutical innovation must be conducted 'extramurally'. He stresses the importance of the 'knowledge value chain' in which intra-industry trading on a global, national and regional multilevel scale occurs. Innovation here occurs in bioregional innovation systems, where innovation is based on intra-industry knowledge trade with specialist knowledge nodes and networks spanning the world and specialized expertise increasingly residing in specific regions. Global key bioregional innovation systems are also identified through geographical analysis of knowledge nodes and networks with points of departure in co-publications and key indicators.

Regional knowledge capabilities are discussed from another perspective in the chapter by Hansen and Serin. Here the possibilities for developing cross border regional clusters in the Öresund region of Denmark and Sweden are analyzed, with the point of departure in the ICT sector. The conditions for establishing cross-border clusters are different and more complicated than establishing national regional clusters, that is, they are, on the one hand, dependent on EU harmonization of policies and institutions and, on the other hand, dependent on the conditions for developing cross border local capabilities related to the specific industry. A central issue of the chapter is if the integration of the ICT industry in the region should be based on agglomeration or on more developed cluster integration. An important conclusion of the study is that it is not fruitful to make a sharp distinction between the two concepts. Instead, agglomeration and clusters should be seen as part of a process and often existing simultaneously on different levels. The most important agglomeration advantage is connected to the fact that the ICT industry is dependent on in-house research and therefore in turn is dependent on a highly educated workforce supplied by universities. Cross-border integration within the Öresund region therefore contributes to developing these agglomeration advantages through Scanian universities supplying Zeeland with highly qualified labour and through cooperation between institutions, thereby developing a critical mass. With regard to the establishment of ICT clusters, it is primarily the market forces, and in this connection the development of front edge capabilities, which defines the segments that will develop into clusters. When these segments have been established, cross-border integration policies can support further development, not only by agglomeration policies in the form of education but also through cluster supporting policies in the form of network and institution building, which often are non-existent in cross border regions. The chapter concludes that the possibilities for developing cross-border clusters are dependent on the ICT firms and on these firms' own innovative capabilities, which are both related to the global level and the regional level. This view of the authors is based on the fact that the advantages of integration more are based on agglomeration advantages than on clusters. This should be seen primarily in the light of the fact that the integration is cross-border integration.

Chapter 5, by Howells, highlights the role of firms' consumption in the process of innovation, therefore focusing on the individual firms' decision-making process. The firm is the unit of the adoption process analysis. Information from the market plays a substantial role in influencing firms' consumerist behaviour and hence the internal process of adaptation of new knowledge. This internal process of adaptation, given the 'community-like' characteristic described by the author of upstream sellers and downstream buyers, leads to an externalization of the adaptation procedure into the 'community' and hence to a diffusion of the new products or processes. Another important aspect highlighted by Howell is that services play a substantial role in filtering and sweetening the adoption process by facilitating the cultural, technical, and economic understanding of the innovation. In this light, and rightly so, though only at the end, the chapter attempts to bring into the discussion the Penrosian approach to firms' capabilities in adopting new ideas and knowledge embedded in services and products purchased by the firm.

Chapter 6, by Pedersen and Pedersen, is instead a 'classical' study on the process of diffusion of innovation. Looking at the introduction of precision farming techniques by some large farmers in Denmark, the United Kingdom and the United States, the chapter addresses the question of why such a complicated technique has been successfully adopted and implemented, in some cases while not in others, and thus if, in this case the farmers, were looking at the right thing. These techniques, using complex satellite positioning systems, enable farmers to have a complete picture of their farm, which allows them to save inputs in some areas and put more where it is needed. It is a system that may increase productivity and reduce cost and negative externalities in the environment. In reality this complex system is doing, in a more sophisticated way, the job that the farmers have always done in their farms for centuries: intervening where and when necessary, avoiding waste and to identify areas in need of more water and fertilizer.

Two aspects were mainly taken into account in the analysis of the factors promoting or discouraging the adoption process: on the one hand, the complexity of this technological system, with many providers of different hardware, software and knowledge and the different decision support systems, which still give the final decision to the farmer, and on the other hand, the economic benefits (the returns from investments) arising from the adoption of the new farming technique. Farms need to be very large and the value added that stems from increased efficiency is not translated into higher prices for the final product paid by consumers (unable to distinguish between a normal corn and a corn produced with precision farming techniques), which renders the investment less attractive. The main result of the survey carried out so far is that the benefits of this technology are very limited in terms of saving inputs and in terms of contribution to the environment following a more rational dispersion of chemical fertilizers in the field. The relation size/innovation or early adoption (see Rothwell & Zegveld, 1982) is definitively confirmed in this case.

The classical problems of selection and adoption, the two ways to look at the diffusion process, are only apparently tackled in the chapter probably due to the limited availability of empirical material. However, the study presents some very interesting hints – the importance for the process of innovation of military research expenditures and the importance of information on its benefit. The case of diffusion studied in this chapter can result in a failure if costs are not sunken with the introduction of more competitors and if information on the alleged advantages of this crop system is not spread in the market. Consumers are reluctant to pay higher prices for little and unknown safety and quality improvements (such as the use of less fertilizer on the crops). But farmers are traditionally one of the slowest adopters of innovations. Size in this case represents another structural limit that can be overcome more easily in the United States than in Europe, where small and medium farmers still predominate. Another interesting hint of the study is the 'fascination' of the possibility offered by this new farming technique. Even farmers today are attracted by the myth of modernity and efficiency embedded in a sophisticated machine born for military purposes. This in turn highlights another largely unresolved issue – the application of this technology in productive systems with high labour surpluses that will be replaced by sophisticated farming machines. While the diffusion of innovation in highly industrialized economies takes into account the environmental surplus, the diffusion of this innovation in more traditional agricultural systems needs to take into account the likely social deficits that it can produce. Modern technologies can and have to be increasingly evaluated for their social and environmental impact and especially in sectors and countries for which the priorities are clearly others.

Bibliography

Audretsch, D.B. & Feldman, M.P. (1996), 'Knowledge spillovers and the geography of innovation and production', *American Economic Review*, 86, pp. 630–40.

Brusco, S. (1982), 'The Emilian Model: Productive Decentralisation and Social Integration', *Cambridge Journal of Economics*, 6, pp. 167–84.

Cooke, P. & Morgan, K. (1998), *The Associational Economy: Firms, Regions and Innovations* (Oxford: Oxford University Press).

David, P.A. (1985), 'Clio and the Economics of QWERTY', *American Economic Review*, 75(2), May, pp. 332–7.

Dodgson, M. & Rothwell, R. (eds) (1994), *The Handbook of Industrial Innovation* (Cheltenham: Edward Elgar).

Fuelhart, K. (1999), 'Localization and the use of information sources: the case of the carpet industry', *European Urban and Regional Studies*, 6, pp. 39–58.

Glaeser, E.L. *et al.* (1992), 'Growth in Cities', *Journal of Political Economy*, 100, pp. 1126–52.

Griliches, Z. (1960), 'Hybrid corn and the economies of innovation', *Science*, 132, pp. 275–80.

Lawson, C. (1999), 'Towards a Competence Theory of the Region', *Cambridge Journal of Economics*, 23(2), pp. 151–66.

Lissoni, F. & Metcalfe J.S. (1994), 'Diffusion of innovation ancient and modern: a review of the main themes' (in Dodgson & Rothwell).

MacKinnon, D. *et al.* (2004), 'Network, Trust and Embeddedness Amongst SMEs in the Aberdeen Oil Complex', *Entrepreneurship and Regional Development*, 16, pp. 87–106.

Malmberg, A. (2002), *Klusterdynamik och regional näringslivsutveckling* (Institutet för näringspolitiska studier).

Mansfield, E. (1961), 'Technical change and the rate of imitation', *Econometrica*, 29, pp. 741–66.

Marshall, A., 'Industrial organization, continued. The concentration of specialized industries in particular localities' in A. Marshall (ed.) (1890 [1960]) *Priciples of Economics* (London: Macmillan).

Martin, R. & Sunley, P. (2003), 'Deconstructing Clusters. Chaotic Concept or Policy Panacea?', *Journal of Economic Geography*, 3, pp. 5–35.

Penrose, E. (1959 [1972]), *The Theory of the Growth of the Firm* (Oxford: Blackwell).

Piore, M.J. & Sabel, C.F. (1986), *The Second Industrial Divide* (New York: Basic Books).

Prahalad, C.K. & Hamel, G. (1990), 'The Core Competence of the Corporation', *Harvard Business Review*, 68(3), May–June, pp. 79–91.

Raines, P. (2002), *Cluster Development and Policy: EPRC Studies in European Policy* (Ashgate: Aldershot).

Rogers, E.M. (1962), *Diffusion of Innovations* (New York: Free Press).

Rothwell R. & Zegveld, W. (1982), *Innovation and the Small and Medium Sized Firm* (London: Pinter).

Swann, P. & Prevezer, M. (1996), 'A comparison of the dynamics of industrial clustering in computing and biotechnology', *Research Policy*, 25, pp. 1139–57.

3
Co-publishing and Innovation. *Bioscience Defies a 'One-Size-Fits-All' Definition*

Philip Cooke

3.1. Introduction

To what extent is innovation comparable across industries? The Schumpeterian literature suggests it is – thus it can be radical, incremental or based on recombination in product, process or organization to name two sets of three of the generic types commonly analyzed in innovation studies conducted from a neo-Schumpeterian perspective. But, as Henderson *et al.* (1999) show, Schumpeterian thinking was driven by an engineering metaphor in which 'gales of creative destruction' removed swathes of industry, and certainly skills, as firms unable to compete with new technologies became bankrupt. This occurred classically in textiles with the handloom weavers and the onset of factory organization and power-loom technology, it happened when sailing ships gave way to steam, and it is happening today as biotechnology replaces synthetic, fine chemistry in pharmaceuticals. Or is it? That is the question that prompts this chapter.

Innovation studies at the national level have declined absolutely and relatively, technological systems studies fluctuate year by year and sectoral studies remain in the minority. But regional innovation studies, judged by number of publications in refereed journals have risen exponentially since 1992. A reasonable deduction is that interest in microanalyses of innovation has grown as that in macro-studies has waned. The chapter suggests a problem of overwhelming complexity in national studies is more tractable, though still difficult, at lower sectoral or spatial scales. Thus it tries to explain the relative success of regional innovation studies, as an intellectual (and policy) field, and contributes research of interest in technological more than sectoral systems studies.

It then moves on to an assessment of ways that these two sub-fields of regional and technological systems analyses may converge, given 'clustering' tendencies of a post-Porterian kind, notably in science-based industry, specifically biotechnology and its two main applications fields of pharmaceuticals and agro-food. From this, it is argued that, on the one hand, manageable research on firm innovation 'capabilities' can be conducted, that, on the other hand, assists understanding of the dynamics of geographical variety in knowledge networks and capabilities that increasingly define places and ways in which innovation is achieved.

3.2. Schumpeter's legacy

Schumpeter showed remarkable prescience that has served the rise in interest and importance of understanding the supposed causal relationship between economic growth, competitiveness, productivity and innovation. Sometimes called the 'Washington Consensus' (Kay, 2003; Capra, 2002) because it is adhered to by the United States, G7, International Monetary Fund, World Trade Organization, and World Bank to name a few, it might as well be called the Harvard Business School Consensus since many of its proponents work there, and one, Michael Porter (1998) has added regional 'clusters' to the recipe for innovative, productive, competitive success. Like Krugman (1995) before him, he realized that economics had been missing an important point for a generation and that geographical location mattered, the world did not spin on the head of a pin, and that innovations usually come from *somewhere*. However, unlike Krugman (2000), who condemns his own 'simplistic two-location models of regional growth', Porter has yet to subject his master concept to auto critique.

We can do it for him. His definition of 'clusters' is ridiculously elastic, comprising anything from neighbourhoods to nations; he never shows the inner workings of a 'cluster' to demonstrate the linkages he asserts exist from maps of macro-data that descriptively reveal geographical concentration or agglomeration of industry; thus he cannot demonstrate what he asserts, namely that clustering raises productivity, hence competitiveness and growth. And he can never show the connection between innovation and clustering for the same reason. Why? Because his is primarily a 'markets' analysis that never goes as deeply into the mechanisms that induce innovation in the manner that even Schumpeter did.

Nowadays, in what many see as a 'knowledge economy' that usually implies science, not just for science-driven industry, but also as Smith (2001) has argued for mundane industries like the food sector. Actually, as we shall see, the food sector is far from mundane in respect of its innovation interactions with science.

This means paying attention increasingly to the sourcing of science by industry. It is widely understood that industry has in recent years reduced the amount of in-house research and development (R&D) it conducts largely on grounds of shareholder outrage at its costs for modest return, but also because of the rise of what Stankiewicz (2001) calls a true 'research industry'. This includes, of course, university research institutes and centres of expertise or excellence as well as public research organizations (PROs) as well as specialist research consultancies, consultant engineers, environmental consultancies and the like, that seem to have burgeoned greatly in recent years.

For example, Schamp *et al.* (2004) show how in Germany in the 1990s engineering consultancy grew so much in scale and so swiftly that it became powerful enough to control large parts of the German automotive supply chain. Suppliers developed the capability to produce modules and systems, increasingly delegating to external engineering consultants. Such outsourcing means the final automotive assembler has the simultaneous problem of safeguarding internal and accessing external knowledge, especially regarding control of model design and development. Accordingly, they adopt a strategy of defining their 'core competencies' through the generation of unique knowledge, which is difficult to imitate, such as a brand or development capability. Concept specification, quality assessment, final model integration, and service provider benchmarking would be included. Schamp *et al.* found that despite this, consultants shared the view that automotive producers no longer have core knowledge of engineering and design. Rather, automotive producer core knowledge became the capability to coordinate and control value chains.

This is not unique to that industry, since it applies for different reasons to pharmaceuticals and is beginning in agro-food biotechnology also, as is shown later. Moreover, for pharmaceuticals there is evidence not only of a substantial outsourcing of basic scientific research but also growing incapability in the development aspects of knowledge generation which, despite claims to the contrary by, for example, Nightingale (2000) that 'big pharma' had mastered high throughput screening (HTS), the supercomputer-based technique by which 'inhibitor' compounds are identified to counter disease-causing small molecules, it seems for many to have proved an expensive investment error causing them to outsource even that core combinatorial chemistry competence. But we know where to look to find from where 'big pharma' gets its science and innovation externally, and some of that activity can be observed quantitatively through joint publication, joint patenting and certain kinds of R&D database information. In this chapter, I devote space to the first and third of those data sources. This is less easy in other industries, such as automotives, metals and materials because they are not heavy scientific research producers, and as we have seen with automotive engineering research, design and development are outsourced to specialist service providers in the market, hence the transaction details are not registered in official statistics. Thus, to determine the extent of innovation in some manufacturing sectors would require examining service sector data on consultancy services.

What can be said with confidence is that unlike bioscience-driven industry, traditional and even high-technology industries such as electronics and software are not heavy investors in university research, at least in the United Kingdom, as the following discussion makes clear. A relatively modestly cited report on co-publication between universities and industry reveals some interesting evidence, albeit for just one EU country (the UK), regarding knowledge sources for innovation (Calvert & Patel, 2002). In their study they investigated which firms and industries were most engaged in research that led to co-publication of scientific articles in respected academic journals. They selected the five leading UK universities in science and technology as judged by their shares of co-publishing of research with industry. Two periods were examined but in the adaptive data re-analysis presented below we need only be concerned with the second period, 1995–2000.

In brief, three things of interest are shown in Table 3.1. First, geography plays a surprisingly strong part in who collaborates with whom and how they rank among all of the university's industrial co-publication partners. Thus the UK's smaller, newer pharma firm AstraZeneca's R&D is near Manchester in the north and is first partner for Manchester and Nottingham but also Imperial (London) that is similarly, a so-called 'redbrick' university. Older and larger (for a time global leader in scale) GlaxoWellcome (now GlaxoSmithKline) are headquartered and do most R&D near Oxford and Cambridge, with which it is first partners. This is also pronounced with biotechnology firms, where British Biotech (now OSI) is a high-ranking co-publication partner with nearby Oxford University, as to a lesser extent is Oxford BioMedica. The West Pharmaceutical Services Drug Delivery & Clinical Research Centre is

Table 3.1.   UK top five co-publishing universities: pharma-food rankings and share of total university–industry co-publications, 1995–2000

Firm	Cambridge	Imperial	Oxford	Manchester	Nottingham
AstraZeneca	3	1	2	1	1
GlaxoWellcome	1	2	1	2	3
SmithKline Beecham	4	3	3	3	2
Unilever	5	–	5	6	–
British Biotech	–	–	4	10	–
Pfizer	–	–	8	9	6
Aventis	–	7	–	–	9
West Pharma	–	–	–	–	4
Oxford BioMedica	–	–	7	–	–
BASF	–	–	–	–	7
Roche	–	–	–	8	–
Johnson & Johnson	–	–	–	–	10
U–I publication share	57.9%	63.0%	68.3%	66.1%	64.8%
U–I articles (N)	170	153	126	120	123
U–I/total: mean	5.0%	5.2%	5.1%	5.0%	5.6%

Source: Derived from Calvert and Patel (2002).

located in Nottingham, where also is its fourth highest co-publication partner. Although BASF's R&D facility in Nottingham was closed and donated to Nottingham's second (Trent) university, it still features high among Nottingham University's co-publication partners. Most of the other lower-ranked partners are not so physically proximate.

Second, probably not too surprisingly, it is still noteworthy that the main university co-publishers co-publish most with indigenous businesses and at relatively lower ranking with less frequency concerning foreign partners. This once again suggests proximity of a national not only a local nature is of some importance despite the hype about globalization, deterritorialization, and the 'death of distance' (Cairncross, 1997). Hence it is clear for the United Kingdom, and as suggested below, other countries in which proximity matters considerably in innovation interactions between research co-publishing partners from industry and university, as Jaffe *et al.* (1993) showed a decade ago, was also the case regarding entrepreneur–academic interactions regarding patent-citations. More to the point, of course, is that this is further evidence of the existence of notable research outsourcing, long-established in pharmaceuticals but being learned later by automotive and, as announced recently as Philips' new 'Open Innovation' (after Chesbrough, 2003) R&D strategy, also in electronics (van den Biesen, 2004).

Table 3.2. Top twenty university–industry publishing collaborator firms, 1995–2000

Firm	Position	Firm	Position
GlaxoWellcome	1*	British Nuclear Fuels	11
AstraZeneca	2*	Roche	12*
SmithKline Beecham	3*	Celltech	13*
Unilever	4*	Merck	14*
ICI	5	Eli Lilly	15*
Pfizer	6*	Shell	16
British Telecom	7	Rolls Royce	17
AEA Technology	8	Novartis	18*
Aventis	9*	Hewlett Packard	19
BP	10	GEC/Marconi	20

Note: * is pharmaceuticals, food and biotechnology.
Source: Derived from Calvert and Patel (2002).

Table 3.3. High and low ranking university–industry co-publishing sectors, 1995–2000

High ranking sectors	Annual average U–I co-publications	Low ranking sectors	Annual average U–I co-publications
1. Pharmaceuticals	659	15. Metals	29
2. Chemicals	128	16. Materials	25
3. Utilities	107	17. Machinery	18
4. Biotechnology	92	17. Software	18
5. Electronics	88	19. Automotive	15
6. Food	82	20. Electrical	11

Source: Adapted from Calvert and Patel (2002).

But third, and most striking of all, is that although co-publications involving university and industry collaboration are on the whole only 5 per cent of total publications in the top collaborating universities, as much as 68 per cent is accounted for by the pharmaceuticals, biotechnology and agro-food industries. The remaining minority, as shown in Table 3.3, covers industries such as electrical and automotive engineering, software, materials, metals and machinery. These industries have very low co-publication statistics with university researchers in the United Kingdom. I inquire if this is a special UK effect later in the chapter, but the high score for pharmaceuticals suggests even hypothetically that this is unlikely to be a mere effect of the United Kingdom having formerly three, now two, indigenous, global pharmaceuticals multinationals on its territory.

This is despite the evidence that both national and local proximity played a far more than accidental role in facilitating co-publications and, presumably, collaborative research upon which publication rests and from which innovation might occur. Table 3.2 lists the top 20 co-publishing firms in the UK in 1995–2000, distinguishing those in pharma, biotech and agro-food from the rest. It reveals in fairly clear and simple terms the overwhelming presence of the pharma-food nexus as important co-publication partners. It also confirms the top linkage between UK pharma-food showing in the first four positions. Foreign pharma is pronounced in the lower half of the table.

Underlining earlier statements regarding pharma dominance in university–industry co-publication patterns, Table 3.3 identifies the sectors in the top and bottom six collaborating co-publishers. It is clear from this that pharmaceuticals easily outperform all of the others added together. But among the laggards, biotechnology and agro-food perform creditably. Hence, pharmaceuticals R&D is far more performed with co-publishing as an output of joint research than might normally be expected. So, finally, for each of the sectors of interest, which firms co-publish with which sectors? To which is added, for further minor interest, the not-too-distant sector of chemicals for simple comparison. The point of this is that it shows new universities and firms coming into the reckoning, but also that the elite universities (i.e., Oxford and Cambridge) are courted most by the elite co-publishing sectors, while the strong research but more 'red-brick' civic universities and the less elite co-publishing firms now find each other. This is especially the case for co-publishing by chemicals firms.

Hence we may conclude three key things about university–industry research collaboration in the United Kingdom, and specifically that, which successfully produces scientific journal articles reporting outcomes and discoveries in the form of co-publications. The first is that proximity matters for universities (Table 3.1) slightly more than for firms (Table 3.4). Thus Cambridge and Oxford both had nearby GlaxoWellcome as their top co-publishing partner, but for GlaxoWellcome its top co-publishing partner was Manchester University. Nearby SmithKline published most with Cambridge University, for whom it was, however, only its fourth most important co-publishing partner. In biotechnology, the partnership pattern is similar, with London-based Celltech favouring Oxford, but for Oxford, Celltech is a minor partner that scores lower than Oxford-based British Biotech and Oxford BioMedica, and is in fact too low to appear in Table 3.1.

Table 3.4.   Top co-publishing partner firms and universities, 1995–2000

Industry	Company	University
Pharmaceuticals	AstraZeneca	Oxford
	GlaxoWellcome	Manchester
	SmithKline Beecham	Cambridge
Biotechnology	Celltech	Oxford
	British Biotech	Cambridge
	Nycomed Amersham	Nottingham
Agro-food	Unilever	Cambridge
	CC Food	Nottingham
	Nestlé	Bristol
Chemicals	ICI	Liverpool
	AkzoNobel	Cardiff
	BASF	London, Imperial

Source: Derived from Calvert and Patel (2002).

Yet British Biotech favours Cambridge, but does not appear in Cambridge's top-ten favoured partners. This shows Cambridge's co-publishing partnership portfolio to be far more substantial than Oxford's, a feature that should not surprise since Cambridge has traditionally been the UK's leading scientific research university. Finally, Nycomed Amersham, based in Cardiff, breaks the mould by favouring Nottingham, strong in diagnostics and platform technology research, whereas Cardiff, at that time was not strong in bio scientific research. In agro-food, the two European giants, Unilever and Nestlé favour Cambridge and Bristol, the Nestlé–Bristol link being geographically proximate. Adding in chemicals merely shows a long historic connection between ICI and nearby city Liverpool, but BASF, also a biopharma company, links to Imperial College on research excellence, as does Dutch pharmaco-chemical company AkzoNobel with Cardiff University (Environmental Water Management Research Centre).

The second, more obvious feature is the dominance of pharmaceuticals in presumably funding research which then produces six times more co-publications between academics and company researchers than the next sector, which is chemicals, closely followed by biotechnology and agro-food. Considering that, except biotechnology, these are all industries dominated by large corporate multinational businesses traditionally possessing in-house R&D capabilities, it is noteworthy that they are especially inclined to outsource so much. Recent estimates of the R&D outsourcing from pharmaceuticals firms put the figure at 30 per cent of total pharma

R&D budgets, with an expectation that this will rise to 50 per cent by 2010. Clearly, it will be increasingly necessary to search for the origin of pharmaceuticals innovation, itself increasingly biotechnology-based, not intramurally but extramurally in specialist, dedicated biotechnology firms (DBFs), university research centres and other PROs.

Finally, *bioregional innovation systems* are thus characteristic of out-sourced knowledge transfer and commercialization in biopharmaceuti-cals, also but to a lesser extent in agro-food and biotechnology sectors. Thus there is clearly no 'one-size-fits-all' pattern to innovation, with many sectors not pursuing such practices, including software and mate-rials industries. However, evidence has emerged that electronics multi-nationals such as Philips have revolutionized their research portfolio along lines pioneered by pharmaceuticals, and automotive firms increasingly complete the outsourcing of R&D, but to specialist design engineering consultancies – a further sign that there is no 'cookie-cutter' reality to innovation across sectors, despite generic models that suggest it can be understood in Schumpeterian vocabularies of 'incremental', 'recombinant',[1] and 'radical' innovation. Where the neo-Schumpeterian school is accurate, is in characterizing innovative as 'interactive'. However, in agro-food and biopharmaceuticals, key interactions involve burgeoning intra-industry trade among producers at distinct points in the knowledge value chain (see Cooke, 2004a). These are geographically proximate to some degree but also significantly global before interaction between producer and final consumer, heavily protected in these sectors by national regulatory systems.

3.3. Where are key bioregional innovation systems, and with what specialization?

Studying globalization through geographical analysis of knowledge nodes and networks, the nodes being in regional innovation systems, is 'ahead of the curve' research currently and to say anything, certain somewhat constrained approaches have to be made. However, the use of co-publication and co-patenting data are of enormous significance. Thus far we can say only a limited amount based upon co-publication data among global bioregional innovation systems. However, the results suggest strongly the correctness of the finding from analysis of single nation (US) biotechnology research collaborations by Powell *et al.* (1996) that innovation no longer lies in codified knowledge held in a place, but in tacit knowledge interactions that reside in networks, increasingly the global networks. As 'open science' evolves into 'open

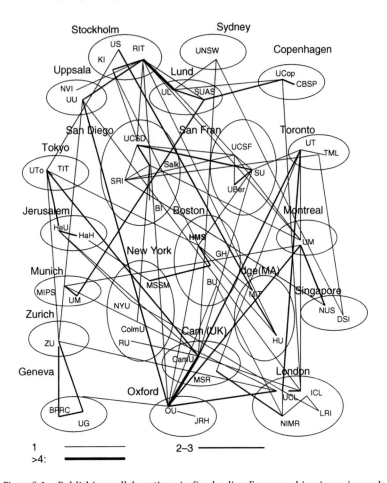

Figure 3.1.   Publishing collaborations in five leading European bioscience journals

innovation' (Chesbrough, 2003), differentiation and specialization come to characterize global regional innovation systems, especially clearly in the case of global bioregional innovation systems.

This is underlined with respect to Figure 3.1 and Figure 3.2, which map collaborative publishing between leading scientists in important or potentially significant bioregions worldwide 1998–2004. Figure 3.1 refers to collaborative publication aimed at the top five European biotechnology journals, and Figure 3.2 registers them for the four leading US journals. Three aspects are of special interest here. First, strong

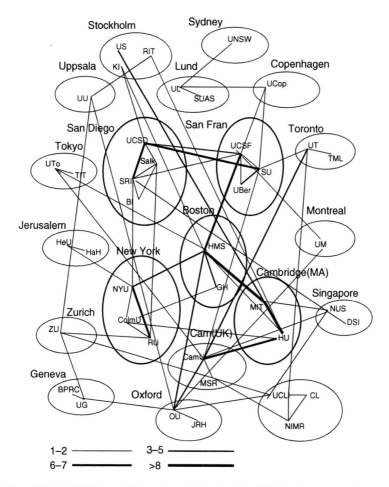

Figure 3.2. Publishing collaborations in four leading US bioscience journals

bioregions in Europe and the United States collaborate significantly and intensely in collaborative publishing in US journals. Second, intensity of collaboration among European (and Canadian) bioregions is more pronounced in leading European journals than US collaborations. Third, collaboration activity for publication in leading European journals (e.g., nature biotechnology) is less intense than for US journals (e.g., *Cell*).

However, in either case the main bioregions listed below are the most active collaborative publishing bases, even though in cases like New York and London, they score less highly regarding commercialization indicators than might be expected. A further point worth noting, which underlines commentary on Japan's weak showing in current bioregion analysis, is that Tokyo is far less active than might be expected, and involved comparably to Uppsala, Zurich or Jerusalem, but far less than Cambridge or Oxford. Figure 3.1 has the nodes and networks for five leading European journals.

In Figure 3.2, the network dynamic is to a considerable extent inverted, in that the US collaborative publishing bioregion 'nodes' are much more active, and the European and other 'nodes' are more active towards them than the reverse in Figure 3.1. This is thus an excellent way of demonstrating the operation of power in network relationships. This is because Boston and Cambridge, Massachusetts, are clearly the most active research publication collaborators, Boston being the location of leading research institutes related to Harvard Medical School. The University of California Scripps Institute and Stanford nodes interact significantly both internally and with regard to each other. Inter-nodal collaborations with Harvard Medical School from UC San Francisco Medical School are strong, but so are those from UC San Diego and Scripps with New York University and Rockefeller University, a specialist medical and bio-scientific campus once headed by retroviruses Nobel laureate David Baltimore.

To characterize the achievement of bioregional success more broadly, I begin with a summary of one US study (Cortright & Mayer, 2002) that guides the effort that follows, to perform broadly comparable indicator-based analysis for key non-US clusters. In Table 3.5, a summary is given of comparative institutional and business strengths in seven leading US biotechnology clusters. This shows in some detail the kinds of network nodes in reasonable proximity that give the possibility of systemic innovation to such locations. The predominance of Boston and San Francisco and the differences between the former (also New York) and the Californian centres are strikingly revealed by these data. Boston's life scientists generate of the order of $285,000 each per annum in National Institutes of Health research funding (New York's generate some $288,000). San Diego's considerably smaller number of life scientists generates $480,000 per capita, substantially more than in Northern California where it is some $226,000. North Carolina, with the smallest number of life scientists in Table 3.5, scores highest at $510,000 per capita, although Seattle, at $276,000 is comparable to Boston, New York and San Francisco. How to interpret these statistics? One way is to note the very large amounts of funding from 'big pharma' going especially to the Boston, and to a lesser extent New York and both Californian centres.

Table 3.5.   Profiles and key indicators of US bioscience clusters

Location	Life scientists (1998)	NIH ($) (2000) (billion)	NIH $ labs (in top 100, 2000)	Pharma alliances ($1996–2001) (billion)	Biotechs (2001)	VC (2000) (million)
Boston	4,980	1.42	10	3.92	141	601.5
New York	4,790	1.38	8	1.73	127	151.6
N. Carolina	910	0.47	2	0.19	72	192.0
San Diego	1,430	0.68	2	1.62	94	432.8
San Fran./SV	3,090	0.70	3	1.21	152	1,063.5
Seattle	1,810	0.50	2	0.58	30	91.1
Wash–Balt.	6,670	0.95	3	0.36	83	49.5

Source: Adapted from Cortright and Mayer (2002). NIH = National Institutes of Health; VC = venture capital.

Table 3.6.   Performance indicators for US bioscience clusters

Location	NIH/life scientist ($)	Pharma/biotech ($) (million)	VC per biotech ($) (million)
Boston	285,000	27.8	4.26
New York	288,000	13.6	1.18
N. Carolina	510,000	2.0	2.66
San Diego	480,000	16.1	4.60
San Fran./SV	226,000	8.0	7.00
Seattle	276,000	19.3	3.03
Wash–Balt.	145,000	4.3	0.60

Source: Developed from Cortright and Mayer (2002). These variables are derived by simple division of columns 2 and 3, 5 and 6, and 6 and 7 in Table 3.1.

A second noteworthy indicator is that Boston and San Francisco/ Silicon Valley captured one half of the venture capital invested in the seven locations listed in Table 3.5 for the year 2000. In other words – it may be a question of maturity versus immaturity as San Francisco and Boston are the earliest biotechnology locations – firms have grown and wider funding opportunities have arisen from private investors, making for less reliance upon NIH grants. Hence, as Table 3.6 shows, while San Diego performs well on all three key indicators, it does much less well than Boston regarding 1996–2001 'big pharma' funding per DBF, faring worse than even relative newcomer Seattle on that indicator, though noticeably better than San Francisco/Silicon Valley. Contrariwise, San Diego marginally outperforms Boston on the venture capital per DBF indicator, but is in turn, outperformed massively by San Francisco/Silicon Valley, as is

Boston. Thus interestingly the USA's three main high-performing biosciences clusters reveal:

- Boston being favoured for 'big pharma' licensing and associated milestone payments;
- San Diego being highly successful in receipt of NIH funding per life scientist;
- San Francisco/Silicon Valley being the most venture capital driven of the three.

Of further interest are the indications that newcomers North Carolina and Seattle most resemble the San Diego and Boston models respectively. Knowledge management and knowledge spillovers may be expected to vary according to these distinctive 'governance' models, with 'pharma' more prominent in the first, research management in the second and venture capital in the third.

Three key aspects have been shown with implications for understanding of knowledge management, knowledge spillovers and the roles of collaboration and competition in bioregions. The first is that two kinds of proximity are important to the functioning of knowledge complexes such as biosciences in Boston and the northern and southern Californian clusters. These are geographical and functional proximity (Rallet & Torre, 1998). The first involves, in particular, medical research infrastructure for *exploration* knowledge as well as venture capital for *exploitation* knowledge, that is, for research on the one hand, and commercialization on the other hand. The second point is that where *exploration* knowledge infrastructure is strong, that nexus leads the knowledge management process, pulling more distant 'big pharma' governance elements behind it. Where, by contrast, *exploitation* knowledge institutions are stronger than exploration, they may, either as venture capital or 'big pharma', play a more prominent role. But in either case the key animator is the R&D and exploitation intensive DBF. The DBFs are key 'makers' as well as 'takers' of local and global spillovers; research institutions are more 'makers' than 'takers' locally and globally, while 'big pharma' is nowadays principally a 'taker' of localized spillovers from different innovative DBF clusters. It is then global marketer of these and proprietorial (licensed or acquired) knowledge, generated with a large element of public financing but appropriated privately.

For obvious reasons to do with scale, especially of varieties of financing of DBFs from big pharma on the one hand, and venture capitalists, on the other hand, we conclude that Boston, San Francisco and San Diego are the top US bioregions that also have the greater cluster characterization of prominent spinout from key knowledge centres, an institutional support set-up such as Boston's Massachusetts Biotechnology Council, San Diego's CONNECT network and San Francisco's California Healthcare Institute, and major investment from both main pillars of the private investment sector. I have attempted to access comparable data from many and diverse statistical sources that justify and represent the successful or potentially successful clusters from outside of the United States, and these are shown in Table 3.7, excluding the four lesser or unclustered of the seven US bioregions.[2]

We saw how public research funding contributed significantly to the advantage enjoyed for basic research by the Cambridge–Boston bioregion compared with San Francisco and San Diego. Recent data taken from NIH allocations for 2002 (Table 3.7) confirm the strengthening of

Table 3.7. Comparison of bioregion NIH research funding, 2002

Rank (Top 300)	Institution	NIH research ($ million)	Rank	Institution	NIH research ($ million)
Massachusetts			San Francisco		
12	Harvard U.	248.6	4	UCSF Med.S.	319.7
18	Mass Gen.	232.1	16	Stanford U.	226.3
22	Brig. & W.	192.4	47	UC Davis	103.1
34	Boston U.	132.3	53	UC Berkeley	81.6
51	Dana-Farber	96.3	117	UC Law.Labs	33.3
52	Beth. Israel	94.8	144	N. Cal. Inst.	22.5
57	Whitehead I.	91.1	169	Chil. Hos. Oakl.	14.7
60	U. Mass. Med.	87.6	206	UC Santa Cruz	11.5
63	MIT	77.8	247	UC Livermore	8.8
76	Children's H.	62.8	253	N. Cal. Cancer C.	5.2
88	Tufts U.	49.9	270	Chiron	2.2
120	N. Eng. M.C.	27.7	San Francisco total		829.0
133	Boston M.C.	27.2			
148	Joslin Diabetes	20.9	San Diego		
166	N. Eng. Rsch. I	14.7	17	UCSD	244.7
200	Mass Eye-Ear	11.9	25	Scripps I.	185.6
210	UM Amherst	11.3	96	Salk Inst.	44.9
228	Boston Biomed.	8.5	108	Burnham I.	37.2
290	Boston College	6.3	167	SD State U.	16.2
Massachusetts total		1,494.2	199	Loma Linda U.	13.3
California total		1,381.5	227	La Jolla Inst.	10.6
			San Diego total		552.5

Source: National Institutes of Health.

the Boston bioregion since 2000. Clearly, the statistics reveal that the Greater Boston bioregion retains its lead over San Francisco and San Diego combined with regard to research funding won from the National Institutes of Health. This is because its institutional base is far broader and deeper. This is revealed in the large number of substantial mid-range institutions that are either independent universities, research institutes, research hospitals and specialist centres such as Dana-Farber, Joslin, Beth Israel, Whitehead and so on. Both California bioregions are heavily dependent upon the University of California system.

We can say quite unexceptionally that Canada's biopharmaceuticals regional innovation systems challenge many elsewhere in the world. The process of bioregional cluster evolution has occurred mainly through academic entrepreneurship supported by well-found research infrastructure and local venture capital capabilities. In Israel, there is a highly promising group of bioregions including also Rehovot and Tel Aviv as well as the main concentration in Jerusalem. Israel is larger quantitatively than all the US clusters, but of course DBFs are lesser in scale. In Europe, those in Table 3.8 are regularly listed as main concentrations in consultancy and governmental reports.[3] In relation to Switzerland, however, new data have been accessed that show Switzerland along with Sweden and possibly Denmark to be high potential bioregions.

Table 3.8.   Core biotechnology firms, 2000: comparative US and European performance indicators

Location DBFs		Life scientists	VC ($) (million)	Big pharma funding ($)
Boston	141	4,980	601.5	800 m/annum 96–01
San Francisco	152	3,090	1,063.5	400 m/annum 96–01
San Diego	94	1,430	432.8	320 m/annum 96–01
Toronto	73	1,149	120.0	NA
Montreal	72	822	60.0	NA
Munich	120	8,000	400.0	54 m (2001)
Stockholm-Upp.	87	2,998	90.0	250 m (2002)
Lund-Medicon	104	5,950	80.0	300 m (2002)
Cambridge	54	2,650	250.0	105 m (2000)
Oxford	46	3,250	120.0	70 m (2000)
Zurich	70	1,236	57.0	NA
Singapore	38	1,063	200.0	88 m (2001)
Jerusalem	38	1,015	300.0	NA

Sources: NIH; NRC; BioM, Munich; VINNOVA, Sweden; Dorey (2003); Kettler and Casper (2000); ERBI, UK; Lawton-Smith (2004); Kaufmann *et al.* (2003).

Based on numbers of DBFs, relations with indigenous and overseas big pharma, and not least rates of publication per head of population (Figures 3.1 and 3.2), these countries are clearly making an active contribution to European biotechnology. Finally, Singapore has been included because it is, after Israel, one of Asia's stronger biotechnology presences and its government is, as we shall see, highly committed to making Singapore a success by investing significant public funds in building a biotechnology presence of global proportions by attracting foreign investment, headhunting foreign 'talent' and stimulating indigenous spinout activity.

3.4. Concluding remarks

The argument herein has been straightforward, namely that innovation is not a generic, universally similar process, nor does it occur in similar places. Rather, I have shown how it is a mistake to expect to find the sources of innovation only or mainly in the firm, even in the large multinational firm. This legacy from the Schumpeterian era is now open to serious questioning. Contrariwise, we now see a 'knowledge value chain' (see Cooke, 2004a), in which intra-industry trading on a global, national and regional multi-level scale habitually occurs. This has been the pattern in biotechnology since 1976 when Boyer and Cohen, funded by Eli Lilly for their insulin research, discovered genetic engineering and, with Robert Swanson the Kleiner, Perkins, Caufield and Byers venture capitalist, created Genentech, the first biotechnology company. The story of how Novartis bought and retains a majority share in Genentech to access gene therapy know-how, and its compatriot Roche did similarly with Chiron, also from San Francisco, is told elsewhere (see Zeller, 2004). That Novartis, in particular, then invested not only in research alliances in San Diego, when the epicentre of bio scientific research moved to immunology after the Aids scare, but also a $50 million partnership with the Scripps Research Institute *and* an even bigger investment in establishing the Genomics Institute of the Novartis Research Foundation (GNF) all in San Diego, shows how the bioregional innovation system exerts reverse power in forcing multinational capital to be a supplicant of research laboratory complexes. Normally, in history small firm DBFs and universities would go cap-in-hand to 'big pharma' for support.

Thus, as the microbiology revolution works its way through to markets, we see bioregions as nodes linked by networks on a global scale targeting each other through pharmaceuticals business leaders, research 'stars' and support institutions according to their special assets or nodal 'capabilities' (see Penrose, 1959; Teece & Pisano, 1996). Thus, to return momentarily to Novartis, their Basel home base consists of many support institutions including DBFs such as Actelion (a Roche spinout), Ecovac (a Novartis spinout), and Speedel Pharma (a Novartis licensee), plus others of the Swiss total as follows. In 2003, Switzerland hosted some 200 DBFs, of which around forty are pure biotechnology firms (DBFs); the others are instrumentation and services firms that nevertheless link to many of the forty. Some 22 per cent of the 200 are located in the Geneva–Lausanne 'BioAlps' region, approximately 26 per cent are in the Basel 'BioValley' region, and about 35 per cent are in the Greater Zurich region.

From the Basel base, Roche and Novartis have been the world's most active acquirers and partners of US, especially Californian, DBFs, although they are not alone in having such links. In San Diego alone, Eli Lilly entered collaboration with the Scripps Institute, gaining rights of first refusal on discoveries in exchange for $50 million. Then, in 1986 Lilly acquired Hybritech, one of the earliest DBFs, only to dispose of it subsequently, thereafter investing in ownership of a leading diabetes therapeutic from Ligand Pharma. In 1996, Lilly entered a collaboration with Neurocrine Biosciences, and in 2001 did the same with Isis Pharma ($200 million). In 1996, Schering-Plough acquired Canji, a gene therapy firm with late-stage clinical trials. Johnson & Johnson also, like Lilly, began interaction early, entering a collaboration agreement with Scripps Institute, then in 1995 taking an 11 per cent stake in Amylin, enlarging this in later years. During 1995–99 it also had collaboration with Neurocrine Biosciences and in 1996 Johnson & Johnson created its integrated Genomics Research Institute in La Jolla, extending it in 2002 after signing a partnership deal with Maxia Pharma in 2001. Warner-Lambert (now Pfizer) acquired Agouron Pharma, the most successful San Diego biotechnology firm, employing 1,000, for $2.1 billion to access its HIV treatment. Pfizer began with a research collaboration in 1991 with Ligand Pharma, integrated Agouron into its worldwide operations in 2000 with the acquisition of Warner-Lambert, and in 2002 opened the first stage of a new research centre ($155 million) in La Jolla on the Agouron site. In 1999, Merck acquired Sibia Neurosciences, invested in its research laboratories expanding them substantially. In 1998, Ireland's Elan Corporation entered partnership with Ligand Pharma and in 2000 acquired Dura Pharma for $1.5 billion, centralizing its biopharmaceuticals operations in La Jolla, before entering eight further biotechnology collaborations. Finally, Japanese pharmas Chugai and Sankyo established research facilities in San Diego in 1995 and 1998 respectively.

It may be concluded that, while there is a general trend in industry, led by biopharmaceuticals,[4] towards 'open innovation' there is no 'one-size-fits-all' style of innovation even among neighbouring multinationals such as Novartis and Roche. Where Novartis and Roche could gain biopharmaceuticals expertise in Basel for *cardiovascular* and *oncology* research and treatments (Carrin *et al.*, 2004),[5] they went with large research investments to San Diego in the Scripps Institute and GNF for *immunology* and *neurosciences* (also some agro-food seed science) expertise, and now to Cambridge, Massachusetts, with an even bigger $4.25 billion investment in the Novartis Institutes for Biomedical Research (NIBR) for *genomics, post-genomics* and *proteomics* research expertise 'ahead of the curve'. That they are not alone is testified to by the arrival there between 1999 and 2003 of a wave of new entries by the likes of Abbott Labs (formerly BASF Bioresearch), Sanofi (formerly Aventis' Hoechst-Ariad Genomics Centre, founded by Nobel Laureate David Baltimore), and Wyeth (formerly Genetics Institute), and openings such as AstraZeneca's Biosciences R&D Centre, Pfizer's Discovery Technology Centre, and Californian firm Amgen's R&D facility (formerly Immunex).

Thus we conclude that innovation operates according to a theory of *regional knowledge capabilities* fairly obviously in bioregional innovation systems, but indicatively for automotive and electronics innovation too (see Cooke, 2004b). Innovation is now based on intra-industry knowledge trade, with specialist knowledge nodes and networks spanning the world and specialized expertise increasingly residing in specific regional innovation systems. Ambitious, competitive businesses must interact with these and their 'open innovation' conventions, for gone are the days when a 'one-size-fits-all' corporate innovation model with a few secretive 'pipeline' contracts to other corporates 'ruled the roost' (Chesbrough, 2003; Owen-Smith & Powell, 2004).

Acknowledgements

This chapter was assisted by the research on international co-publication conducted in CESAGen by Ann Yaolu. I am also grateful to Olivier Crevoisier of the University of Neuchâtel for connecting me to his biotechnology research colleague Alex Mack, who supplied important information on the Swiss biopharmaceuticals sector.

Notes

1   On 'recombinant' innovation and its differences from 'radical' and 'incremental' innovation, see Cooke and Schall (1997). Our empirical analysis of this phenomenon – where a firm adapts a core technology for multiple, highly distinctive sectoral users – differs from the recent efforts of Hargadon (2003) who reduces all innovation to recombination thus rather throwing the innovation, as well as the invention and discovery, babies out with the bathwater.
2   It is arguable that they should stay in Table 3.5, but they can in any case be compared by those who are interested. The justification for including these bioregions is argued in Cooke (2004b).
3   For example they appear in the UK government (DTI, 1999) report as well as those published annually by Ernst & Young on *Entrepreneurial Life Sciences Companies (ELISCOs)*.
4   In December 2004, it was reported that the global top ten pharmaceuticals firms generated 35 per cent of their revenues from in-licensed research from DBFs in 2003, and forecast that this would rise to 50 per cent by 2008 (Lyall *et al.*, 2004).
5   Notably the celebrated *Glivec* drug that is the first to cure a cancer, namely chronic myeloid leukaemia, researched in Cambridge and Boston, Massachusetts, in the Whitehead Institute (by retroviruses Nobel Laureate David Baltimore) and Dana-Farber Cancer Research Institute, but developed in Basel.

Bibliography

Cairncross, F. (1997), *The Death of Distance* (Boston: Harvard Business School Books).

Calvert, J. & Patel, P. (2002), *University–Industry Collaborations in the UK* (Brighton: SPRU).

Capra, F. (2002), *The Hidden Connections* (London: Flamingo).

Carlsson, B. (ed.) (2001), *New Technological Systems in the Bio-Industry: an International Comparison* (Dordrecht: Kluwer).

Carrin, B., Harayama, Y., Mack, A. & Zarin-Nejadan, M. (2004), *The Competitiveness of Swiss Biotechnology* (Geneva: JETRO and University of Neuchâtel).

Chesbrough, H. (2003), Open Innovation: The New Imperative for Creating and Profiting From Technology (Boston: Harvard Business School Press).

Clark, G., Gertler, M. & Feldman, M. (eds) (2000), *The Oxford Handbook of Economic Geography* (Oxford: Oxford University Press).

Cooke, P. (2004a), 'Rational drug design, the knowledge value chain and biosciences mega centres', *Cambridge Journal of Economics*, 23, pp. 167–185.

Cooke, P. (2004b), 'Globalization of biosciences: knowledge capabilities and economic geography', paper presented to the Centennial Conference of Philadelphia, *American Association of Geographers*, 16 March.

Cooke, P. & Schall, N. (1997), 'How Do Firms Innovate?', *Regional Industrial Research Paper 29* (Cardiff: Centre for Advanced Studies).

Cortright, J. & Mayer, H. (2002), *Signs of Life: the Growth of Biotechnology Centres in the US* (Washington, DC: Brookings Institute).

DTI (1999), *Biotechnology Clusters* (London: Department of Trade & Industry).

Dorey, E. (2003), 'Emerging market Medicon Valley: a hotspot for biotech affairs', *BioResource*, March, at <www.investintech.com>.

Hargadon, A. (2003), *How Breakthroughs Happen: The Surprising Truth About How Companies Innovate* (Boston: Harvard Business School Press).

Henderson, R., Orsenigo, L. & Pisano, G. (1999), 'The pharmaceutical industry and the revolution in molecular biology: interactions among scientific, institutional and organisational change' (in Mowery & Nelson).

Jaffe, A., Trajtenberg, M. & Henderson, R. (1993), 'Geographic localisation of knowledge spillovers as evidenced by patent citations', *Quarterly Journal of Economics*, 108, pp. 577–98.

Kaufmann, D., Schwartz, D., Frenkel, A. & Shefer, D. (2003), 'The role of location and regional networks for biotechnology firms in Israel', *European Planning Studies*, 11, pp. 823–40.

Kay, J. (2003), *The Truth About Markets* (London: Allen Lane).

Kettler, H. & Casper, S. (2000), *The Road to Sustainability in the UK & German Biotechnology Industries* (London: Office of Health Economics).

Krugman, P. (1995), *Development, Geography & Economic Theory* (Cambridge, MA: MIT Press).

Krugman, P. (2000), 'Where in the world is the 'new economic geography?' (in Clark, Gertler & Feldman).

Lawton-Smith, H. (2004), 'The Biotechnology Industry in Oxfordshire: enterprise and innovation', *European Planning Studies*, 12, pp. 985–1002.

Lyall, C., Bruce, A., Firn, J., Firn, M. & Tait, J. (2004), 'Assessing End Use Relevance of Public Sector Research Organisations', *Research Policy*, 33, pp. 73–87.

Mowery, D. & Nelson, R. (eds) (1999), *Sources of Industrial Leadership* (Cambridge: Cambridge University Press).

Nightingale, P. (2000), 'Economies of scale in experimentation: knowledge and technology in pharmaceutical R&D', *Industrial & Corporate Change*, 9, pp. 315–59.

Owen-Smith, J. & Powell, W. (2004), 'Knowledge networks as channels and conduits: the effects of spillovers in the Boston biotechnology community', *Organization Science*, 15, pp. 5–21.

Penrose, E. (1959), *The Theory of the Growth of the Firm* (Oxford: Oxford University Press).

Porter, M. (1998), *On Competition* (Boston: Harvard Business School Press).

Powell, W., Koput, K. & Smith-Doerr, L. (1996), 'Interorganisational collaboration and the locus of innovation: networks of learning in biotechnology', *Administrative Sciences Quarterly*, 41, pp. 116–45.

Rallet, A. & Torre, A. (1998), 'On geography and technology: proximity relations in localised innovation networks' (in Steiner).

Schamp, E., Rentmeister, B. & Lo, V. (2004), 'Dimensions of Proximity in Knowledge-based Networks: The Cases of Investment Banking and Automobile Design', *European Planning Studies*, 12(5), pp. 607–24.

Smith, K. (2001), *What is the 'knowledge economy'? Knowledge-intensive industries and distributed knowledge bases* (Oslo: STEP Group).

Stankiewicz, R. (2001), 'The cognitive dynamics of technology and the evolution of its technological system' (in Carlsson).

Steiner, M. (ed.) (1998), *Clusters and Regional Specialisation* (London: Pion).

Teece, D. & Pisano, G. (1996), 'The dynamic capabilities of firms: an introduction', *Industrial & Corporate Change*, 3, pp. 537–56.

van den Biesen, J. (2004), 'University-industry relations and innovation strategy in Philips worldwide: an R&D outsourcing approach', (paper presented to the EU Conference *The Europe of Knowledge 2020: a Vision for University-based Research and Innovation*), 25–28 April, Liège.

Zeller, C. (2004), 'North Atlantic innovative relations of Swiss pharmaceuticals and the proximities with regional biotech areas', *Economic Geography*, 80, pp. 83–111.

4
Agglomeration or Cross-border ICT Cluster? *The Öresund Region*

Povl A. Hansen and Göran Serin

4.1. Introduction

Following the recent intense debate about clusters and cluster development, consensus has emerged that innovation and firm's competitive powers are not only based on the firm's own ability to develop knowledge into technological solutions, but are also dependent on the firm's relations to other firms and local capabilities and infrastructure. The character of these external relations and the forms which best suit innovation and productivity growth are however still under discussion. It is of prime importance whether these external relations can be characterized as agglomerations or clusters, not the least for policy development. It is, therefore, a central issue in this context whether the ICT (information communication technology) sector in the Öresund region is characterized by agglomeration or clusters. Because the Öresund region is a cross-border region (Sjaelland (Zealand) in Denmark and Skåne (Scania) in southern Sweden), the second issue that will be discussed is the possibilities and barriers for integrating the region's ICT sector. Despite the EU's support for cross-border regionalization, there has been little academic interest in the possibilities for developing clusters or agglomerations in cross-border regions. In contrast our agglomeration and cluster discussion focuses on cross-border issues and the consequences for policy.

The chapter is structured as follows. In section 4.2, the concepts of agglomeration and cluster are discussed as is the relationship between the two. At this point, the analytical approach employed here is presented. In section 4.3, the problem of what constitutes an ICT agglomeration and a cluster is discussed, especially in relation to defining their borders. In the following section (section 4.4), we go into greater depth concerning the existence, or otherwise, of an agglomeration or clusters in the Öresund region, where we first review previous cluster investigations and then investigate the possibilities for cross-border ICT clusters or agglomeration. Section 4.5 presents an analysis of research and development (R&D) and education within ICT in the region, while section 4.6 discusses policies for cross-border integration in relation to the characterization of the region. The chapter ends by summarizing the character of integration in the Öresund region and the policy implications.

4.2. Agglomeration or cluster?

The central issue concerning the ICT sector in the Öresund region is whether there is an ICT cluster or just an agglomeration of ICT activities. This is important in relation to the discussion of the possibilities for developing an ICT policy for the cross-border region and the role played by public support to infrastructure and interaction between ICT firms. The agglomeration of firms has traditionally been discussed in terms of industrial districts, agglomeration advantages and most recently in the context of clusters. Traditionally, location theory has focused on the externalities defined by cost reductions and knowledge spillovers for firms located in the same place (Marshall, 1890 [1960]). Many theorists within geography have discussed and defined such localization externalities.

Objections have been raised against the idea that these externalities, especially knowledge externalities, should only exist in relation to firms within the same industry (see Feldman & Audretsch, 1999). The idea that knowledge spillovers only occur within an industry ignores the important sources of knowledge in the form of inter-industry spillovers. Jacobs (1969), for example, asserts that the most important form for knowledge spillovers are external to the industry in which the firm operates. Of course, these external industries are not arbitrary. There must be some basis for interaction between the industries and, thereby, knowledge spillovers. According to Jacobs, and Feldman and Audretsch, a common science base constitutes such a basis. Feldman and Audretsch classify industry into six groups that rely on similar academic disciplines. One of these groups is 'high-tech computing.'[1]

In relation to the ICT sector, which consists of many different industries, it is necessary to investigate whether or not its constituent parts have the same possibilities for cost reductions and knowledge spillovers by locating close to each other. Although there is a large agglomeration of ICT firms in the region, this must not imply that all the different firms benefits from the same type of agglomeration advantages. Here agglomeration externalities can be defined by cost reductions by economies of scale, scope and in transacting (Malmberg & Maskell, 1999). In relation to the ICT sector, this will be cost reductions by externalities in relation to other firms in the ICT sector or externalities related to public infrastructure and institutions. The discussion about clusters has been conceived in terms of close interaction between firms and has taken its point of departure in Porter's work where he defines a cluster as a 'geographically proximate group of interconnected companies, suppliers, service providers and associated institutions in a particular field, linked by externalities of various types' (Porter, 2003). Porter stresses the interconnectedness and thereby the interaction between firms in a cluster.[2] A cluster is therefore characterized by an active role for the participant firms, while the firms in an agglomeration can benefit from externalities while being passive. A cluster is, therefore, a more ambitious form of agglomeration.

In their criticism of Porter's cluster theory, Martin and Sunley (2003) have pointed out that his definition of a cluster especially lacks industrial and geographical boundaries. They question the level of industrial aggregation defining a cluster and the range of related and associated industries and activities that should be included. They also raise the issues of how strong the links between the firms have to be and how economically specialized a local concentration of firms has to be to constitute a cluster. In short, they assert that Porter's definition seems intentionally opaque and fuzzy. Porter (1998) is also conscious of this as he writes that drawing borders is often a matter of degree and involves a creative process.

Here Malmberg's (2002) distinction between functional or firm clustering and geographical clustering can contribute to increased clarity, as a firm's functional linkages, especially for larger firms, more go beyond the regional perspective, implying that a functional or firm cluster need not be restricted to a narrow geographical region. In the case of the ICT sector, large telecom firms often have a functional clustering that goes beyond the region. This will often also be the case for ICT industrial production while, for example, many smaller ICT consultants have more local linkages. Although many of the latter have been going international in recent years, a large part of their market is still within the firm's home region, based on close ties between the consultant firm and the industrial structure. It is therefore not useful to separate agglomeration advantages from cluster development, where the latter can be seen as a dynamic form of agglomeration.[3]

Therefore, we prefer to discuss geographical space in relation to inputs in the production process connected to different technological levels, in terms of different agglomeration advantages on different levels. The character and the depth of the agglomeration process, hereunder tendencies to cluster development, in the Öresund region can thus be analyzed taking a point of departure in the following factors (implying a more institutional and learning approach to agglomeration and clusters):[4]

- The different parts of the ICT sector's ability to take advantage of public institutions, especially research and development (R&D) and education.
- The connection to technologically related industries on different levels and the role of geographical space in different parts of the ICT sector.
- The importance of new firms through entry and spin-offs in the different parts of the ICT sector.
- The continuous development of more specialized inputs and services by industries located in the same area.

The focus of our analysis is on the relation between externalities and the structure of the ICT sector. This is in order to separate the agglomeration advantages from the effects of networking and public cooperation especially concerning education and R&D across the border of the Sound separating Zealand from Scania. The four factors above imply a comprehensive analysis, which is too ambitious within this framework. Instead, we focus on the first two factors and especially the contributory role of education and R&D institutions.

4.3. What constitutes ICT agglomerations and clusters?

There are many studies confirming the existence of ICT clusters at the international level. (see Swann & Prevezer, 1996; Swann, Prevezer & Stout, 1998; Söderström *et al.*, 2001; Quah, 2001; Koski, Rouvinen & Ylä-Antilla, 2002). A central issue in this connection has been whether the ICT sector is now so large that it is no longer meaningful to talk about ICT clusters (Quah, 2001). However, in their study of the US and British computer industry, Swann and Prevezer identified clear linkages between the different segments of the industry. The study showed that the firms were specialized in specific segments; that is, components, hardware, software, peripherals and systems and they were dependent on each other for producing the end-product, which resulted in positive feedback between the firms in the different segments. The linkages between firms in the computer industry were, for example, stronger than in the biotech sector, where the dependence on research institutions was stronger. Although we can identify linkages between the different segments of the computer industry on a general level, the question remains of whether these define relevant boundaries of the cluster. Other studies indicate that a common science base may be more important for defining an ICT cluster.[5]

If we return to our study of the ICT industry in the Öresund region, it is therefore not certain that the strongest linkages are between the four segments of telecommunications, electronics industry, trade and ICT consultants which constitute the Organization for Economic Cooperation and Development (OECD) definition of the ICT industry. Although there is a strong concentration of all these sectors in the Öresund region, it is not certain that this concentration is due primarily to the linkages between these sectors. For example, it is very likely that the linkages between ICT consultants and their customers, often located in the capital region, are stronger than those between other segments of the ICT sector and therefore account more to a clustering of ICT consultants in the Öresund region than do linkages to other ICT segments.

The importance of the customer in the innovation process in ICT is also indicated by the fact that 28 per cent of the R&D costs in Denmark lie within customer adapted software and 34 per cent within integrated software (The Danish Institute for Studies in Research and Research Policy, 2004). Both of these categories indicate customer participation in the development processes in one way or another. This indicates important ties to firms outside the ICT sector. A study made by the Danish Ministry of Science, Technology and Innovation also shows that there are large differences between industries using ICT in their production. The sector with the largest integration of ICT is the business services sector where 77 per cent of the firms have integrated ICT into their production, while the sector with the smallest degree of ICT integration is industrial production with only 40 per cent integration (The Ministry of Science, Technology and Innovation, 2003).

The Danish examples above indicate that you cannot just identify one cluster border for the ICT sector. Instead, the different parts of the industrial structure are integrated in different ways with the different segments of the ICT sector.

4.4. Is there a cluster or an ICT agglomeration in the Öresund region?

4.4.1. Investigations of ICT clusters in the Öresund region

The ICT sector has been considered a core for developing a high-tech sector across the Sound. It is a sector characterized by innovation and rapid technological change. The ICT sector also plays an important role in the development of sophisticated production in other parts of the industrial structure. This raises the questions of the importance of the ICT sector in the Öresund region, its composition, and the possibility of the sector contributing to developing a more knowledge based and advanced industrial sector in the region.

In an attempt to strengthen regional industrial policy on the Danish island of Zealand as well as in the Swedish county of Scania, an attempt was made by political organizations to map possible clusters in the region. In this process, some ICT clusters were identified on Zealand (Oxford Research 2002; The National Agency for Enterprise and Construction, 2002). The National Agency for Enterprise and Construction has analyzed cluster developments in the Danish part of the Öresund region. The definition of a cluster was that of agglomeration together with performance and interaction and coordination between firms.[6] The study identified clusters in Copenhagen and the northern part of Zealand within hearing aid manufacturing, optical communications and sensor technology, and data processing within the field of ICT.[7] The Oxford Research report found clusters within optical communication, sensor technology, e-learning, bioinformatics, nanotechnology (under development) and wireless communication.[8] Although there are methodological differences between the two reports, we can identify some overlap of identified cluster industries. However, we must keep in mind that some of the clusters in the region are very small. In Scania there was only a potential cluster related to the food industry but no clusters related to the ICT sector were found (Nilsson *et al.*, 2002).

On the basis of these analyses of clusters within the ICT sector on Zealand and in Scania, we can ask what are the opportunities for establishing cross-border clusters within the ICT sector in the Öresund region – the ultimate goal of authorities as well as industrialists of the region. Before we discuss this question, we first discuss whether or not there is an agglomeration of ICT employment both within industry and research and development in the region, including the areas on both sides of the Sound, and second what possibilities and potentials there are for such agglomerations and, in their extension, clusters. Lastly, we discuss and evaluate the policies developed to establish a cross-border cluster in the ICT industry in the Öresund region. This is done in the light of the ongoing discussion concerning cluster policies.

4.4.2. The agglomeration of ICT in the Öresund region

If we look at the ICT sector in the Öresund region based on the definitions used by OECD statistics, we find that it is large indeed, even larger than more internationally well-known ICT regions such as Kista in the Stockholm region of Sweden.[9] In 2000, the Öresund region had 104,734 people employed in the ICT industry, compared with the Stockholm region's 100,208.[10] If we look at the number of ICT firms too, there are 11,044 in the Öresund region – slightly fewer than in the Stockholm region, which had 12,682 in 2000.[11] In the past few years, the Stockholm region has been mentioned as one of the better known and developed clusters within the ICT sector. If we look at agglomeration alone, we would therefore be justified in talking about a cluster in the Öresund region too.

However, employment in ICT is not evenly distributed between the two parts of the Öresund region. It is concentrated in Zealand, which has 80 per cent of the employment in ICT in the region, while only 20 per cent is in Scania (Hansen & Serin, 2003). This concentration in Zealand is greater than employment figures in general would justify. For

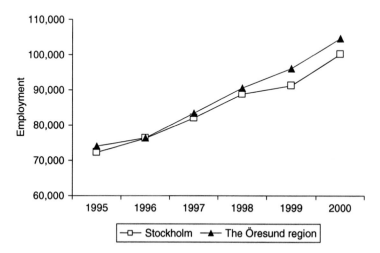

Figure 4.1.   Employment in ICT in Stockholm and in the Öresund region

Sources: Statistics Denmark and Statistics Sweden, special task.

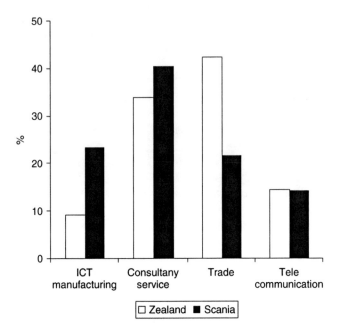

Figure 4.2. The employment structure in the ICT industry in the two national parts of the Öresund region as percentage of total ICT employment, 2000

Sources: Statistics Denmark and Statistics Sweden, special task.

Scania's share of total employment in the region is 28 per cent. This suggests that the percentage of employment in ICT of total employment is lower in Scania than Zealand. As discussed above, it is hardly meaningful to analyze the ICT sector on such a general level. The sector was therefore divided into sub-sectors according to the statistical definitions made by the OECD, because it is not likely that the different sub-sectors are connected in the same way to the industrial structure. The following picture of the ICT sector on Zealand and Scania then appears.

Although the employment in absolute terms is larger in all segments of the ICT sector on Zealand compared with Scania, the figure above shows that the employment structure differs between the two parts; ICT trade is especially strong on Zealand. The importance of trade is due to the fact that the headquarters of large international ICT companies are located in the Copenhagen area and these firms are registered in this category. However, these firms also play an important role in developing and diffusing technology in the region by consulting and technological support. If we look at Scania, we find an ICT sector that is in many ways different from Zealand's. Here we find that the ICT industry is, in percentage terms, stronger than on Zealand. This also accords with the fact that industry as a whole has a stronger position in Scania than on Zealand. ICT consultancy and services are also, in percentage terms, larger in Scania than on Zealand. This reflects the fact that this sub-industry is larger in Sweden than in Denmark.

We can thus conclude that there are clear differences in the structure of the ICT sector in the two national parts of the Öresund region according to the classification made by the OECD.[12]

4.5. R&D and education in the ICT sector in the Öresund region

4.5.1. R&D and the relationship between firms and public institutions within the ICT sector

A decisive factor in the analysis of the possibilities of agglomeration and the establishment of clusters is the existence of educational and R&D institutions. This is especially true for a sector such as ICT, which traditionally has been considered a knowledge-based industry. This dependence on R&D can be split up into the industry's own R&D and external R&D. This latter category includes both public sector R&D and R&D collaboration with other firms.

If we first look at public sector R&D[13] in relation to the ICT industry in the Öresund region we find, precisely as we do with employment in ICT, a large agglomeration. If we compare the number of researchers in the Öresund region with the so-called Kista cluster in the Stockholm region, we find a larger number in the Öresund region.

Hansen and Serin (2003) found that there were 458 public ICT researchers in the Öresund region compared to 233 in the Kista cluster in Sweden. But as we were able to conclude concerning ICT employment, they are not equally distributed. Seventy-five per cent of the ICT researchers are on the Zealand side, while 25 per cent are in Scania. In 2000, the Scania share of total employment within the region's ICT industry was 20 per cent. However, employment in public ICT research is disproportionally larger. A large part of the research is basic research that is more closely related to the educational system than it is to industry. A characteristic feature of industry-related ICT research is that, to an increasing extent, it has been moved out and is now developed in research parks connected to the universities in the region. This has resulted in 104 ICT firms being established in research parks in the region

(Hansen & Serin, 2003). However, a Danish study has shown that the ICT industry collaborates far more often with private partners in relation to R&D than with public research institutions (Graversen & Mark, 2002; The Danish Institute for Studies in Research and Research Policy, 2004). This finding is also in agreement with international research that also stresses the importance of technology interdependence, in the form of, for example, software and component inputs, compared to public research in the ICT sector. This is in contrast with, for example, biotechnology where public research has a more central position (Swann & Prevezer, 1996; Swann *et al.*, 1998).

Another Danish study also shows that ICT industries have fewer joint innovation activities with other firms than firms in general (The Danish Ministry of Science, Technology and Innovation, 2003). Other research shows that the collaboration agreements between private firms in the ICT sector increased in the period from 1975 up to the end of the 1980 and thereafter diminished to very low levels (Palmberg & Martikainen, 2003). Danish Research Statistics also show that the firms' own research accounts for the main part of the research in the ICT sector in Denmark (The Danish Institute for Studies in Research and Research Policy, 2002). This shows that the ICT sector is more dependent on its own innovation processes, and thereby on a highly educated workforce, than on R&D collaboration with the universities. This is based on the fact that university research is more oriented towards basic research than to technological development (Gravesen & Mark, 2002). Eighty per cent of total R&D costs of Danish ICT firms are also attributed to development (The Danish Institute for Studies in Research and Research Policy, 2004). The minor importance of collaboration with public R&D institutions is shown by the fact that only 0.2 per cent of the firms running R&D expenses could be attributed purchase of public R&D (The Danish Institute for Studies in Research and Research Policy, 2002). However, if we look at the number of ICT firms that have collaboration with universities in projects we find 24 per cent of the firms engaged in collaboration with universities and 9 per cent with other R&D institutions (The Danish Institute for Studies in Research and Research Policy, 2004).[14]

But is cooperation on the whole conducive to R&D efficiency? This issue together with the geographical extension of R&D collaboration has been the subject of investigation by Fritsch (2004). In the investigation of 11 regions in Europe, where R&D cooperation was not restricted to ICT, the conclusion was that R&D cooperation, which included both private and public partners, was not more common in densely populated regions. It also concluded that there was no support for the suggestion that cooperation or a relatively pronounced cooperative attitude in a region was conducive to innovation activity. Instead, the investigation suggests that R&D spillovers are effective independently of cooperative relationships. This could point to other factors such as mobility of labour, normal market relations and the education system. This still stresses the importance of agglomeration for R&D efficiency, which is also supported by a Hungarian study of regional knowledge spillovers (Varga & Schalk, 2004).

4.5.2. ICT education and cross-border integration in the Öresund region

One of the advantages of agglomeration is the possibility for economies of scale in relation to education. A study by Quah (2001), where the clustering of ICT in the United States is caused by its dependence on a highly educated workforce and that it is a growth industry, points to the importance of a highly educated workforce. Also an analysis of the telecom cluster in Helsinki stresses the importance of higher education for the development of the cluster (van den Berg, Braun & van Vinden, 2003). The proximity to educational institutions facilitates collaboration between these and the ICT industry. This impression is conveyed by the number of students who utilize local corporate internships in connection with their end-thesis writing. This proximity also facilitates recruitment by pre-selection of staff. Further evidence can be found in a British analysis of local development policies in relation to information and communication technologies that stresses the importance of education. This study found that besides lack of finance, lack of qualified personal was the major obstacle to developing ICT initiatives locally (Gibbs & Tanner, 1997). Also Danish statistics confirms the importance of a highly educated workforce in the ICT sector. Here we find that the importance of academic manpower is different from private industry in general. R&D's share of turnover is only 1 per cent in the industry in general in 2001, while the share was 2.8 in the ICT industry in the same year. This is also in line with the fact that 14.9 per cent of the employees in the ICT industry have university degrees, compared with only 5.8 per cent for industry in general (The Danish Institute for Studies in Research and Research Policy, 2002).

However, it is important to keep in mind that the ICT sector is not homogeneous in relation to educational structure, and it cannot be characterized as a sector that is altogether dependent on a highly educated workforce. Analyses made by Swedish Statistics and Danish Statistics show that, on the contrary, the educational structure of the ICT sector is very differentiated. The Danish study shows that the share of direct ICT jobs in the ICT sector is small – considerably less than 50 per cent. The sector with most direct ICT jobs was consultancy with about 49 per cent. Consultancy was also the sector which employed most academic labour. A similar conclusion was reached in a Swedish investigation (Hansen & Serin, 2003; Nutek/SCB, 2002).

Although the conclusion is that the workforce in the ICT sector cannot be reduced to a highly educated academic workforce, this does not mean that access to academic labour is of minor importance. These jobs are often of strategic importance to the firm. An executive survey made by *The Economist*, where different factors are ranked according to how important they are in making particular regions attractive to business as places to invest, shows that availability of R&D talent ranks number three in the Copenhagen–Öresund region (Economist Intelligence Unit, 2003).

Given the fact that the ICT sector is more dependent on a highly educated workforce than industry in general, it is therefore primarily ICT research related to the development of high levels of education, rather than R&D collaboration with the private sector, that is of special importance.

A higher level of education supported by advanced R&D is also important for the development of closer collaboration between ICT firms and public research institutions. To be able to collaborate with public research institutions, the general knowledge level of the firms must be increased. Focusing on the universities as primarily suppliers of academic manpower, has therefore a double effect, on the one hand, by supplying the firm with in-house R&D, but on the other hand also stimulating increased R&D collaboration with public institutions. The existence of many universities and, thereby, university qualifications is therefore one of the main agglomeration advantages of the Öresund region. The integration of the two sides of the region also implies a further exploitation of these agglomeration advantages, where Zealand can benefit from access to a larger, highly skilled, ICT workforce. This is because 35 per cent of total ICT graduates come from Scanian universities, while Scania only counts for 20 per cent of employment in the ICT sector (Hansen & Serin, 2003). We can thus conclude that one of the primary agglomeration factors in the ICT sector in the Öresund region is access to a well-qualified workforce based on a large common science base, especially if we look at the region as a whole.

4.6. Policies for ICT cluster development and its implications for the Öresund region

4.6.1. Policies for cluster development

In relation to the discussion of the concept of 'cluster', there has been intense discussion on policies for promoting the establishment and development of clusters, both generally and for specific industries and regions (The National Agency for Enterprise and Construction, 2003). In this section, we discuss the attempts to develop a cross-border strategy for the development of an ICT cluster in the Öresund region. This is done against the background of both a theoretical discussion and concrete experiences of cluster policies.

A central issue here is whether we can identify a specific cluster policy, and if this is the case, how this policy differs from traditional policies such as industrial and regional policies and innovation policies. Closely related to this issue is also the issue of whether clusters on the whole can be built by policy (Cooke, 2002). Many writers who focus more on market failures in cluster building assign policy intervention an influential role. This can be in the form of supporting interaction within the cluster, attracting external investment, developing research excellence and developing awareness and branding of the cluster (Raines, 2002). In Cooke's writings (Cooke & Morgan, 1998; Cooke, 1998, 2002), clusters are closely related to 'the learning region'. Here political intervention plays an important role on a regional level. In this connection, Cooke refers to regional-learning systems where firms seek competitive advantages through externalization and specialization and where we also can see a regionalization of innovation as a part of a decentralization of industrial policy (Cooke & Morgan, 1998). Here the political institutions have more the roles of animateurs (Raines, 2002). Raines has identified three characteristics to distinguish cluster policy as a specific form for industrial policy, namely a focus on networks instead of individual firms. Second, these networks are in turn selected to support a growth strategy. This strategy is reminiscent of Perroux's 'growth poles'. Third, and last, there is a priority of learning and innovation in the cluster strategy (ibid.).

The above characteristics of cluster policies are also much in line with the cluster policy developed in the Öresund Region. In the following we focus on policies for the ICT sector. A decisive factor in policy formulation is whether one is to focus on agglomeration or clusters where the conditions for development differ between the two forms. Although, as pointed out before in this chapter, it is not possible or desirable to make a sharp distinction between an agglomeration and a cluster, we concluded that a cluster was a more dynamic form of agglomeration that included an active interaction between the firms of the cluster in contrast to the passive agglomeration advantages of an agglomeration. This understanding has also implications for policy, where a policy focusing on cluster building should give priority to supporting the strengthening of the ties between the actors of the cluster, while a policy focusing on agglomeration primarily should focus on developing social and material infrastructure. To support integration in the Öresund region, it is important to differentiate between these two policies. If we look at the region, we find a slightly complicated picture of both clusters and agglomeration. If we look at the ICT sector as a whole, we concluded that on this level we could not find a cluster but could find important agglomeration advantages especially in relation to education that is grounded on a common science base for the different parts of the ICT sector. But if we look at specific parts of the ICT sector, we found clusters or cluster tendencies within, for example, hearing aid manufacturing, optical communication and sensor technology, bioinformatics, and possibly nanotechnology. This calls for a differentiated policy where cluster support directed towards specific fields or industries are combined with building agglomeration advantages.

4.6.2. Policies for cross-border development in the Öresund region

How then have the regional policies within the ICT sector in the Öresund region been related to our main issue, namely agglomeration or the establishment of clusters in the region? The establishment of the network organization Öresund IT Academy indicated an ambitious approach to the cross-border integration of the sector in the region. The organization is a cooperative organization in the area for Danish and Swedish ICT actors. The board consists of important representatives from the region's ICT sector.

The organization has recognized that the ICT sector is too large for establishing a basis for cluster development in the Öresund region. The consequence of this insight is that the organization has realized that a cross-border integration policy within the ICT sector must be built on a broader policy approach including the development of clusters as well as agglomeration. Concerning cluster policy, Öresund IT Academy has identified areas where the region can develop front-edge competencies. These are areas such as optical communication, mobile technology, software development, micro- and nanotechnology and Bio + IT. These areas roughly correspond to the clusters identified in the above mentioned cluster studies. In these chosen areas, Öresund IT Academy supports cross-border cluster collaboration.

One form of such a cross-border cluster policy is the support of a 'virtual reality network' on both the Zealand side and the Scanian side. In the region, there are many research institutes and hundreds of companies with an interest in virtual reality, simulation, visualization, etc. Another cluster supported by Öresund IT Academy is the 'Vision in Scania Network'. The purpose of the network is to connect the companies and the research groups in the Malmö/Lund area that have special competencies within the field of vision, which includes imaging technology, and hooking them up with the Danish side thus developing a cross-border network (see <www.oresundit.org>).

Also, the support of increased interaction between firms and between firms and public institutions can, in a wider sense, be seen as an expression of this effort to develop an ICT cross-border cluster policy. This means interaction in both physical and virtual space. Besides arranging conferences and seminars, Öresund IT Academy also supports interaction among the actors in the region by having established a database called 'Find IT', which is an electronic service for business, organizations, universities and service providers in the ICT field. These network activities also support the mobility of labour across the Sound, which is a decisive factor in the cross-border integration process.

But, as mentioned above, developing cluster policies within specially chosen areas is only one part of Öresund IT Academy's integration policy. The main advantage as discussed in previous sections remains that of agglomeration. One important role for a cross-border organization is, therefore, to support agglomeration through marketing the region and thereby the individual firms worldwide. The most important factor, however, relates to the support of agglomeration development in relation to research and education within ICT through cross-border cooperation. Through closer cross-border cooperation it is possible to build up a critical mass and thereby scale advantages within more areas than would have been possible within the two sides separately. With this critical mass, R&D and education can contribute to agglomeration by supplying a broad scientific base for the ICT sector, which is a condition for the supply of a highly educated workforce in the region. However, the policy within R&D cannot be confined to agglomeration advantages only. Within special fields where the region has front-edge capabilities, it is possible to develop closer collaboration between the R&D and educational institution of the region. One example that can be mentioned is the Bio+IT Post Doc program, a joint initiative of the Öresund IT Academy and Medicon Valley Academy, an organization in the region with the same function as Öresund IT Academy, but within the medical and biomedical fields.[15] This again shows that it is hard to draw a distinct line between agglomeration advantages and clusters.

Integration policies both in the form of policies supporting agglomeration as well as cluster policies within specific areas are therefore important for the establishment of cross-border integration. This is especially true for cross-border regions where new functional relations have to be built up and, in relation to this, new local capabilities based on two different national regional institutions. A central problem is that organizations such as Öresund IT Academy work in a vacuum, with lack of public regional authorities and with few public regional tools. These types of organizations can be important in two ways. On the one hand, they show the necessity of creating cross border instruments and, on the other hand, the experience gained by organizations is important for the development of such instruments. Organizations such as Öresund IT Academy are particularly important in such cases where resources on both sides of the Sound are required for developing strong local capabilities in the region.

4.7. Conclusion

An important conclusion of the study of the ICT sector in the Öresund region is that it is not fruitful to make a sharp distinction between agglomeration and clusters. On the one hand, the two concepts should be seen as part of a process where agglomeration can often be seen as a condition for the development of clusters, where a well functioning agglomeration is a condition for the development of a cluster. On the other hand, agglomeration and clusters can be seen as existing simultaneously on different levels. In the case of the Öresund region, we find strong agglomeration advantages related to the ICT sector as a whole, while there simultaneously exist clusters or cluster tendencies in specific segments of the sector where the region has front-edge capabilities. The most important agglomeration advantage is connected to the fact that the ICT sector is dependent on its own research within the firm and therefore in turn is dependent on a highly educated workforce and therefore is primarily dependent on universities for the supply of labour. Cross-border integration in the Öresund region therefore plays an important role in developing these agglomeration advantages through the Scanian universities supplying Zealand with highly qualified labour. Most important, without doubt, is to connect the ICT industry and the institutions across the border and thereby exploit the great possibilities for agglomeration advantages in the form of cooperation, not least between institutions in the two national parts of the region.

Cross-border integration policy in the Öresund region therefore plays an important role for the development of agglomeration advantages primarily through developing a critical mass in relation to education in the region. Concerning the establishment of ICT clusters, it is primarily the market forces, and in this connection the development of front-edge capabilities, that define the segments that will develop into clusters. When these segments have been crystallized, cross-border integration policies can support further development not only by agglomeration policies in the form education but also through cluster supporting policies in the form of network and institution building, because these are often non-existent in cross-border regions. The experience from the Öresund cross-border integration shows that it is only through both supporting agglomeration advantages and cluster supporting policies in specific areas that a successful integration can be accomplished.

Notes

1 This group is according to Feldman and Audretsch (1999) based on material sciences, computer science, physics and chemistry.

2 In contrast to this, Porter mentions static agglomeration economies, which consists of a local concentration of customers (or downstream firms) sufficient to permit suppliers achieving economies of scale in production or distribution, large enough for local firms to amass sufficient demand to warrant the provision (usually by or via local governments) of specialized infrastructure, and large enough to realize a specialized local division of labour (Porter, 2000).

3 This is also in line with the approach developed in *The Cluster Policies Whitebook* (Andersson, Schwaag-Serger, Sörvik & Wise Hansson, 2004) where clusters in their life cycle go through different stages starting with agglomeration.

4 The following factors are based on Söderström *et al.* (2001).

5 This was discussed in the previous section, where Feldman and Audretsch (1999) defined high-tech computing clusters by a common science base. They also assert that the most important knowledge spill overs often are external to the industry.

6 The National Agency for Enterprise and Construction (2002, p. 4).

7 Ibid., p. 57.

8 Oxford Research uses three indicators for identification of clusters: (1) On the basis of electronic newspapers; (2) industry analysis; (3) firm identification on the basis of accounts.

9 A Swedish investigation of the so-called 'Kista cluster' (Sandberg *et al.*, 2004), shows that the R&D collaboration between firms and universities is low, despite geographical proximity, and the collaboration between firms is mostly

in 'open networks' and not locally based. Also an investigation by Fritsch (2004) points out that R&D collaboration between firms as well as between firms and institutions is limited in Stockholm county. Both of these investigations thus question if there really is a cluster in the Stockholm region.

10   In this chapter, we take our point of departure in employment. In the report (Hansen & Serin, 2003) both turnover and value added are presented. With few exceptions, turnover and value added give the same picture of the development as employment.

11   These numbers do not include telecommunications, which are not included in the material from Statistics Denmark. However, the numbers for the Öresund region are systematically underestimated because Statistics Denmark do not include firms with six months, work or less.

12   This is in line with another analysis of the industrial structure of the Öresund region and which also stresses the importance of the relation between the industrial structure of the two national parts of the region and their respectively national industrial structure (Lundquist & Winther, 2002).

13   There are many problems related to defining research within ICT. Today there are few, if any, fields where there is no ICT research. In the report referred to in this article (Hansen & Serin, 2003), a narrow definition was chosen. ICT research only includes institutions whose primary activity lies within the ICT field, not institutions where ICT is often used.

14   This investigation was only a sample of 300 firms, compared to the former, which was an analysis of the total population. It is also an important difference between purchasing R&D and participating in common projects, because participating in common projects cannot result in commercial products if the public institution does not get paid for their participation. Public institutions cannot participate in projects with commercial results without payment. This would distort competition. Common projects must thus include collaboration on a more general level.

15   Nine positions will be established within three key areas: System Biology, 3D Modelling of Molecular Structures, and Nanobiotechnology.

Bibliography

Andersson, T., Schwaag-Serger, S., Sörvik, J. & Wise-Hansson, E. (2004), *The Cluster Policies Whitebook* (Malmö: International Organisation for Knowledge Economy and Enterprise Development).

Braczyk, H.J., Cooke, P. & Heidenreich, M. (eds) (1998), *Regional Innovation Systems – The Role of Governances in a Globalized World* (London: UCL Press).

Clark, G.L., Feldman, M. P. & Gertler, M. S. (eds) (2000), *The Oxford Handbook of Economic Geography* (Oxford: Oxford University Press).

Cooke, P. (1998), 'Global clustering and regional innovation. – Systemic integration in Wales' (in Braczyk, Cooke & Heidenreich).

Cooke, P. (2002), *Knowledge Economics: – Clusters, Learning and Cooperative Advantage* (London and New York: Routledge).

Cooke, P. & Morgan, K. (1998), *The Associational Economy – Firms, Regions and Innovation* (Oxford: Oxford University Press).

The Danish Institute for Studies in Research and Research Policy (2002), *Tabelsamling: Erhvervslivets forskning og udviklingsarbejde* (Forskningsstatistik).

The Danish Institute for Studies in Research and Research Policy (2004), *Danske Virksomheders forsknings- og udviklingsarbejde inden for informations- og kommunikationsteknologi 2003* (Århus).

Economist Intelligence Unit (2003), 'Perspectives on the Copenhagen–Øresund Region', *The Economist* (Economist Intelligence Unit).

Feldman, M.P. & Audretsch, D.B. (1999), 'Innovation in cities: Science-based diversity, specialization and localized competition', *European Economic Review*, 43(2), pp. 409–29.

Fritsch, M. (2004), 'Cooperation and the efficiency of regional R&D activities', *Cambridge Journal of Economics*, 28, pp. 829–46.

Gibbs, D. & Tanner, K. (1997), 'Information and Communication Technologies and Local Economic Development Policies: The British Case', *Regional Studies*, 31(8), pp. 765–74.

Graversen, E.K. & Mark, M. (2002), 'Bestemmende faktorer for danske virksomheders valg af forskningssamarbejdspartnere' (Working Papers 2002/14, Danish Institute for Studies in Research and Research Policy).

Gustafsson, H. (ed.) (2002), *På Jakt efter Öresundsregionen* (Lund: Öresundsuniversitetet).

Hansen, P.A. & Serin, G. (2000), 'Industriens teknologistruktur i Öresundsregionen' (Research paper, Department of Social Sciences, Roskilde University, no. 9).

Hansen, P.A. & Serin, G. (2001), 'Regionala näringslivsstrukturer i Öresundsregionen – mellan centrum och periferi' (Forskningsrapport, Roskilde University, no. 122).

Hansen, P.A. & Serin, G. (2002), 'Regionerne i regionen – om Öresundsregionens regionalstrukturelle udvikling' (in Gustafsson).

Hansen, P.A. & Serin, G. (2003), 'IT – sektorens udviklingsmuligheder i Öresundsregionen – en analyse af erhverv, forskning og uddannelse' (Öresund IT Academy København).

Jacobs, J. (1969), *The Economy of Cities* (New York: Random House).

Koski, H., Ruovinen, P. & Ylä-Antilla, P. (2002), 'ICT clusters in Europé. The great central banana and the small Nordic potato', *Information Economics and Policy*, 14, pp. 145–65.

Lundquist, K.J. & Winther, L. (2002), 'I korsdrag mellan Danmark och Sverige – Öresundsområdets industriella struktur och dynamik' (in Gustafsson).

Malmberg, A. (2002), *Klusterdynamik och regional näringslivsutveckling* (Stockholm: ITPS).

Malmberg, A. & Maskell (1999), 'Localized Learning and Industrial Competitiveness', *Cambridge Journal of Economics*, 23(2), pp. 167–85.

Marshall, A. (1890), 'Industrial organization, continued. The concentration of specialized industries in particular localities' (in Marshall, 1890 [1960]).

Marshall, A. (1890 [1960]), *Principles of Economics* (London: Macmillan, 1890 [1960]).

Martin, R. & Sunley, P. (2003), 'Deconstructing clusters: chaotic concept or policy panacea?', *Journal of Economic Geography*, 3, pp. 5–35.

Ministry of Science, Technology & Innovation (2003), *Værdi. En værdiskabende sektor – Fokus på de danske IT erhverv* (Copenhagen: Ministry of Science, Technology & Innovation).

The National Agency for Enterprise & Construction (2002), *De danske kompetenceklynger* (Copenhagen: National Agency for Enterprise & Construction).

The National Agency for Enterprise & Construction (2003), 'European Cluster Policy', European Seminar in Copenhagen, 10 June.

88   *Contemporary Management of Innovation*

Nilsson, M., Svensson-Henning, M. & Wilkenson, O. (2002), *Skånska kluster och profilområden – en kritisk granskning* (Malmö: Region Skåne, 2002).
Nutek/Statistics Sweden (2002), *Elektronikindustri- och IT relaterade tjänsteföretag i Sverige* (Sweden: Nutek/Statistics).
Oxford Research (2002), *Kompetenceklynger i Hovedstadsregionen* (Copenhagen: HUR).
Palmberg, C. & Martikainen, O. (2003), 'The Economics of Strategic R&D Alliances – A review with focus on the ICT-sector', *ETLA paper*, no. 881.
Porter, M.E. (1998), 'Clusters and the New Economic Competition', *Harvard Business Review*, Nov.–Dec., pp. 77–90.
Porter, M.E. (2000), 'Locations, Clusters and Company Strategy' (in Clark, Feldman & Gertler).
Porter, M.E. (2003), 'The Economic Performance of Regions', *Regional Studies*, 37(6–7), pp. 549–78.
Quah, D. (2001), *ICT Clusters in Development: Theory and Evidence* (London: London School of Economics).
Raines, P. (2002), *Cluster Development and Policy – EPRC Studies in European Policy* (Aldershot: Ashgate).
Sandberg, Å., Lintala, A. & Augustsson, F. (2004), *IT-företagen i Kista – Verksamhet, nätverk, kompetens och platsens kvalitet* (Stockholm: Kungliga Tekniska Högskolan CID 253).
Söderström, H.T. *et al.* (2001), *Kluster.se* (Stockholm: SNS Förlag).
Swann, P. & Prevezer, G.M. (1996), 'A comparison of the dynamics of industrial clustering in computing and biotechnology', *Research Policy*, 25, pp. 1139–57.
Swann, P., Prevezer, G.M. & Stout, D. (1998), *The Dynamics of Industrial Clustering* (Oxford: Oxford University Press).
van den Berg, L., Braun, E. & van Winden, W. (2003), *Growth Clusters in European Metropolitan Cities* (Aldershot: Ashgate).
Varga, A. & Schalk, H.J. (2004), 'Knowledge Spillovers, Agglomeration and Macro-economic Growth: An Empirical Approach', *Regional Studies*, 38(8), pp. 977–89.

5
Innovation and Firm Consumption.
A New Perspective?
Jeremy Howells

5.1. Introduction

There continues to be an overwhelming supply-side focus in the study of innovation and the firm. There have been a number of exceptions, notably around the work of von Hippel and others, which emerged in the mid 1970s in relation to the role of the user on new product development and the innovation process (von Hippel, 1976, 1978, 1988; Parkinson, 1982; Foxall, 1987). However, even here the focus on use and its relationship with innovation was on the *supplier* rather than that on the consumer. The role of demand and consumption in the innovation process still remains largely neglected in the literature. This chapter seeks to redress some of this imbalance by exploring the role that consumption plays in the innovation process. More particularly, it seeks to explore the firm as a consumer and how this may shape the innovation process. Consumption and the way firms consume intermediate goods and services forms an important, but neglected, part of a firm's capability set. The focus of the chapter is, therefore, primarily on the consumption of intermediate goods and services by firms, rather than on the role of final consumption by individuals and households.

Research into consumption and innovation in relation to the firm remains undeveloped. Despite a number of useful studies, the role of consumption and demand in the innovation process still remains largely neglected. There has also been little discussion about consumption by the firm in comparison to individual or household consumption. However, in particular, the role of consumption in relation to services, rather than consumption of goods, has only been briefly commented upon (see Gershuny, 1978; Gershuny & Miles, 1983). In this latter context, introducing a service dimension to the discussion on innovation also helps shed a new perspective on the process of consumption and its relationship with firm-level innovation for several interrelated reasons. It is suggested that services are important in the consumption of new goods (and services). The way firms consume intermediate goods (and services), yields service-like attributes and these form important and distinctive capabilities for the firm. Consumption and the development of routines associated with it can in turn be seen as forms of disembodied, organizational innovation.

5.2. Industrial consumption

From a period of relative stasis in terms of academic interest and progress, there have been several recent studies that have sought to review and critique existing consumption theory from neoclassical (see Lancaster, 1966, 1971, 1991; Stigler & Becker, 1977) and other reformulated economic studies (Ironmonger, 1972; Scitovsky, 1992; Earl, 1986; Woo, 1992) to much more complex and interdisciplinary perspectives (Ackerman, 1997, p. 651). These studies have sought to develop and integrate consumption theory within a wider socio-economic context, in particular focusing on consumption as a change agent.

These analyses have highlighted several characteristics of consumption building upon the existing body of literature that have not been readily acknowledged in the past (see Table 5.1). Table 5.1 highlights the seed change in thinking about the nature, value and importance of consumption in shaping economic change and including innovation. Such studies stress that to be an effective consumer involves time and resources, and is not merely a passive process (McMeekin *et al.*, 2002, p. 8). Some of these studies develop Lancaster's theory of consumer choice (Lancaster, 1966, 1971, 1991), in that the consumer needs to be an active agent and invest in time and resources to build up capabilities to consume effectively. By emphasizing the acquisition and development of consumer competences and routines, such studies also echo and build upon Stigler and Becker's (1977, p. 78) neoclassical concept of the accumulation of 'consumption capital'. Just as innovations require considerable investment to produce things, so do consumers need to invest in new capabilities and routines to consume them.

The studies listed above, although significant in the conceptualization of consumption, have a number of limitations. They only tangentially discuss the role of consumption in the process of innovation. The issue of innovation and technology, if noted at all, is within the broader context of the search for new tastes or in the desire for novelty. The search

Table 5.1. Firm consumption: as a capability and stimulant to innovation

	New perspectives on firm consumption	*Authors*
1.	Consumption is an active, rather than passive, process.	Hirschman, 1980, p. 284; Bianchi, 1998a, p. 65; Fournier & Mick, 1999, p. 15.
2.	Consumers actively seek novelty to satisfy needs and tastes.	Hirschman, 1980, p. 286; Oliver, 1989; Oliver & Swan, 1989.
3.	Consumers act as interactive agents in the wider competitive environment.	Gualerzi, 1998, p. 59.
4.	Effective consumption patterns require time and resources to develop, but which for this reason also sets constraints for such development.	Loasby, 1998, p. 94; Metcalfe, 2001, p. 44.
5.	As consumption requires time and resources it should be seen as forming a key capability of the firm.	Langlois & Cosgel, 1998, pp. 110–11.
6.	Consumption requires a process of learning and this is reflected in the development of efficient routines for successful consumption.	Loasby, 1998, p. 98; and Robertson & Yu, 2001, p. 90.
7.	Competences and routines are built around the consumption process and this requires a whole set of attributes in investment, knowledge and enterprise in the consumption process. This is associated with the notion of the 'enterprising consumer', 'skilled consumption' and the development of 'consumption knowledge'; in turn linked with wider notion of 'market knowledge'.	Earl, 1986, pp. 53–4; Scitovsky, 1992, p. 225; Metcalfe, 2001, p. 38; Li & Calantone, 1998.
8.	Consumption, in seeking different wants and novelty, creates incentives for innovation and has an important influence on the selection of new technologies and the new combinatorial use of them.	Ironmonger, 1972, p. 13.

for novelty and the development of new tastes are important issues but their impact on innovation is not pursued. These studies make little or no specific reference to the consumption of services or to intermediate goods, but instead remained focused on final consumption patterns by the individual or households. The literature remains centred on the behaviour of the 'atomistic' individual or (at best) household consumer and their consumption of final goods. Thus, Earl's detailed analysis of consumption, focuses on the car as the consumer durable 'par excellence' (Earl, 1986, pp. 20–1), even though it is based on an adapted model of business strategy developed by Kay (1982, 1984) reworking it to analyze household consumption patterns rather than directly exploring how firms may seek to consume (Earl, 1986, pp. 63–5, 74–6). There are a few exceptions to this neglect of intermediate goods and services, most notably by Langlois and Cosgel (1998) and Langlois (2001) in their development of a 'capability model' of consumption associated with the development of consumption routines.[1] This chapter therefore seeks to explore some of these central issues in more detail. Thus, what do we mean by the firm being a consumer and more generally the term 'industrial consumption'? Can we talk about industrial consumption in any meaningful sense? In what way does it differ from personal or household consumption? And, what processes are involved in industrial consumption? Each of these questions is be examined in turn.

5.3. Industrial consumption: a framework

Firms and other organizations can clearly be seen to 'consume': they purchase, use, manipulate and incorporate goods and services to run their business and to produce new goods and services. Thus, they not only 'consume to use', but also they 'consume to produce'. Consumption is therefore an integral part of production and vice versa. Firms gain direct utility from their consumption, but consumption should not be seen in terms of these direct utilitarian benefits. They gain other more indirect and complex benefits from consumption. Thus, they generate wider benefits ('psychic income') from consumption in terms of, for example: (a) recognition (or 'classification' as Holt (1995) would put it, in relation to generating status); (b) the development of key trading relationships (relating in turn to power dependency issues); and, (c) articulation of what the organization is.

How might firms be said to consume? There has been little, if any, real articulation of firm-level consumption processes. How useful is it to apply notions from individual or household consumption (final consumption) and apply it to firm or organizational consumption (intermediate consumption)? It would be easy to argue that industrial consumption is a more collective, rational, objective and 'depersonalized' process. However, we should be wary of making such simple comparisons. Let us focus on the initial process of the decision to buy, as the first step in the consumption process. Industrial decision making is certainly outwardly by its nature a more collective process, but equally purchases of personal and household goods associated with family involvement are often collective in nature. Moreover, the actual decision making process within the firm is effectively undertaken only by a small group of key individuals (rarely larger than a family group). Similarly, the decision making process in not necessarily any more rational or objective in its decision-making despite the growth in decision making models and procedures deployed by companies when they buy or outsource goods and services. Studies have shown that decision making within firms is a just as personal, subjective and irrational as in most personal buying situations (Klein, 1989). There is also the issue of the 'depersonal' nature of corporate buying because of its supposed formulaic and objective process. Paradoxically, therefore, because industrial 'buyers' and 'sellers' of industrial goods and services form relatively small communities, they often know each other very well and personally. The extreme may be large, specialized industrial equipment, such as power plants or aircraft, where the effective number of buyers and sellers may be very small indeed and where long-term personal relationships may build up. Even with more routine, lower value goods specialist buyer and seller teams will still know the customer/supplier very well. Compare this with personal purchasing. Close personal involvement may still hold for the local corner shop, but for shopping in major multiple chains, such personal relationships and knowledge may now be very much more distant.

The most significant difference between individual and corporate consumption may however be in the demarcation between buyer and seller and their associated roles. For household durable goods, the division of roles and responsibilities between buyer and seller are largely clear-cut, but for complex projects involving the generation of a new good or service the role between producer and consumer may be much more ambiguous and indeterminate (Rosenberg & Stern, 1971). This is especially the case where introducing a technological innovation requires close cooperation between consumer and supplier (Vaaland & Håkansson, 2003).

In relation to answering the question of what processes are involved in industrial consumption, what studies there have been, have only tangentially covered the relationship between consumption and innovation, have concentrated on examining what may be viewed as the very 'front end' of consumption, namely the purchasing and buying of (new) goods and services. Existing studies, therefore, where they relate to consumption, have tended to focus on the demand process, associated with the buying and purchasing process (see Figure 5.1). This has particularly centered on the (a) 'buyer-supply' or (b) 'user-producer' relationships. However, even here the focus has been supply-led and discussion largely centred on implications for production and the producer. Thus buyer–supplier relations (as indicated as (a) in Figure 5.1), centred on essentially the supplier and supply networks and how firms established supply networks for their production process (see, e.g., studies of the automotive industry during the 1980s and the 1990s; see, e.g., Sabel *et al.*, 1989).

The focus of these studies has, moreover, been more on the relations themselves rather than specific functions. However, there have been studies investigating the activity of buying in terms of the purchasing function within the firm (and within this role of purchasing on new product development and innovation; see, e.g., Burt & Soukup, 1985; Thomas, 1994; Wynstra *et al.*, 2003). They, however, remain centred on the *initial* act of buying and how technical inputs can be incorporated into new product developments rather than wider consumption activities (see Figure 5.1.).

User–producer relations (see (b) in Figure 5.1) have been examined more specifically within the context of innovative activity. The role of users in the innovation process was fairly extensively studied during the 1970s and the 1980s (see von Hippel, 1976, 1978; Parkinson, 1982;

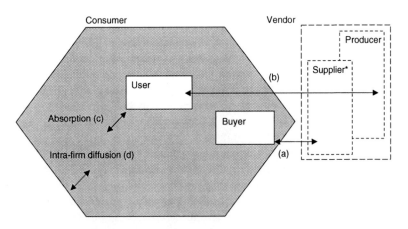

Figure 5.1.   Industrial consumption: fragmented conceptions

Notes: * A supplier may not always be a producer; they can include non-manufacturing firms such as factors, wholesalers and component stockholders.

Shaw, 1985, 1987; Holt, 1987; Foxall, 1987; and Lundvall 1988, 1992a). Here the important role that users play with producers was highlighted, and in particular the links or relationships between them. However, the focus was mainly on the impact of users *on* producers in terms of what innovations they produce rather than so much on the actual use and shaping of innovations by consumers (however, see Foxall, 1988). Apart from these studies, which have a bearing on consumption, there have been several studies that have highlighted issues to do with absorption, most notably Cohen and Levinthal's work on absorptive capacity (Cohen and Levinthal, 1990), and diffusion (Roger, 1995). Discussion about absorption has, however, been on a rather abstracted level. In relation to diffusion, studies have sought to map out the diffusion of innovations within the firm (after the initial purchase and adoption) and reveal that this is far from an instantaneous or homogenous process (Pae *et al.*, 2002). Finally, here there are more general studies associated with the impacts of buying equipment in terms of their benefits to operational efficiency. This can be related to a whole literature on productivity and improving yields, particularly in relation to materials use (see Heshmati, 2003).

These studies, however, provide a rather disparate picture of the 'demand' side of innovation in the context of buying new goods and services. There are much wider range of functions and activities associated with the consumption of new intermediate goods and services (see Figure 5.2). These relate to activities such as the installation and testing of goods and services once purchased, training in the use of goods and services, the maintenance and upgrading of them once in use and their final disposal. These activities and relationships associated with consumption within the firm are complex, interrelated, interactive (that is role of feedback processes) and contested. This moves well beyond the fragmented picture so far described by existing studies. For example, one common and continuing misconception is the frequent conflation of the role of buyer (or purchaser) with user within the firm. This more fundamentally involves confusing buying with use (Lundvall, 1988, p. 365) and the often frequent individualistic and personalized notion of the firm as a single knowing entity. This is despite studies highlighting conflicts between the purchasing department and user departments (Howson & Dale, 1991), or in the case of new product development between the R&D/product development department and purchasing (Faes, 1986).

Between the initial purchase of a new good or service and its disposal there is a series of complex activities and processes within the firm, and

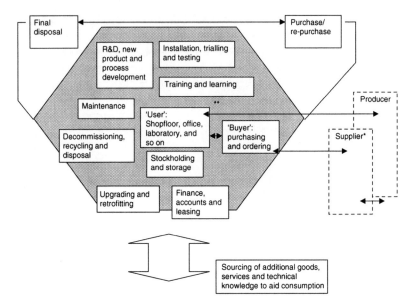

Figure 5.2.   Industrial consumption: sphere of consumption

Notes: * A supplier may not always be a producer; they can include non-manufacturing firms such as factors, wholesalers and component stockholders; ** Only a few of the links between the activities and functions within the firm are not shown on the diagram.

associated with the consumption process. It may also involve the sourcing of additional goods, services and knowledge from outside of the firm to help consume the initial material or equipment (see Figure 5.2). There will also be feedback between previous rounds of consumption between the initial purchase and its final disposal.

There is a constant round of feedback information loops and iterations over the consumption life cycle between the consumer firm and the producer or supplier firm. This is particularly important in relation to the transfer of information and knowledge by the user firm about the good or service being consumed, to the supplier firm which produced the good and the creation of complex knowledge structures which co-evolve between producer and consumer.[2] It should be stressed that this is not just about the user firm feeding back information on the consumption process to the supplier; it may involve the user initiating new products and asking a supplier to bid to produce it (see Foxall, 1988). There is often a complex interplay between producers and users in the innovation process; changes in one sphere often 'sparking off' changes in the other sphere. This can lead to constant rounds of new interaction (von Hippel, 1994, pp. 432–4), with the innovation process between producers and users creating its own innovative dynamic. Indeed, staff from the user organization may form part of the production function (O'Farrell & Moffat, 1991; O'Farrell, 1995) helping to co-produce services (Bettencourt *et al.*, 2002; Lovelock & Young, 1979; Sundbo, 1998). Strong behavioural forces also come into play here in terms of how consumers interact with products and how these change with the introduction of something radically new (Cooper, 2000) and creates the indistinctness of production and consumption noted earlier (Rosenberg & Stern, 1971).

Care must be taken not to assume that there is a single feedback path between disposal and purchase. Feedback within the consumer firm itself is often likely to be fragmented and sometimes contradictory. Consider the decision to replace a current piece of equipment with a newer model from the same supplier firm. This is often seen as a 'simple' replacement decision by the 'firm', where the supplier and the good are already familiar to the firm as consumer. But is the decision that simple? The decision to buy a replacement will obviously involve the key user unit or department, a particular factory or manufacturing department, but will also include often many other functions and activities within the firm. Here are just a few main functions:

(a) the purchasing department who handled the order (considerations on how easy it was to find alternative suppliers, processing the previous order with the supplier firm and so on);

(b) the finance department (what finance or leasing arrangements were offered, for example);

(c) the maintenance and engineering department (ease and cost of maintenance, possibility of upgrades or retrofitting);

(d) human resources department (training requirements to use the equipment effectively); and,

(e) environmental and disposal issues associated with running and replacing the equipment (increasingly associated with end-of-life legislation).

These are just a few functions and activities that could be involved in making the 'simple' replacement decision. For larger pieces of equipment or for shared facilities there may, in addition, be several user units within the firm that have differing views about whether the upgraded model supplied by the existing supplier firm should be given the go

ahead or another model and supplier should be considered. The latter
may involve substantial 'switching costs' but may be preferred not for
reasons of the quality and attributes of what is being consumed, but
rather in terms of strategies over who is supplying the good or service
(e.g., to reduce dependence on a single dominant supplier) or to encourage innovation by attracting in new suppliers (Helper, 1989). In this case
the 'simple' decision may not be about direct, short-term consumption
issues, but about establishing longer-term consumption trajectories in
the future.

5.4. Industrial consumption as a distributed process

Consumption within the firm in terms of the different (and distributed)
elements that are associated with it has been reviewed above. However,
the analysis so far has centred on viewing consumption largely in terms
of the life cycle of a single element – a single good being purchased and
consumed. Consumption, though, should not be restricted to viewing it
as a single event or element, but rather should also be considered as a
continuing process associated with combining different elements –
other goods, services and resources – to yield a more complete or ultimate consumption experience (see Figure 5.2). This more dynamic view
in relation to the consumption of new goods is be outlined in more
detail below. Interestingly, it links up with more traditional notions
about utility derived from more traditional theories about consumption.
Although neoclassical economic theory has many limitations, the
notion of utility is useful in helping to uncover what consumption,
especially industrial consumption, is essentially about.

The concept of utility helps highlight the distinction between desires
and the satisfaction of wants.[3] What discussion there has been about
industrial consumption, has been in a very one-dimensional and direct
sense associated with the 'act of buying' a specific product, and this is
particularly true of industrial goods and services. However, as economists have long recognized in relation to buying goods in general, these
goods satisfy certain wants and therefore yield a utility in satisfying
these wants. This basic notion has been reflected more recently in marketing literature with identifying, for example, the 'core benefit' of a
product or service (Kotler, 1984). In this context many services may be
seen as 'purer' in utilitarian terms as they are often nearer in the spectrum of satisfying ultimate wants, whereas goods may be seen as being

more about an interim milestone on the road to such satisfaction (or more specifically provide a solution to a problem). What this suggests is that consumption has a strong temporal quality (and with it, dynamic and evolutionary qualities). Consumption is rarely an instantaneous process (i.e., when a good or service is actually purchased) in the sense of satisfying immediate wants (Robinson, 1962, pp. 122–3), but rather more prolonged process seeking some kind of underlying satisfaction (Ackerman, 1997, p. 663). Consumption is, therefore, a much richer, but also more time-consuming process about satisfying more fundamental wants rather than a more 'one-off' and one-dimensional experience. This is difficult to illustrate adequately, but even for such a seemingly ephemeral and transient, personal consumer matter of whether watching a film at the cinema is a case in point. Should its 'consumption' solely be seen as watching the film or does it encompass the much wider consumption experience of discussing the film with friends and colleagues afterwards and remembering it in connection with other films and books after the event? With the exception of Greenfield (1966) and Hill (1977) in the field of services, few researchers have recognized the temporal and durable notions of the consumption process.

However, this leads into a discussion about the similarity and inter-linked nature of goods and services (rather than their distinctiveness raised earlier). This can be seen on two levels. First, if one is interested in consumption as satisfying ultimate wants, goods therefore fulfil essentially service-like attributes (Howells, 2004). This issue is developed by Saviotti and Mectalfe's (1984) work on attempting to measure technical change of products, that is material artefacts. Saviotti and Mectalfe, building upon Lancaster's work (Lancaster, 1966), stress that a product can have both internal properties, that is those relating to the internal structure of the product, and external properties, relating to wider issues associated with the type of service being offered to users as part of that good. Second, goods not only have service-like qualities in their consumption and utility, but more fundamentally they are interlinked more directly in their consumption (de Brentani, 1995) and hence often 'co-consumed'. Thus, as far back as 1892, Alfred Marshall highlighted the issue of derived demand and joint demand for goods and services (Marshall, 1892 [1899], pp. 218–23), exemplified in his notion of composite demand. More specifically this has been explored in more detail by Swann (1999) in his analysis of 'Marshall's consumer' and the increasing levels of sophistication that consumers can present in the consumption process.

Consumption is therefore rarely, if ever, the consumption of a good or service at a single point of time. In the case of a piece of machinery or equipment, consumption is rarely about a simple, one-off purchase but involves a much more complex and longer-term process of buying (or increasingly leasing), using, maintaining, upgrading and eventual disposal. This shift in focus has major implications for firms that sell such products and services in terms of how they address consumers' needs and satisfy their ultimate demand. Consumption is therefore not a one-off contact, via the sale of a product, but a continuing process involving long-term customer contact. This is to be expected if consumption shifts from a single, one-off act to long-term user support; that is, from selling a good at a single point in time to supplying better and more efficient service-like effects over a period of time.

5.5. Consumption and innovation: the interlinked nature of goods and services

If the above emphasized that industrial consumption should not be seen as a 'one-off' but rather a longer-term process, it is also important to recognize the important combinatorial aspects of the consumption process, particularly in relation to the consumption of new goods and services. The combinatorial aspects of the consumption process, when a firm consumes a good and combines it with the consumption and use of other goods and services, has been recently outlined (Howells, 2004). In short, services often 'encapsulate', or act as 'wrappers' to, goods and resources. This will not be explored in detail here, but there are some aspects that are worth discussing as they help illuminate the consumption process within firms.

In order to consume a new good, (a), firms frequently consume multiple sets of goods and services to create a consumption experience and to yield some kind of utility. This involves not only purchasing goods and services from other suppliers/producers to help consume the initial good, (b), but also may involve the generation of in-house goods and services from other parts of the firm as well. The consumption of a good therefore can involve multiple sets of other consumption and production activities. The consumption capability of a firm therefore resides not just in consuming the initial product and absorbing it within the firm, but also in combining other goods and services to aid consumption.

This combinatorial aspect in the consumption process can be seen in the way that services can help in the consumption of new goods (and services). This can be seen to operate in several different ways (Howells, 2003):

- Existing, familiar services encapsulate new goods (or services), in turn, providing a:
  - ○ *familiarizer effect* – by providing a familiar, trusted service to a new good, making it more acceptable for consumers to adopt the innovation;
  - ○ *buffer effect* – once the good has been adopted enabling the consumption of a new good in exactly the same consumption service format as the former, old good (that is earlier vintage) was consumed;
  - ○ *facilitator effect* – by encouraging and helping consumers to learn new practices and routines through an existing service 'window' or framework to use a new good. As noted earlier, learning plays an important role in the consumption of new innovations.
- New services encapsulating existing goods (or services). Here services are used to improve the acceptability, flexibility and performance of existing goods and these attributes are outlined in more detail below, using some simple examples. As such, new services encapsulating existing goods can provide a number of revitalizing and innovative roles in terms of a:
  - ○ *sweetener effect* – by improving the acceptability of a good through a new service format, which may overcome obstacles to the adoption, or use of a good or service before. This may involve better set-up and operational instructions, which to the consumer may involve simple changes, but to the provider may involve complex, disembodied technical changes to routines and practices in the presentation of the good. Thus technical documentation, including product configuration data, maintenance and operating instructions for use, may involve changes in highly complex organizational and operating routines both for the service being sold and the purchasing company using such new documentation.
  - ○ *flexibility effect* – new services associated with an existing good (or service) may improve flexibility of use. Thus better maintenance practices and fault diagnostics may allow the good to be made available to the user over longer periods of time or during periods when it was previously not possible to use it.
  - ○ *performance effect* – a new service may improve the performance of the good. The most obvious example here is a new software

program (with improved performance and functionality) being loaded to run on existing information technology equipment. However, another example is the development of a whole new area of services associated with 'predictive support services', which both improve the efficiency of a good, but also reduces 'downtime' in its use.

○ *functionality effect* – new services may allow an existing good to be used in a different way (Robertson & Yu, 2001, p. 188). Thus a piece of testing equipment, or scientific instrument (von Hippel, 1976), may be used to test for things in different environments or conditions it was previously not initially designed for. However, this in turn may involve modifications to the existing good, generating a new round of innovation.

Combining services in this way can be seen as playing an important role in the consumption of innovations by enabling firms as consumers to interact and accommodate these new goods and services more easily. Through mechanisms such as branding, they can reassure consumers and act as pointers to quality standards that were experienced through previous rounds of consumption. However, services also provide conduits through which innovations are adopted and learning mechanisms through which innovations are used. On the basis of Scitovsky's (1992) notion of skilled consumption, adopting a new good requires some of its attributes to be recognized and understood (and in this context, facilitated by services) if the consumption of the innovation is to be successful.

The shift from a single one-off consumption event to a more long-term combinatorial process in turn suggests that firms' develop practices and routines surrounding the process of consumption. This picks up the general theme outlined earlier of what Langlois and Cosgel (1998, p. 59) and Langlois (2001, p. 90) saw as the development of efficient routines by firms for successful consumption. This can be seen to parallel Warde's (2003) outline of consumption practices by individuals, and can also be traced back to earlier work in industrial economics associated with the notion of the development of firm routines and capabilities as they relate to the capacities of firms to change the resources they consume. Edith Penrose (1959 [1995], pp. 78–9) in her book *The Theory of the Growth of the Firm* noted in relation to consumption by firms that:

Physically describable resources are purchased in the market for their known services; but as soon as they become part of a firm the range of services they are capable of yielding starts to change. The services that resources will yield depend on the capacities of the men using them, but the development of the capacities of men is partly shaped by the resources men deal with. The two together create the special productive opportunity of a particular firm.

As such, the distinctive way which firms *consume* and use physical goods and resources in terms of their service utility, forms a key, but neglected element within a firm's repertoire of capabilities (Richardson, 1972; Swann, 2002). Consumers must learn about and correctly use a product to realize its benefits (Wood & Lynch, 2002, p. 425). Indeed, how firms *translate* goods and resources into *services* may form an important component and attribute in this whole process. The process of consumption as a capability can form a powerful complementary asset in innovation that consumers can use to exert control over the producer (Foxall, 1988, pp. 242–3). To be effective, consumption requires the development of a set of routines, which can form distinctive capabilities for the firm (Langlois & Cosgel, 1998, pp. 110, 112). These capabilities not only include better communication of a firm's needs to suppliers capabilities, but perhaps more fundamentally identifying and articulating what these existing and new needs are to itself (Robertson & Yu, 2001, p. 190).

Firms need to develop successful routines and procedures in order to successfully compete. However, we need to caution against such routines being undertaken in a necessarily coordinated or harmonized way. As noted above, it has been recognized that purchase decision-makers and product users are often not the same group within a firm (Pae *et al.*, 2002, p. 720) and that lack of adequate linkages between purchasers and users within an organization can often lead to poor purchasing decisions with regard to new goods and services. A fractured and departmentalized process to the buying, use and more general consumption of goods and services can lead to lost opportunities in terms of harnessing a firm's potential capabilities in terms of consumption. Firms need to provide a more integrated consumption knowledge framework from which they can harness in distinctive ways to form a core capability of the firm.

5.6. New directions

This chapter has sought to explore and analyze how firms consume. The chapter has reviewed previous literature in this field and has shown that there has been very little discussion about firms as consumers and more particularly what processes are involved in firm or organizational consumption. What mention there has been of consumption in industrial terms has been in terms of a narrow interpretation centred on buying or use. By contrast, the above discussion has revealed that firm consumption should be considered as a much more intricate process involving a distributed set of functions and activities which are seeking to satisfy a variety of complex needs and wants which are both immediate and longer term. Here it is useful to conceptualize consumption as a single event but rather as a longer-term, dynamic process. Firms do not consume products or services in isolation, but combine them to achieve both their short-term and long-term requirements. This combinatorial approach can be seen in how firms 'encapsulate' a good or service with other goods and services as part of the consumption process. This approach is also evident in the consumption of new products and services and can be seen as being an important, but neglected, element in a firm's wider set of practices and strategies associated with innovation. Indeed consumption, and the practices and routines surrounding these processes, should be viewed as part of a firm's development of its strategic capability.

Even here, although the discussion has attempted to move away from the consumption process of a firm as a single act of consuming a single good and service towards a much more complex, interlinked and distributed process both internal to the firm but also externally. In this latter context, we should start conceiving firms as being in networks or chains of consumption. The notion of a 'supply chain' has proved a valuable concept to both managers and academics alike in terms of articulating and describing a firms relations and linkages with other firms and organizations in the supply process. Could the notion of a *consumption chain* be developed to provide an equally valuable tool and concept? At the very least, the notion of a 'consumption chain' could provide an alternative (and indeed diametrically opposite) perceptive to the supply chain approach. However, more fundamentally it could have the potential to become a much more powerful tool highlighting new areas that firms could address and develop to gain and sustain long-term competitive advantage. In order to achieve this, though, much more research is required to provide a truer and more holistic view of this industrial consumption process and how it fits in with the wider strategic operations of the firm. In developing this new research avenue we could, at the very least, provide a counter-balance to the overwhelmingly supply oriented business and innovation models that dominate the literature.

Acknowledgement

This chapter arises out of research funded by the UK Economic and Social Research Council.

Notes

1 This is echoed in an earlier work by G. Katona, *The Powerful Consumer: Psychological Studies of the American Economy* (New York: McGraw-Hill, 1960) pp. 58–9, who talks about habitual problem-solving frameworks which steer decisions in a certain direction.
2 In terms of Pfaffman's terminology, this would involve the exchange of substantive knowledge about how a product is produced and functional knowledge, the knowledge about how it is applied and used; E. Pfaffman, 'Knowledge maturity of products, modularity, and the vertical boundaries of the firm', in N. Foss & V. Maluke *Competence, Governance and Entrepreneurship* (Oxford: Oxford University Press, 2001), pp. 250–75.
3 Although as Joan Robinson noted in her analysis of neoclassical theory of utility: '*Utility* is a metaphysical concept of impregnable circularity; *utility* is the quality in commodities that makes individuals want to buy them, and the fact that individuals want to buy commodities shows that they have *utility*.' J. Robinson, *Economic Philosophy* (London: Penguin, 1962), p. 48.

Bibliography

Acker, M. & McReynolds, P. (1967), 'The need for novelty: a comparison of six instruments', *Psychological Record*, 17, pp. 177–82.
Ackerman, F. (1977), 'Consumed in theory: alternative perspectives on the economics of consumption', *Journal of Economic Issues*, 31, pp. 651–64.
Baker, M.J. & Parkinson, S.T. (eds) (1986), *Organizational Buying Behaviour: Purchasing and Marketing Implications* (London: Macmillan).
Bettencourt, L.A., Ostrom, A.L., Brown, S.W. & Roundtree R.J. (2002), 'Client co-production in knowledge-intensive business services', *California Management Review*, 44(4), pp. 100–28.
Bianchi, M. (1998a), 'Taste for novelty and novel tastes: the role of human agency in consumption' (in Bianchi 1998b).
Bianchi, M. (ed.) (1998b), *The Active Consumer* (London: Routledge).
Burt, D.N. & Soukup, W.R. (1985), 'Purchasing's role in new product development, *Harvard Business Review*, Sept.–Oct., pp. 90–97.
Callahan, J. & Lasry, E. (2004), 'The importance of customer input in the development of very new products', *R&D Management*, 34, pp. 107–20.
Cattell, R.B. (1975), *Personality and Motivation: Structure and Measurement* (New York: Harcourt, Brace & World).
Cohen, W. & Levinthal, R. (1990), 'Absorptive capacity: a new perspective on learning and innovation', *Administrative Science Quarterly*, 35, pp. 128–52.
Cooper, L.G. (2000), 'Strategic marketing planning for radically new products', *Journal of Marketing*, 64, pp. 1–16.

de Brentani, U. (1995), 'New industrial service development: scenarios for success and failure', *Journal of Business Research*, 32, pp. 93–103.

Dosi, G., Freeman, C., Nelson, R., Silverberg, G. & Soete, L. (eds) (1988), *Technical Change and Economic Theory* (London: Pinter).

Dow, S.C. & Earl, P.E. (eds) (1999), *Economic Organization and Economic Knowledge: Essays in Honour of Brian J. Loasby* (Cheltenham: Edward Elgar).

Earl, P.E. (1986), *Lifestyle Economics: Consumer Behaviour in a Turbulent World* (Brighton: Wheatsheaf).

Earl, P.E. (1998), 'Consumer goals as journeys into the unknown' (in Bianchi, 1998b).

Faes, W. (1986), 'Singler Chemicals: purchasing's contribution to new product development – a case history in the pharmaceutical industry' (in Baker & Parkinson).

Farley, F. & Farley, S.V. (1967), 'Extroversion and stimulus-seeking motivation', *Journal of Consumer Psychology*, 31(2), pp. 215–16.

Foss, N. & Maluke, V. (eds) (2001), *Competence, Governance and Entrepreneurship* (Oxford: Oxford University Press).

Fournier, S. & Mick, D.G. (1999), 'Rediscovering satisfaction', *Journal of Marketing*, 63, pp. 5–23.

Foxall, G.R. (1987), 'Strategic implications of user-initiated innovation' (in Rothwell & Bessant).

Foxall, G.R. (1988), 'The theory and practice of user-initiated innovation', *Journal of Marketing Management*, 4, pp. 230–48.

Foxall, G.R., Murphy, F.S. & Tierney, J.D. (1985), 'Market development in practice: a case study of user-initiated innovation', *Journal of Marketing Management*, 1(3), pp. 201–11.

Gershuny, J. (1978), *After Industrial Society: The Emerging Self-Service Economy* (London: Macmillan).

Gershuny, J. & Miles, I. (1983), *The New Service Economy* (London: Pinter).

Greenfield, H.I. (1966), *Manpower and the Growth of Producer Services* (New York: Columbia University Press).

Griffin, A. & Hauser, J.R. (1993), 'The voice of the customer', *Marketing Science*, 12, pp. 1–27.

Gualerzi, D. (1998), 'Economic change, choice and innovation in consumption' (in Bianchi, 1998b).

Helper, S. (1989), 'Strategy and irreversibility in supplier relations: the case of the US automobile industry, Working Paper No. 89–22, School of Management, Boston University, Boston, MA.

Heshmati, A. (2003), 'Productivity growth, efficiency and outsourcing in manufacturing and service industries', *Journal of Economic Surveys*, 17, pp. 79–112.

Hill, P. (1977), 'On goods and services', *Review of Income and Wealth*, 4, 315–38.

Hirschman, E.C. (1980), 'Innovativeness, novelty seeking and consumer creativity', *Journal of Consumer Research*, 7, pp. 283–95.

Holt, D.B. (1995), 'How consumers consume: a typology of consumption practices', *Journal of Consumer Research*, 21, June, pp. 1–16.

Holt, D.B. (1997), 'Poststructuralist lifestyle analysis: conceptualizing the social patterning of consumption in postmodernity', *Journal of Consumer Research*, 23, pp. 326–50.

Holt, K. (1987), 'The role of the user in product innovation' (in Rothwell & Bessant).

Howells, J. (2003), 'Innovation, consumption and knowledge: services and encapsulation', ESRC Centre for Research on Innovation & Competition Discussion Paper, No. 62 (Manchester: University of Manchester).

Howells, J. (2004), 'Innovation, consumption and services: encapsulation and the combinatorial role of services', *Service Industries Journal*, 24, pp. 19–36.

Howson, T.G. & Dale, B.G. (1991), 'An example m of the purchasing function in a sales-oriented company', *International Journal of Operations & Production Management*, 11(5), pp. 71–82.

Ironmonger, D.S. (1972), *New Commodities and Consumer Behavior* (Cambridge: Cambridge University Press).

Katona, G. (1960), *The Powerful Consumer: Psychological Studies of the American Economy* (New York: McGraw-Hill).

Kay, N.M. (1982), *The Evolving Firm* (London: Macmillan).

Kay, N.M. (1984), *The Emergent Firm: Knowledge, Ignorance and Surprise in Economic Organisation* (London: Macmillan).

Klein, G.A. (1988), 'Recognition-primed Decisions', *Advances in Man-Machine Systems Research*, 5, pp. 47–92.

Kotler, P. (1984), *Marketing Management: Analysis Planning and Control* (London: Prentice-Hall).

Lancaster, K.J. (1966), 'A new approach to consumer theory', *Journal of Political Economy*, 14, pp. 133–56.

Lancaster, K.J. (1971), *Consumer Demand: A New Approach* (New York: Columbia University Press).

Lancaster, K.J. (1991), *Modern Consumer Theory* (Aldershot: Edward Elgar).

Langlois, R.N. (2001), 'Knowledge, consumption, and endogenous growth', *Journal of Evolutionary Economics*, 11, pp. 77–93.

Langlois, R.N. & Cosgel, M.M. (1998), 'The organization of consumption (in Bianchi, 1998b).

Li, T. & Calantone, R.J. (1998), 'The impact of market knowledge competence on new product advantage: conceptualisation and empirical examination', *Journal of Marketing*, 62, pp. 13–29.

Loasby, B.J. (1998), 'Cognition and innovation' (in Bianchi, 1998b).

Lovelock, C. & Young, R. (1979), 'Look to consumers to increase productivity', *Harvard Business Review*, 57(3), pp. 168–76.

Lundvall, B.-Å. (1988), 'Innovation as an interactive process – from user-producer interaction to the National Systems of Innovation' (in Dosi, Freeman, Nelson, Silverberg & Soete).

Lundvall, B.-Å. (1992a), 'User-producer relationships, national systems of innovation and internationalization' (in Lundvall, 1992b).

Lundvall, B.-Å. (ed.) (1992b) *National Systems of Innovation: Towards a Theory of Innovation and Interactive Learning* (London: Pinter).

Macdonald, S. (1995), 'Too close for comfort? The strategic implications of getting too close to the customer', *California Management Review*, 37(4), pp. 8–27.

Marshall, A. (1892 [1899]), *Elements of Economics of Industry* (London: Macmillan).

McMeekin, A., Green, K., Tomlinson, M. & Walsh, V. (eds) (2002), *Innovation by Demand: An Interdisciplinary Approach to the Study of Demand and its Role in Innovation* (Manchester: Manchester University Press).

Metcalfe, J.S. (2001), 'Consumption, preferences, and the evolutionary agenda', *Journal of Evolutionary Economics*, 11, pp. 37–58.

Midgely, D.F. (1976), 'A simple mathematical theory of innovative behavior', *Journal of Consumer Research*, 3, pp. 31–41.

Midgely, D.F. & Dowling, G.R. (1978), 'Innovativeness: the concept and its measurement', *Journal of Consumer Research*, 4, pp. 229–42.

O'Farrell, P.N. (1995), 'Manufacturing demand for business services', *Cambridge Journal of Economics*, 19, pp. 523–43.

O'Farrell, P.N. & Moffat, L.A.R. (1991), 'An interaction model of business service production and consumption', *British Journal of Management*, 2, pp. 205–21.

Oliver, R. (1989), 'Processing of the satisfaction response in consumption: a suggested framework and research propositions', *Journal of Consumer Satisfaction/ Dissatisfaction and Complaining Behavior*, 2, pp. 1–16.

Oliver, R. & Swan, J.E. (1989), 'Consumer perceptions of interpersonal equity and satisfaction in transactions: a field survey approach', *Journal of Marketing*, 53, pp. 21–35.

Pae, J.H., Kim, N., Han, J.K. & Yip, L. (2002), 'Managing intraorganizational diffusion of innovations: impact of buying center dynamics and environments', *Industrial Marketing Management*, 31, pp. 719–26.

Parkinson, S.T. (1982), 'The role of the user in successful new product development', *R&D Management*, 12, pp. 123–31.

Peck, H., Payne, A., Christopher, M. & Clark, M. (1999), *Relationship Marketing: Strategy and Implementation* (Oxford: Butterworth-Heinemann).

Penrose, E. (1959), *The Theory of the Growth of the Firm* (Oxford: Oxford University Press).

Pfaffman, E. (2001), 'Knowledge maturity of products, modularity, and the vertical boundaries of the firm' (in Foss & Maluke).

Richardson, G.B. (1972), 'The organisation of industry', *Economic Journal*, 82, pp. 883–96.

Robertson, P.L. & Yu, T.F. (2001), 'Firm strategy, innovation and consumer demand', *Managerial and Decision Economics*, 22, pp. 183–99.

Robinson, J. (1962), *Economic Philosophy* (London: Penguin).

Rogers, E.M. (1976), 'New product adoption and diffusion', *Journal of Consumer Research*, 2, pp. 290–301.

Rogers, E.M. (1995), *Diffusion of Innovations* (New York: Free Press, 4th edn).

Rosenberg, L.J. & Stern, L.W. (1971), 'Conflict measurement in the distribution channel', *Journal of Marketing*, 8, pp. 437–42.

Rothwell, R. & Bessant, J. (eds) (1987), *Innovation: Adaptation and Growth* (Amsterdam: Elsevier).

Sabel, C.F., Kern, H., & Heerigel, G. (1989), 'Collaborative manufacturing: new supplier relations in the automobile industry and the redefinition of the industrial corporation', *International Motor Vehicle Program International Policy Forum* (Cambridge, MA: MIT Press).

Saviotti, P.P. & Metcalfe, J.S. (1984), 'A theoretical approach to the construction of technological output indicators', *Research Policy*, 13, pp. 141–51.

Scitovsky, T. (1992), *The Joyless Economy: The Psychology of Human Satisfaction*, Second Edition (Oxford: Oxford University Press).

Shaw, B. (1985), 'The role of the interaction between the user and the manufacturer in medical equipment innovation', *R&D Management*, 15, pp. 283–92.

Shaw, B. (1987), 'Strategies for user-producer interaction' (in Rothwell & Bessant).

Shostack, G.L. (1977), 'Breaking free from product marketing', *Journal of Marketing*, 41(2), pp. 73–80.

Stigler, G.J. & Becker, G.S. (1977), 'De gustibus non est disputandum', *American Economic Review*, 67, pp. 76–90.

Storer, C.E., Holmen, E. & Pedersen, A.C. (2003), 'Exploration of customer horizons to measure understanding of netchains', *Supply Chain Management*, 8, pp. 455–66.

Sundbo, J. (1998), *The Theory of Innovation* (Cheltenham: Edward Elgar).

Swann, G.M.P. (1999), 'Marshall's consumer as an innovator' (in Dow & Earl).

Swann, G.M.P. (2002), 'There's more to economics of consumption than (almost) unconstrained utility maximisation' (in McMeekin, Green, Tomlinson & Walsh).

Thomas, R. (1994), 'Purchasing and technological change: exploring the links between company technology strategy and supplier relationships', *European Journal of Purchasing and Supply Management*, 1, pp. 161–8.

Tiger, L. & Calantone, R.J. (1998), 'The impact of market knowledge competence on new product advantage: conceptualisation and empirical examination', *Journal of Marketing*, 62, pp. 13–29.

Tzokus, N. & Saren, M. (1997), 'Building relationship platforms in consumer markets: a value chain approach', *Journal of Strategic Marketing*, 5, pp. 105–20.

Tzokus, N. & Saren, M. (2004), 'Competitive advantage, knowledge and relationship marketing: where, what and how?', *Journal of Business and Industrial Marketing*, 19, pp. 124–35.

Vaaland, T.I. & Håkansson, H. (2003), 'Exploring interorganizational conflict in complex projects', *Industrial Marketing Management*, 32, pp. 127–38.

von Hippel, E. (1976), 'The dominant role of users in the scientific instrument innovation process', *Research Policy*, 5, pp. 212–39.

von Hippel, E. (1978), 'Successful industrial products from customer ideas', *Journal of Marketing*, 42, pp. 39–49.

von Hippel, E. (1986), 'Lead users: a source of novel product concepts', *Management Science*, 32, pp. 791–805.

von Hippel, E. (1988), *The Sources of Innovation* (Oxford: Oxford University Press).

von Hippel, E. (1994), 'Sticky information and the locus of problem solving: implications for innovation', *Management Science*, 40(4), pp. 429–39.

Warde, A. (2003), 'Consumption and theories of practice', *Mimeo* (Manchester: ESRC Centre for Research on Innovation & Competition, University of Manchester).

Witt, U. (2001), 'Learning to consume – a theory of wants and the growth of demand', *Journal of Evolutionary Economics*, 11, pp. 23–36.

Woo, H.K.H. (1992), *Cognition, Value, and Price: A General Theory of Value* (Ann Arbor: University of Michigan Press).

Wood, S.L. & Lynch, J.G. (2002), 'Prior knowledge and complacency in new product learning', *Journal of Consumer Research*, 29, pp. 416–26.

Wynstra, F., Axelsson, B. & van Weele, A. (2000), 'Driving and enabling factors for purchasing involvement in product development', *European Journal of Purchasing and Supply Management*, 6, pp. 129–41.

Wynstra, F., Weggeman, M. & van Weele, A. (2003), 'Exploring purchasing integration in product development', *Industrial Marketing Management*, 32(1), pp. 69–83.

6
Innovation and Diffusion of Site-specific Crop Management

Søren M. Pedersen and Jørgen L. Pedersen

6.1. Introduction

The concept and philosophy behind precision farming is not different from traditional farm management, namely that the field should be cultivated according to the temporal and variation on the field and with an ultimate goal of obtaining better gross margins. In principle, farmers have been practising precision farming for centuries. Most farmers possess site-specific knowledge about soil conditions and expected yields and they often know where to expect areas with weeds, drought and scarce water resources in the field. Precision farming is taking place all over the world either with or without global positioning systems (GPS). Currently, about 400 Danish farmers are expected to use GPS on their farms (Pedersen, 2003). Even in developing countries, such as Tanzania, simple precision farming systems occur. At the local tea plantations, small field plots are registered and the yields related to a given sub-unit are measured during harvest by weighing each tea yield individually. By doing so the farmer is able to point out where to plant new tea bushes. A similar approach was prevalent in Denmark and Europe years ago, when the individual peasants had small and nearly subsistence-based family holdings. Each field was divided into sub-units according to soil type and yield potentials – often divided with hedges and stone fences. Often the individual sub-fields were devoted to a particular arable crop (Blackmore *et al.*, 2002).

Modern farming is to a large extent specialized and focuses on scale advantages. Most of the stone fences have been removed to allow for large uniform areas that are easy to handle with large modern farm vehicles. The size of a combine harvester is about 20–30 feet and a boom sprayer is between 24 and 36 metres. Fields are seldom below 10 hectares.

In this respect some spatial variation will often occur within the field. Compared with previous farming traditions, the major progression in modern precision farming is that farmers are able to register and save documentation about spatial variation due to GPS and GIS (geographical information systems), advanced sensor systems and other electronic remedies. Precision farming is a management concept, which is highly information intensive. Several new technologies for gathering data on the field have been developed during the past decade. Many of them seem to be fully developed and commercialized. Even so, only a few of these systems seem to be sufficient for decision making on the field. It is still the farmer who is going to make the final decision about management strategy and this approach seems to be even more important than ever before, simply as a result of an enormous pool of data and information. Until now, most trials have only shown little yield improvements from variable fertilizer application or mixed results at best (see Pedersen, 2003).

6.2. Innovation and precision farming

The development from the first idea to practical application on the market can be defined as a process in three steps: *invention, innovation* and *diffusion*. Invention usually related to the first idea of using a new technique. A good example is the first attempt to map the site-specific yield on the field by using the GPS system. A technical innovation is defined as the first commercial application or production of a new process or product (Freeman, 1974), and innovation has also been defined as a change of decision rules to fit with the surrounding requirements (Coombs *et al.*, 1987). An innovation includes all activities that create technological change. It may depend on several activities, such as research and development, product design, process engineering, distribution and marketing. Diffusion is related to the widespread adoption of an innovation. What causes a successful diffusion and how can we expect a general adoption among the users?

Innovation scholars have discussed the driving forces of innovations for several years. The Austrian and, later, American economist Schumpeter (1883–1950) argued in his early work that the entrepreneurs are the key actors within the development of innovations. The entrepreneurs were responsible of the introduction of new products, process and systems based on their business decisions. These processes provide opportunities for new supply and markets (Freeman, 1991). New entrepreneurs are willing to develop new technologies and are able to run a risk to get a temporal monopoly on the market. Later, Schumpeter put more emphasis on the big established monopolies and recognized that those companies would be the driving forces for growth. One reason for that is the large profits related to monopolies, which enable large companies to invest in research and development (Schumpeter, 1943 [1966]). Later, the demand pull view gained recognition by economists. The American economist Schmookler, among others, argued from empirical studies, that market demand and customers had a significant impact on development of new technologies.

With these two theories – demand pull and technology push – several compromising theories have been developed and of which several studies have focused on the demand side. In fact, it is very difficult to distinguish between these two schools. Innovation involves two sides. On the one hand, innovation involves new technical knowledge, which may require technical and scientific knowledge. On the other hand, it involves the market and a certain need for a new product. These two approaches have been known as the *technology push theories* and *demand pull theories* of innovation (Freeman, 1974). As indicated, an innovation process is a complex process that involves demand- and supply-side parameters. It seems to be the case that 'technology push' is often important in the early development phase of an innovation, whereas the market demand is becoming more important while the innovation matures over time (Coombs *et al.*, 1987). The agricultural sector comprises of many small firms that cannot afford to invest a large share of their income from production into innovation research, simply because the potential gains are proportionally small. In this respect, agricultural research is carried out by public research or large companies that sell to the sector.

6.2.1. Interdependences between different technologies

A new technique or innovation is often developed in an isolated process regardless of the surrounding environment. In several cases the innovation can be used as an isolated item that is useful in itself. In many situations, however, the innovation has to fit into a larger system. An innovation implies that specific fittings and adaptations have to be made in order to use the technology in its current form. Sometimes it might be necessary to adapt existing technologies and structures in order to fit with the new innovation.

In a technical system that is made up of many different components, it is vital that all items are able to function in an easy way. In other words, each component has to be compatible with the other components in the system. The development of the assembly line by Henry Ford is regarded as a *systemic innovation*, since it requires a new design of much known special-purpose machinery. All of the machinery has to be adjusted or modified in order to fit with the assembly line (Boon, 2001). The application of the positioning systems (GPS and GIS) in the agricultural sector can also be considered as a systemic innovation because tractors, tractor tools and combine harvesters have to be modified in order to receive and use GPS signals. Moreover, electronic equipment, cables and plugs have to be compatible with other systems. It is pointed out that a successful innovation often requires the development or investment in other parameters, such as marketing, services, logistics, financing and economics. If the actors involved solely focus on the core technology without paying attention to the other elements in the system, then it is likely that the commercialization will be jeopardized (Boon, 2001).

One of the most comprehensive studies of success and failure among entrepreneurs and their development of new innovations was the SAPPHO project, which concluded that in addition to well-functioning technology, a key criteria for successful innovation was that marketing of the product was in place. An understanding of the market and user need is essential for commercial success (Freeman, 1974). In this respect the interdependence between different components or special purpose machinery should be considered in an economic perspective. Some systems are just a part of an overall economic system but others might be so comprehensive that they can be considered as a complete self-contained economic system. Whether or not the system consists of one or several interactions, it is important when looking at industrial innovations and interrelated production chains that all partners or the overall chain get an economic benefit from participating (Gylling *et al.*, 1999; Boon, 2001), otherwise it is impossible to commercialize and market the innovation successfully. A study (Mohamed & Rickards, 1996) concluded that firms that interact among other firms and their external environment tends to encourage creativity and innovation. These innovative firms also have a higher degree of computerization than less innovative firms. This study was based on a given industrial environment but the tendency might be similar in the agricultural sector, although market conditions in the farm business is highly competitive focusing on traditional price reductions.

A final element to describe the process of technological change and innovation is the organizational environment in which the producer operates (Coombs, 1987). This environment can either be a public sector or a private market. In the private market, the firm or producer has to buy capital goods, raw materials, labour and so on and sell its products on the market in competition with other companies. The influence of many factors and a high degree of complexity implies that different innovations will have different criteria for success and failure. Innovations in the agricultural sector must often act according to the private market mechanism and environmental regulations imposed by the government. In addition we have seen that the European agricultural policy has a major impact on the Danish agricultural sector.

6.3. Methodology

In order to assess the advantages and disadvantages of precision farming (PF) as a new technology and management system it is relevant to analyze the impact on users. A holistic approach with interviews of users and stakeholders, farm surveys and a formal assembling of experts and stakeholders was therefore organized. The validity of information varies depending on the information source. It is essential that the external validity is high and that the findings are not too biased and subjective. Otherwise, it may be difficult to generalize the conclusions and make suggestions beyond this study.

6.3.1. Farm survey

The farm survey was designed to collect information about the farmers' view and adoption of precision farming technologies. In total, 102 questionnaires were sent to Danish PF farmers with 78 responses in October 2000; 103 were sent to UK farmers with 51 responses and 144 were sent to farmers in Nebraska, United States, with 77 responses. The survey list was provided by Massey Ferguson (AGCO), LH-Agro and University of Nebraska Cooperative Extension in the United States.

A survey is an excellent information source for statistical comparisons and it is possible to handle a larger group of stakeholder/participants compared with interviews. All participants are treated uniformly and should also be regarded as such. A problem regarding the validity of these data could arise from misunderstandings in which individual respondents have not responded to the questions in the way that they were intended. The survey design and total number of respondents to each question also have an impact on the output quality.

6.3.2. Interviews

Interviews enable the analyst to get a deeper knowledge about specific issues from key respondents. The respondents represent stakeholders and experts who have experience and inside knowledge about different precision farming practices. We have tried to cover a relatively broad group of stakeholders, which represents farmers', manufactures', researchers' and consultants' views on PF technologies.

Most of the questions were 'open-ended' and prepared in advance but often the interviews were carried out in an explorative manner in the sense that they allowed for new angles and issues to be commented on. The reason is that most issues are technically complex and the interviewees are often highly specialized in a certain topic. In the beginning, it was difficult to prepare and focus on the key issues in advance. The questions in the first interviews were fairly general, but as long as more interviews were conducted it was possible to get more specialized knowledge of the various technologies, which led to more detailed and focused interviews.

The following issues were discussed:

- Technical advantages and disadvantages of PF practices.
- Costs of electronic devices and so on.
- Potential environmental impact from specific technologies.
- Time consumption and requirements from new technologies.

The interviewees were notified in advance about the topics of discussion. After the interview, a written summary of the discussions (minutes of meeting) was returned by mail or e-mail to the interviewee in order to correct any misunderstandings. The validity of the interviews depended on the interviewees' knowledge about the issues and their degree of interest in the topic. The opinion of stakeholders who have no economic or other potential gains from the technology might be more objective than stakeholders who are deeply financially involved. The interview gives an in-depth knowledge of technical issues and perception of the technology among stakeholders and helps to find likely barriers for adoption.

6.4. Interactive workshop

The farm survey and individual interviews were followed up by a one-day workshop/seminar with focus group meetings where the individual stakeholders had the opportunity to discuss technical and sociological issues with other stakeholders in small focus groups. To introduce each topic, an oral presentation was made by different experts with different views on precision farming. Papers on these presentations were mailed in advance to all of the participants. This allowed the participants to be prepared before the discussions in the focus group. The outcome from these discussions can be regarded as information of high validity since many stakeholders and experts have been involved in the discussions and conclusions. However, this information often become fairly general and it is difficult to agree upon specific conclusions and actions according to the discussions. This seminar was partly based on the ideas from scenario workshops (Teknologirådet, 2000; Mayer, 1997) and focus group meetings. The design of this forum was relatively operational in the sense that the outcome was quite specific.

The number of participants that are highly expert oriented (35) also seem to be appropriate to evaluate technologies in different regions. The workshop was based on different scenarios that were pointed out as barriers in the previous interview and which were discussed among different interest groups. At this seminar, we chose to look at different issues regarding the role of the advisory service, consumer interest and user experiences. These issues/questions had been prepared and made in advance.

6.5. Results

The introduction of precision farming is to some extent aiming at large holdings with a structure that enables them to invest in new management systems. These systems should ideally enable the farmer to replace labour-intensive practices with efficient sensing techniques that can increase productivity and reduce costs. In that sense the GPS follows previous labour-reducing innovations, although it might in addition include an environmental dimension.

Precision farming has primarily been adopted in cereal producing areas, particularly in Northern Europe and the United States. In Denmark, less than 10 per cent of the area with cereals (wheat, barley and rye) has been yield mapped. Some farmers in the United Kingdom as well as Denmark have used PF practices since the early 1990s. A general trend is that large producers with more than 300 hectares, tend to be the first to invest in the new technology, whereas small producers are more reluctant to invest in GPS equipment. There is, however, some divergence in the adoption speed between North European countries. To date, the adoption rate in France and Germany has been relatively slow compared with Denmark, the UK and Sweden. A relatively high adoption rate in Denmark is probably related to an early domestic production of combine harvesters with GPS equipment. Massey Ferguson (formerly Dronningborg Combine Harvesters) was a pioneer in the development of commercial yield monitors with GPS.

A nationwide survey in the United States concluded that the adoption of PF technologies has been related to farm size. To date, less than 5 per cent of all US farmers have adopted some aspects of PF, however the total cereal area, which is managed with PF techniques is expected to cover more than 12 per cent. It has been grain and oil seed farmers who have been aware of these technologies and adoption has primarily been carried out by large farmers (Daberkow & McBride, 2001). Compared with other farm technologies, such as GMOs (genetically modified organisms), the adoption of PF practices has been relatively slow in the United States (Daberkow, 2001). It seems, however, that the adoption rate has been a little faster in North America compared to Europe. A reason for that is likely to be larger farm sizes and specialization in certain cash crops, whereas European crop producers traditionally have been smaller in terms of farm size and less specialized compared with their American colleagues.

The adoption of yield monitors and especially satellite pictures have been relatively popular in the United States when compared with Europe – probably because of large areas with cash crops and less cloudy days in the landlocked areas. Variable treatment with fertilizers and weed detection seems however to be well adopted in Europe. In the United States, the application of yield monitors without GPS positioning is a rather common practice in most states. Currently there are about 20,000 farmers (in 2001) who have adopted yield monitors.

6.6. Farm survey

Findings from the farm survey need to be considered in the light of this being a targeted, rather than a random, survey. In particular, the mailing lists in the United Kingdom and Denmark were derived from customer lists of manufacturers of yield mapping combines. Consequently, a high adoption of yield mapping as a precision practice was to be expected. The US survey was conducted only in Nebraska, and represents primarily producers who use irrigation. This survey provides a summary of the opinions of early adopters of PF technologies, and does not necessarily represent the opinions of the broader producer population in any of the three countries evaluated.

Producers in all three countries use a range of precision technologies on a variety of crops, but mostly on crops that are combine-harvestable – cereals, corn and soybean. Participants are generally quite optimistic about increased profitability with precision agriculture, but figure it will take 5–10 years to achieve their expected level of profitability. Variable rate application of fertilizer was the practice most commonly cited as likely to increase profits on their farm – either through decreased total applications of phosphorous and potassium (Denmark and the UK) or increased total application of phosphorous (United States). Participants in all three countries felt that total nitrogen use on their farms would remain unchanged with the use of PF practices.

Generally, producers found PF to be useful in their interactions with consumers, landlords and government agencies. They were somewhat concerned about the use of PF data by others (government, lenders, and so on) – more so in the United States and the UK than in Denmark. They felt the greatest disincentive to adoption of precision agriculture was the cost of the equipment coupled with a current lack of evidence of increased profit with PF. Despite this, producers were generally optimistic about the potential for increased profit with PF in the future. The second major disincentive to the use of precision practices is the time required, although many admit an incentive to adopting PF was a fascination with the technology. A majority of farmers feel that the use of precision practices will help the use of inputs more efficiently and reduce the environmental impact of crop production.

We categorized into seven categories responses when producers were asked what they would recommend for future improvements in precision technologies (Table 6.1). Each user had the opportunity to respond with one recommendation. This allowed the comparison of general categories for improvement by country. In all countries, there seems to be a general concern that different technologies are not always compatible. Respondents were interested in standards where software and hardware

Table 6.1. Recommendations to improve the further development of precision farming technology

Recommendation	Denmark	UK	USA
		%	
More accuracy	6	0	15
Better advice	13	28	2
Compatibility	23	31	15
Less expensive equipment and profitability	10	19	34
Other specific technological developments	32	11	22
User friendly technology	13	6	5
Other recommendations	3	6	7

Source: Pedersen *et al.* (2001).

can 'speak together' with ease. Better advice on the use of precision technologies, and evidence of profitability and economic returns are also recommended.

When asked who the primary data processor for PF-related data should be, the majority recommended that the farmer should play a key role in the data processing. Especially in Denmark, respondents felt that it would be helpful to have a crop consultant involved in processing PF data. This difference may be connected to the availability and use of consulting services in Denmark and Nebraska relative to the United Kingdom.

In summary, these early adopters of PF remain optimistic about precision farming technologies, but are cautious about encouraging others to jump into it, given the cost, a current lack of economic return, time required, incompatibility, advice and extension and the depressed farm economy. This was particularly the case in the United Kingdom and Denmark. The apparent lack of scientific evidence is still a key issue in all three countries. More thorough and scientifically based advice about input application is needed as well as development of compatible technologies.

6.6.1. Findings from workshop and interviews

An overall objective of the workshop was to assess the benefits and advantages of precision farming and potential barriers according to economic viability, environmental concerns, user-friendliness and consumer preferences. A total of 35 farmers, consultants, researchers and manufacturers, as well as representatives from consumer organizations, participated at the workshop. The workshop included a combination of oral presentations and focus group meetings, in which issues such as economics, environmental impact and consumer preferences were discussed. Conclusions from the working groups were followed up with a presentation of the results in a plenary session. This approach implied that all participants and stakeholders had a chance to interact and discuss the various issues and perspectives of different PF systems. The outcome from the focus group workshop was contained in a report with conclusions and recommendations by the stakeholders and participants (Pedersen, Pedersen & Gylling, 2002).

The following sections present the outcome and conclusions from the workshop and enhanced with the personal interviews covering impact on environment, economy, user requirements, advisory service, retailers and consumers.

6.6.2. Environmental impact

The potential environmental benefits from precision farming are primarily obtained from better utilization of nitrogen and reduced application of pesticides. So far, there seems to be a general agreement among participants that there has not been any continuous Danish trials, which indicates that variable rate application of nitrogen enables the farmer to increase yields in cereals.

More focus should also be put on the link between site-specific application of nitrogen and nitrate leaching. Several participants felt that a better utilization of sensors could improve the application of fertilizers in the future. They also argued that emphasis should be put on variable rate pesticide application and patch spraying. New methods with sensor technologies, such as weed eye, are important in order to conduct fast and efficient detection of weeds and fungi on the field. Furthermore, site-specific application might also enable the farmer to point out certain areas that are environmentally vulnerable or, for instance, suitable for set aside and to minimize structural damages from tillage. One participant argued that different authorities, including EU and national governments might be interested in promoting precision farming as an environmental farming practice. Such policies could be implemented by reducing subsidies for farmers who practice conventional farming methods or uniform applications. This raises another question – whether small farmers are able to pay for such investments.

Finally, the potential disadvantages according to the environment could be an increase in fuel consumption and possible damages on fauna and crops caused by mistakes and errors in GIS software, GPS and other decision-support systems.

6.6.3. Economy

A presumption for adoption of PF practices is that the technology is economically viable, which depends on numerous still unproven parameters. Most participants were sceptical about the potential economic benefits from variable fertilizer application. The main issue was the difficulties in obtaining higher yields from variable nitrogen application compared with uniform application. Given the daily change in weather conditions, an application strategy should rely on dynamic data rather than historic data and the application strategy should involve slurry and manure with mineral fertilizers. It is important to minimize the uncertainty caused by weather fluctuations. Real-time sensing could be relevant for coping with these uncertainties.

A variable rate application of pesticides and lime seem to be practices that most participants found useful, even though the potential benefits cannot cover the extra costs. For some farmers, especially with large farm areas, it might be economically viable to conduct variable lime application. Likewise, farmers who use contractors for this purpose might gain an economic benefit. The costs of patch spraying and the investments are still too high compared with the minor potential benefits from reduced chemical application. In addition, several participants were also sceptical whether traceability and documentation with GPS could obtain a higher market price for the farm commodities. On the contrary, several participants perceived that more focus should be put on additional benefits such as drainage, logistics and better farm management.

6.6.4. User requirements

Global positioning systems and precision farming seems to provide a tool for better management on the farm. In the near future we will see improvements with better and standardized software, integrated computers, and reduced investments in additional accessories and equipment. In this regard, the different farm practices will be less monotonous and farm vehicles will be easier to handle.

There are still several obstacles that need to be resolved to make these technologies convenient for the users. Many farmers lose contact with reality by using high-tech methods and feel dependent on the technology, which could cause problems if the system breaks down. Data collection is still too difficult to handle with different and often non-compatible software programs. There is a need for education and training to interpret different presentations, yield maps and application maps. In this respect, time seems to be a matter of concern for the farmer, especially since the potential economic benefits are modest compared with other farming practices. Many activities have moved from the field into the farm office, which is time consuming and costly. In this respect, farmers seek for practical and simple and 'easy to handle' solutions. To resolve many of these issues, it is important to design simple, low-cost and robust systems, which are easy to implement and handle for the farmer. Research that can prove the positive effects and further research into decision-support systems is therefore required. It was suggested that a databank, from which the advisory service and farmers can draw information, could be an important tool.

6.6.5. Advisory service

Many participants felt that the advisory service will have a significant impact on the development and adoption of precision farming. In order to increase the adoption rate, it is important to focus and point out successful experiences from PF practices. In this respect, it is vital that cooperation between all elements in the advisory chain is established and integrated. New field trial designs, which are linked to economic evaluation methods, are required. A vital limitation is still a lack of professional and technical experience with many PF practices. Currently, there is no national uniform coverage by advisors offering precision farming services. This might be caused by traditions, geographical and local differences.

6.6.6. Retailers and consumers

Some wholesale companies have already introduced 'concept agreements' and contractual agreements with farmers who will use precision farming. These agreements involve economic compensation for practising variable rate treatment on the farm. In this respect, there is a risk that individual farmers will be locked up in certain contractual arrangements that are difficult to terminate. If any such agreements are introduced, it is important that the wholesale companies are involved and willing to pay an extra price for documentation.

Beyond specific quality parameters, such as increasing protein content in the kernels from better nitrogen utilization, many participants found it hard to believe that documentation and traceability eventually will result in higher prices at the farm gate. It is a presumption that value added occurs in the production chain if higher prices at the farm gate are to be expected. Otherwise, the adoption of PF practices will stagnate in the future. In this respect, it is necessary to introduce documentation and certification for such treatment. More research that describes and explains the relationship between consumer needs and potential possibilities within precision farming, is needed. Finally, it was argued that the consumer would find it difficult to understand and distinguish the difference between conventional farming practices and site-specific farming practices.

6.7. Conclusions

It is likely that some farmers will benefit from precision farming, especially the large producers that are able to absorb and cover the investments. However, to do so it is a prerequisite that some spatial soil variation occurs on the field.

An important finding is that the use of PF practices should be user-oriented and decision-support systems should be simple, robust and clear. According to the results of focus groups and personal interviews with stakeholders in Precision Farming, it seems that most farmers remain unconvinced regarding the use of PF techniques. Simple and plain decision and management systems are necessary to prove the benefits of precision farming. Farmers and users should be more involved in the planning process about spatial application. Software programs should be user-friendly and farmers should be involved when designing the nitrogen-application strategies and application maps. Farmers' inherent knowledge about weed patches on the field should be considered when designing the programs. Each farmer has often individual needs depending on his crop rotation, technical insight and management strategies. The various technologies should be used for several purposes at the same time in order to distribute the costs of basic equipment (e.g., GPS equipment and tractor computers) on many applications. The costs of implementing PF practices are high and technical functionality and hardware compatibility is a concern among farmers. Otherwise, manufacturers should strive to provide low-cost options for producers interested in precision agriculture but are unable to afford large-scale investment. Precision farming may also enable retailers and the final consumer to trace and control each action on the field. Consequently, 'traceability' has been regarded as an important incentive for implementing precision farming.

To improve the adoption of variable nitrogen application, crop scientists, advisors and farmers should continue the development of scientifically sound decision-support systems based on real-time sensing, weather forecasts, soil structures and the field history. Farmers need clear proof that shows yield improvements from variable rate technologies. More focus should be put on integrated decision support based on historic yields, soil and site-specific fertilizer applications should integrate manure, slurry and mineral fertilizers. Moreover, manufacturers should focus on the development of compatible, reliable and low-cost hardware and advisors should coordinate experiences and establish common databases with PF information. So far, about 400 farmers have adopted some PF practices in Denmark but only a few farmers practise full-scale variable rate application. The findings above cover issues concerning potential losses from not taking a holistic PF system approach and potential losses by not taking risks.

Bibliography

Blackmore, B.S., Griepentrog, H.W., Pedersen, S.M. & Fountas, S. (eds) (2002), *Precision Farming in Europe* (Binghamton, NY: Haworth Press).

Boon, A. (2001), 'Vertical Coordination of Interdependent Innovations in the Agri-Food Industry' (Institute of Industrial Economics and Strategy, Copenhagen Business School, PhD series 6).

Coombs, R., Saviotti, P. & Walsh, V. (1987), *Economics and Technological Change* (Totowa: Rowman & Littlefield).

Daberkow, S.G. (2001), address to 3rd European Conference on Precision Agriculture, Montpellier).

Daberkow, S.G. & McBride, W.D. (2001), 'Farm and operator characteristics affecting the awareness and adoption of precision agricultural technologies in the US', Proceedings of the 3rd European Conference on Precision Agriculture, Montpellier.

Freeman, C. (1974), *The Economics of Industrial Innovation* (Harmondsworth: Penguin).

Freeman, C. (1991), 'The nature of innovation and the evolution of the productive system, Technology and productivity, The challenge for economic policy' OECD Paris, pp. 303–14.

Gylling, M., Pedersen, S.M. & Boon, A. (1999), 'Non-food produktion fra land-brugsafgrøder' (Frederiksberg: SJFI; Report No. 112).

Mayer, I. (1997), *Debating Technologies, A Methodological Contribution to the Design and Evaluation of Participatory Policy Analysis* (Tilburg: Tilburg University Press).

Mohamed, M.Z. & Rickards, T. (1996), 'Assessing and comparing the innovativeness and creative climate of firms', *Scandinavian Journal of Management*, 12(2), pp. 109–21.

Pedersen, S.M. (2003), 'Precision farming – Technology assessment of site-specific input application in cereals' (PhD dissertation, IPL, DTV).

Pedersen, S.M., Ferguson, R.B. & Lark, R.M. (2001), 'A multinational survey of Precision Farming early adopters' *Farm Management*, 11(3), Oct., pp. 147–62.

Pedersen, S.M., Pedersen, J.L. & Gylling, M. (eds) (2002), 'Perspektiverne for præcisionsjordbrug', *Danish Research Institute of Food Economics*, FOI working paper no. 6.

Schumpeter, J.A. (1943 [1966]), *Capitalism, Socialism and Democracy* (London: Unwin University Books, 11th edn).

Srinivasan, A. (2002), 'Precision farming – A global perspective' (in Blackmore *et al.*).

Teknologirådet (2000), *The Methods of the Danish Board of Technology*, <www.tekno.dk/eng/methods>, 11 Sept.

Part III: Organization of Innovation

Introduction

The Organizational or 'Soft' Aspects of Innovation

Jon Sundbo

Behavioural approach to innovation

The chapters in Part III take a behavioural approach to innovation. They look at what could be called its 'soft' factors: organizational, psychological and individual-oriented factors. There are many such factors that influence the innovation process, which thus becomes complex. The chapters emphasize variables other than those that have been central to mainstream innovation theory over the past few decades. The analyses and discussions presented in this part challenge the institutional approach, which is based on fixed, repetitive patterns of behaviour such as learning (cf. Cohen & Sproull, 1996), routines (cf. Nelson & Winter, 1982) and expert-based formal organizations, for example research and development (R&D) departments (e.g., Kay, 1979). It is claimed that the innovation process is more varied than the picture presented by the institutional approach, and is guided more by personal and managerial intervention and decisions throughout the process than is often supposed in the mainstream theory. This perspective is mainly produced because the chapters take a sociological, and partly psychological, approach in contrast to mainstream innovation theory, which often takes an economic approach (e.g., Dosi *et al.*, 1988; Freeman & Soete, 1997). In the economic approach, there is a tendency to see social factors in a somewhat rigid fashion as, for example, institutional social patterns that are repetitive and routine. The chapters in this part put forward more actor-based, situational views, as a supplement to the traditional institutional view.

The innovation process and management of innovation is seen as non-rational. Process-oriented phenomena such as entrepreneurship (cf. Pinchot, 1985), creativity (cf. Nyström, 1979), roles (cf. Sundbo, 2001; Darsø, 2001)) and innovative organizational climate (cf. Ekvall, 1996) are introduced. These micro-organizational factors are in the chapters introduced as a supplement to more rational management ones such as organization of learning, conscious organizational design (centralized or decentralized organization) and so on. The innovation process is also seen differently as being guided from below by the employees, who are conceptualized as being creative and entrepreneurial.

The non-rational, actor-based approach, which is also stressed by strategy, is a central issue in several of the chapters. The notion of strategy has been introduced in innovation theory (e.g., Horwitch, 1985; Tushman & Anderson, 1997) as a goal-seeking, rational behaviour that leads to routines that directly lead to the development of innovations. Strategy can, however, also be seen as a more interpretative and non-rational choice of direction into an unsure future (e.g., Sundbo, 2001). Strategy thus becomes more actor based, which means that the management chooses a certain strategy, upon which the management and the whole organization will reflect, also in relation to innovation. The strategy and concrete innovation projects may be changed if they do not seem to lead to the desired goal, or the goal may even be changed. The strategic choice overrules routines such as learning and traditional ways of organizing innovation processes. All this is summed up in the suggestion that if we want to understand the innovation process, we should look at the strategy and the strategy-making process more than at institutional routines such as organizational learning systems and R&D-based expert organization.

The approach of the chapters is not to produce a general attack on the concept of institution in innovation theory and the concept is used in some of the chapters. However, the chapters introduce a broader and 'softer' concept of institution in which choice processes and entrepreneurship play a main role. The organization of innovation has been treated in the literature before (e.g., Hage, 1998; and Burgelman & Sayles, 1986), also by introducing micro-organizational variables (e.g., Kanter, 1983; Pinchot, 1985; Ekvall, 1996). However, particular organizational factors which have not been emphasized much in the previous literature on the organization of innovation are discussed in the following chapters. This is, for example, the case with interpretative strategy, creativity, roles, the environmental embeddedness of the innovation and interaction within the organization.

Several of the chapters also refer to innovation in services, which to a large degree follows patterns other than those traditionally observed in manufacturing. Studies of service innovations have discovered new organizational and behavioural variables (e.g., Boden & Miles, 2000), and this has again led to new general views on innovation that may be universally valid. For example, service innovations are rarely based on R&D, and are often small improvements developed by employees in close consultation with clients. This new knowledge has also been a background for the challenging approaches of some of the chapters. The research into service innovation has also pointed to the fact that new kinds of measurement to measure innovation of service products and of the innovations processes are needed. Such new measurements could also be useful in investigating the relevant 'soft' aspects of manufacturing innovations.

The chapters challenge conventional wisdom and suggest new, 'soft' factors and views, which should be further investigated in research. Management comes more into power. Innovation is an intentional process that does not need to be dependent on institutionalized patterns or heavy organizational apparatuses such as R&D departments, formalized organizational learning systems and so on. The chapters argue, based on empirical research, that a more flexible strategic goal system and organization of the process is developing in firms. This system is based on the involvement of the employees and a high degree of embeddedness in the environment. The development of the firm in the classic Schumpeterian sense (cf. Schumpeter, 1934) can be understood in terms of many small improvements, either as the only development mechanism or as a supplement to more radical innovations as they have been considered in traditional innovation theory. This view makes the innovation process complex and even the outcome of the process – the innovations understood as a new product (whether a new service or a new good) – becomes complex. This complexity also means that the statistical measurements that have been developed over the past decade (e.g., European Community Innovation Survey) are not able to measure the organizational and 'soft' aspects of the innovations, and are consequently invalid. Complex measurements are required – a viewpoint that challenges the attempts to create simple standard innovation measurement instruments that have been used within the past decade.

The chapters

Meeus, Faber and Oerlemans investigate the classic issue of how strategy affects structure in relation to innovation. Will an innovation-oriented strategy create a structure that is learning-oriented and innovation promoting? They introduce the distinction between short-term exploitation and a long-term exploration of innovative ideas and they emphasize learning as an intermediate variable to explain the effect of strategy on structure. In their chapter, they develop a structural equation model to answer the following questions: To what degree do combinations of exploratory and exploitative learning and innovation strategies induce patterns of structures, and will such strategies lead to a greater interaction with the environment (external embeddedness)? They assume that a clear strategy leads to a more decentralized structure and this leads to exploratory learning that amplifies exploitative learning. Further, they assume that high levels of strategic goals in the field of innovation cannot be achieved without learning. The model is tested in a survey of Netherlands companies. The result is that their hypotheses are not completely confirmed. An innovation-oriented strategy leads to explorative learning, but has only indirect effect on the short-term exploitative learning. Explorative learning pushes the structure towards centralization, while exploitative learning pushes it towards decentralization. Learning did not affect external embeddedness. Meuss *et al.*'s analysis thus challenges conventional wisdom by concluding that learning is perhaps not the central factor that can explain innovative success.

Sundbo and Fuglsang continue the theme by discussing, theoretically, how the environment drives innovation and to which structure innovation strategy leads. They introduce the concept of strategic reflexivity to explain the firm's relation to the environment. They see innovation as being very much determined by the strategy, which is the framework for innovative activities in the firm. However, firms are cautious because innovation is risky, thus the strategy and the attempts at innovation are continuously considered in a reflexive process in which employees and managers are involved. The firm can be more adaptive to the environment, which means that it introduces incremental innovations. The employees are highly involved in that as well as in reflections on whether the firm is on the right path to success. The firm can also attempt to create the environment's competitive conditions. This demands more radical innovations that are developed in expert departments, such as R&D. Even that process is reflexive. Sundbo and Fuglsang discuss the organizational structure and state that different roles are developed in the strategic reflexive innovation system. They suggest four core roles and two outside roles. Their chapter suggests a model for understanding the relation between environment and strategy, on the one hand, and the organizational microstructure on the other hand. It challenges the strong emphasis on institutionalized innovation structures such as R&D departments and instead points to micro-sociological processes as decisive for innovation.

Guia, Prats and Comas also emphasize learning and cognition and the complexity of innovation processes seen from an organizational perspective. They also continue the micro-organizational perspective by introducing the paradigm of identity difference as a framework for understanding innovation. This paradigm implies that individual differences between the employees are a source of innovative creativity. Guia, Prats and Comas introduce two organizational factors – routines that determine the coordination pattern, and values that are seen as individual and varied throughout the organization. Routines do not lead to innovation because most members of an organization are not seeking change but stability. Values produce a complex organizational pattern. Guia, Prats and Comas discuss how individuals are driven into creativity and entrepreneurship by psychological factors such as curiosity, wondering and communicating. Innovation is created by interaction processes between people with different values in the organization. Even the formalized innovation process in R&D departments can be seen as the final materialization of such interaction processes. Guia, Prats and Comas' article challenges the institutional view that innovative and evolutionary paths are determined by rational choice or functions such as routines. They are, instead, the result of value-based interaction processes.

Den Hertog Poot and Meinen investigate how 'soft', or non-technological innovations can be measured. A problem is that there are numerous competing concepts and the organizational structures that may produce innovations are mixed with the innovations in analyses. Den Hertog *et al.* make criticisms of the official innovation surveys (such as the EU's CIS). They have introduced new questions in a survey of Netherlands firms. In their chapter, they discuss the results of this and how we can measure 'soft' innovations. They conclude that it is relevant to ask about innovation in marketing, organization and external relations because many firms in all sectors make innovations in these fields. However, many respondents also had difficulties in separating the technological and the non-technological aspects of innovations. Den Hertog *et al.* discuss the outcome of the measurement experiment. They stress one problem, namely whether the 'soft' sides concern real innovations or just ordinary adjustments that every entrepreneur has to make regularly to stay competitive. However, this dilemma challenges the conceptualization of innovation since many small adjustments together might develop the firm. Further, den Hertog *et al.* conclude that 'soft' innovations are perceived differently in manufacturing and services, which suggests that different measurement instruments must be developed. The chapter points out that we cannot just continue developing the measurements used hitherto, but we must also develop new instruments.

Bibliography

Boden. M. & Miles, I. (eds) (2000), *Services in the Knowledge-based Economy* (London: Continuum).

Burgelman, R.A. & Sayles, L.R. (1986), *Inside Corporate Innovation: Strategy, Structure and Managerial Skills* (New York: Free Press).

Cohen, M.D. & Sproull (eds) (1996), *Organizational Learning* (London: Sage).

Darsø, L. (2001), *Innovation in the Making* (Copenhagen: Samfundslitteratur).

Dosi, G., Freeman, C., Nelson, R., Silverberg, G. & Soete, L. (eds) (1988), *Technical Change and Economic Theory* (London: Pinter).

Ekvall, G. (1996), 'Organizational Climate for Creativity and Organization', *European Journal of Work and Organizational Psychology*, 5(1), pp. 105–23.

Freeman, C. & Soete, L. (1997), *The Economics of Industrial Innovation* (London: Pinter).

Hage, J. (1998), *Organizational Innovation* (Aldershot: Dartmouth).

Horwitch, M. (ed.) (1985), 'Special Issue: Technology in the Modern Corporation. A Strategic Perspective', *Technology in Society*, 7(2/3).

Kanter, R.M. (1983), *The Change Masters* (London: Unwin).

Kay, N. (1979), *The Innovating Firm: A Behavioural Theory of Corporate R&D* (London: Macmillan).

Nelson, R. & Winter, S.G. (1982), *An Evolutionary Theory of Economic Change* (Cambridge, MA: Belknap).

Nyström, H. (1979), *Creativity and Innovation* (Chichester: Wiley).

Pinchot, G. (1985), *Intrapreneuring* (New York: Harper & Row).

Schumpetes, J. (1934), *Theory of Economic Development* (Boston: Harvard University).

Sundbo, J. (2001), *The Strategic Management of Innovation* (Cheltenham: Elgar).

Tushman, M. & Anderson, P. (1997), *Managing Strategic Innovation and Change* (Oxford: Oxford University Press).

7
Do Network Structures Follow Innovation Strategy? *Chandler Revisited with Learning as an Intermediary Variable*

Marius T.H. Meeus, Jan Faber and Leon A.G. Oerlemans

7.1. Introduction

In the literature on learning and innovation, a substantial amount of theorizing on the combination of exploration and exploitation has been conducted (March, 1991; Nooteboom, 2001; Volberda & Lewin, 2002). Two observations can be derived from this literature. On the one hand, the conceptual and theoretical development outpaced the empirical research so far (e.g., the volume of Dierkes *et al.* (2001) on organizational learning). There is an old, but profound theoretical literature on innovation and structure (Hage, 1980, 1998; Alter & Hage, 1993; Damanpour & Gopalakrishnan, 1998). Until recently these literatures on learning and structuring have been rather detached. Only some researchers (Boisot, 1998; Nooteboom, 2001; Volberda, 1998; Volberda & Lewin, 2002) aimed at synthesis, nevertheless the empirical part remains underdeveloped. On the other hand, learning is considered too often as an exogenous variable. In the organizational learning literature, there is a tendency to consider learning as a process without a context, which implies that important related aspects remain underanalyzed. In this chapter, we want to combine learning with the Chandlerian (Chandler, 1962) notion of structure follows strategy, in which structure is not conceptualized as internal organizational structure but as external network structure.

Empirically, the starting point of this study lies in the findings of Pettigrew *et al.* (2000). In the four-year period 1992–96, substantial structural dynamics in European firms were reported and these are summarized in Table 7.1.

Table 7.1. Aspects of structural dynamics in European companies, 1992–96

Aspects of structural dynamics	1992 %	1996 %
Structures		
Mean number of Layers	3.5	3.2
Median	3.0	3.0
Project form	19.6	41.6
Operational decentralization	40.7	61.0
Strategic decentralization	15.3	18.9
Processes		
Vertical linkages	10.3	31.8
Horizontal linkages	10.8	25.6
Information technology	7.2	38.8
New HR practices	Not asked	34.9
Boundaries		
Strategic alliances	10.2	31.1
Downscoping: single core business	34.3	23.7
Dominant core business	25.4	34.3
Set of related businesses	25.6	29.9
Wide range of businesses	14.7	12.1

Source: Pettigrew *et al.* (2000), p. 264.

As far as dynamics of organizational structures are concerned, two major developments can be noted, namely a growing importance of the use of inter- and intra-organizational project form, and of operational decentralization. In the same period, vertical and horizontal linkages as well as information technology were processes that received far more attention in organizations, whereas a stronger focus on the core business in combination with a substantial increase in strategic partnering turned out to be important structural trends as far as organizational boundaries are concerned.

Of course these structural dynamics seek an explanation. Why do they occur? Unfortunately, Pettigrew *et al.* do not give an empirical analysis. Several factors that could potentially account for these trends in structural dynamics are suggested by Pettigrew *et al.* (2000): for example environmental dynamics (Salançik & Pfeffer, 1976; Khandwallah, 1972; Duncan, 1972; Gopalakrishnan & Damanpour, 1998), past performance (Miller, 1999; Miller & Friesen, 1977, 1982, 1984; Meeus & Oerlemans, 1993), learning (March, 1991; Levinthal & March, 1993; Levitt & March, 1988; March & Olsen, 1975), and of course strategic choice (Carr, 1993).

Some of these factors are taken on board in this chapter. First, we take the old Chandlerian perspective (Chandler, 1962) – 'structure follows strategy' – as a starting point. However, we concentrate on a specific part of firm strategy, namely the innovation strategy. This restriction is important because especially in innovation strategy, specific learning goals are defined, and to achieve these goals structures must be (re)considered. Second, we consider the mediating effect of learning between strategy and structure. Recently, several authors (e.g., Wolf & Egelhof, 2002; West, 2000) recouped the chandlerian 'structure follows strategy' discussion, advancing an information processing perspective. As in the debate on the M-form (Freeland, 1996) and the A-form versus the J-form (Aoki, 1986), changes in the intensity of information processing account for the adaptation of intra-organizational structures (West, 2000).

An important restriction in this literature is that the external organization of research and development (R&D) and innovation is somewhat ignored. In our theoretical model, external organizational structure is included, because of the emergence of the networked organization – the *N-form* – and the growth of the number of strategic alliances (see Table 7.1). As a theoretical starting point for the analysis of learning processes, we concentrate on a specific type of outcome: relative embeddedness in networks of organizations with varying learning efforts and innovation strategies. To us it seems that this is not only important to be able to develop more analytical accounts of organizational behaviour, but also that it opens up possibilities for a more differentiated set of interventions enabling successful learning.

Another important issue is the conceptualization and measurement of learning. In the seminal work of March (1991), exploration and exploitation are considered to be more or less unrelated – as an either/or category – whereas many organizations probably combine both exploratory and exploitative learning activities. From an empirical point of view, this is important because in terms of resource allocation, the two types of adaptive processes are exclusive, whereas it cannot be set aside that the exploratory part feeds the exploitative part of organizational learning. So an additional question is: to what extent does exploratory learning affect exploitative learning? Despite the interest in the strategic implications of inter-firm networks, there is a need for additional theories of how networks evolve and change over time (Borgatti & Foster, 2003). The tradition in network analysis has been to consider network embeddedness as an exogenous variable – a given context for action – rather than being endogenized (Madhavan *et al.*, 1998). Before being able to develop theories in the temporal dimensions of network evolution, one first needs a theoretical and empirical starting point, and that is our main goal here. Therefore, our research questions read as follows:

- To what extent does the level of strategic innovative activity of innovating firms impact directly on the embeddedness in networks?
- To what extent is this relation mediated by distinct levels of exploratory and exploitative learning?
- To what extent does exploratory learning affect exploitative learning?

The aim of this chapter is threefold. First, it tries to refine the rather linear and simplified discussion on the strategy – structure nexus by introducing mediating variables of a process nature. Second, it tries to extend the structure debate by adding a focus on external structuring. Third, it is one of the few efforts to analyze empirically the interrelatedness of distinct learning activities.

7.2. Toward a research model

The innovation and organization literature does not suggest any hypotheses on the intermediary effects of learning, on the relation of levels of activity in innovation strategy and network structures. Therefore, the model advanced here is more an inductive effort pursuing theory development, rather than that it is an explanatory approach.

7.2.1. An exploratory theoretical model

Our theoretical model (see Figure 7.1) contains three building blocks that cover the issues raised in the introduction of this chapter: the first block is innovation strategy, the second is the Marchian conceptualization of exploratory and exploitative learning, and the third consists of two types of external structuring, that is to say, the level of embeddedness of the focal firm in the value chain and in the knowledge infrastructure, respectively.

A model with six variables in it allows for many model specifications. Our model basically tells the following story.

In this model, we concentrate not on strategy in the broadest sense but focus on innovation strategy in particular, because this is a special knowledge intensifying activity. If strategic innovative actions are intensified, organizational goals and ambitions are adapted and this implies stronger information exchange and monitoring activities. That is also the basic mechanism that links strategy with structure (Wolf & Egelhoff,

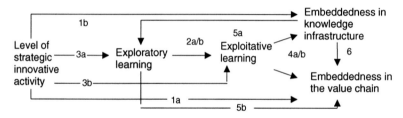

Figure 7.1. An exploratory model of innovation strategy, learning and external structuring

2002). Relatively higher levels of strategic innovative activity cannot be achieved without learning, and since learning implies more intense information processing this would demand for specific internal and external organizational structures enabling intensified information and knowledge processing. This leads to a first proposition:

P1. If the level of strategic activity of innovating firms increases, the level of external monitoring grows, and hence the external embeddedness is stronger.

The reviewed literature suggests several types of structural adaptations. As was shown in the introduction of this chapter, the growth of operational decentralization is one of the most significant structural dynamics among the European organizations in 1992–96 (Pettigrew *et al.*, 2000), although external structuring also changed significantly. The general trend is towards more strategic alliances, in tandem with a growing focus on core business. Empirical research (Meeus, Oerlemans & Hage, 2001a, 2000b, 2004) and theoretical considerations (Lundvall, 1992; Nooteboom, 1999) on the nature of innovation has shown that more complex innovative activities induce more intense monitoring and utilization of external knowledge resources due to a need to reduce input and output uncertainty. Hence, we expect that if strategic activity is augmented that foremost the linkages in the value chain are strengthened and additionally that the linkages with the knowledge infrastructure accrue. Ample empirical research reports a strong focus of innovator firms on their suppliers and buyers as their main knowledge sources (Oerlemans & Meeus, 2001; Freel, 2003; Poot, 2004). These arguments allow for a further specification of proposition 1, namely:

P1a. The higher the level of strategic innovative activity, the higher will be the level of embeddedness in the value chain.

P1b. The effect of levels of strategic innovative activity on the level of embeddedness is stronger in case of the value chain, as compared to embeddedness in the knowledge infrastructure.

The second part of our research question concerns the relationship between different types of learning. Theoretically, March's notion of organizational learning serves as a basis for our ideas. In his seminal paper, James G. March (1991) introduced the dichotomy of exploration – exploitation in organization learning. In this dichotomy, two types of adaptive processes were conceptualized. Exploration includes aspects of learning captured by terms such as variation, risk taking, experimentation, play, flexibility, discovery and innovation. Exploitation includes refinements, choice, production, efficiency, selection, implementation or execution. March presents the problem related to this dichotomy as a trade-off (ibid., pp. 71–2).

> Organizations engaging in exploration to the detriment of exploitation are likely to find that they suffer the costs of experimentation without gaining many of its benefits. They exhibit too many undeveloped new ideas and too little distinctive competence. Conversely, systems that engage in exploitation to the exclusion of exploration are likely to find themselves trapped in suboptimal stable equilibria. As a result, maintaining an appropriate balance between exploration and exploitation is a primary factor in system survival and prosperity.

March's ideas offer an interesting research challenge: the extents into which exploratory and exploitative learning are related. March (1991) suggests that in terms of resource allocation there is a problem of balancing between the short-term benefits of exploitation and the more long-term benefits of exploration. According to this line of reasoning, exploration would hamper exploitation. However, if seemingly exclusive behavioural alternatives would turn out to have a positive effect on each other, this could imply that these behavioural alternatives are complementary, creating positive feed forwards. For instance, a positive effect of exploration on exploitation would mean that organizations investing in radical new technologies, obviously daring to experiment heavily, systematically accrue organizations' capabilities of improving their existing products and processes. These arguments yield two competing propositions:

P2a. Higher levels of exploratory learning are associated with higher levels of exploitative learning (March's idea).

P2b. Higher levels of exploratory learning are associated with lower level of exploitative learning (a contrasting notion).

The next issue is the mediating effect of learning in the relation between innovation strategy and network structure. To identify a mediating effect implies that the mediator is theoretically and empirically associated with the antecedent variable – in our case the level of strategic innovative activity – and an outcome variable – in our case external structuring. Central in learning is, on the one hand, the information and knowledge processing capabilities and, on the other hand, the development of external monitoring capabilities. If levels of strategic activity go up, it is a routine activity to develop new goals and set targets at the strategic and operational level. The more these targets are removed from the targets in former periods, the higher the inducement to search for radically new techno-economic options in the long run and incremental innovation for the short term.

P3a. The higher the level of strategic innovative activity, the higher the level of exploratory learning.
P3b. The higher the level of strategic innovative activity, the higher the level of exploitative learning.

The more firms combine processes of exploration and exploitation, the more they have to structure themselves in such a way that they can easily process and distribute knowledge and information needed for their learning processes. One way to do this is to try to get access to information that is critical for product development, and that is from users and producers (Lundvall, 1992). Therefore, we expect that:

P4a/b. The higher the level of exploitative learning, the stronger the embeddedness in the value chain, and in the knowledge infrastructure, respectively.

The effects of more intensive exploratory learning are specified in a different way. Exploratory learning draws much more than exploitative learning on state-of-the-art scientific knowledge. So it is interesting to see whether stronger embeddedness of innovator firms in the knowledge infrastructure induces higher levels of exploratory learning on the one hand. On the other hand, higher levels of exploratory learning can also induce more embeddedness in the value chain in terms of identifying crucial new user needs. Recently, Belderbos *et al.* (2004) presented empirical evidence that substantiates this line of reasoning. Based on CIS data of the Netherlands, it was found that innovating firms with strong links with universities tend to have higher levels of novel or radical innovations (exploratory learning). Moreover, they showed that customers and universities are important sources of knowledge for firms aiming at radical innovations. This enables us to formulate the propositions:

P5a. A stronger embeddedness in the knowledge infrastructure induces more exploratory learning.
P5b. A higher level of exploratory learning is associated with a higher level of embeddedness in the value chain.

Finally it is interesting to see to what extent patterns of embeddedness – the external structuring of firms – are associated. Looking into this association captures the idea that innovating firms that network tend to partner with a wide variety of actors, since networking is a default mode of structuring their innovation processes.

P6. To what extent does a higher level of embeddedness in the knowledge infrastructure co-vary with a higher level of embeddedness in the value chain?

In our inductive search for backing of our ideas, propositions 1 to 4 form the basis of our analysis and try to reveal the direct effects of innovation strategies on internal and external structures of organizations. In addition, we explored several possible indirect relations between the variables included in our model. The propositions in this section indicate our interest in the existence of both direct effects and indirect effects indicating the intermediate function of learning in the effects of strategy on structure.

7.3. Research design

7.3.1. Data source

This chapter draws on a survey on R&D, innovation, networks, management practices (financial, knowledge and human resource management) and changes in organizational structures in the Netherlands. The survey was held in 1997 (relating to firm behaviour covering the five-year period 1992–96) among some 2,200 manufacturing and service companies. A non-random convenience sample was taken from a database of fast growing firms at the Netherlands Ministry of Economic Affairs. A paper version of the survey questionnaire was mailed to the selected firms. Subsequently, firms were contacted by telephone and supported by a research project assistant, a knowledgeable firm representative (mostly CEOs) filled out the questionnaire. The response was 13.6 per cent

Table 7.2. Responding firms by size and sector

Firm size	%	Sector	%
<50 employees	21.8	Manufacturing	49.8
50–<100 employees	29.5	Services	25.7
>100 employees	48.7	Trade	14.5
		Other	10.0
Total	100.0	Total	100.0

and the dataset contains survey results of some 300 firms. The characteristics of the population have been described extensively in Oerlemans and Meeus (1998). In Table 7.2, a brief description of the responding firms is provided.

7.3.2. Measurement of variables

In this chapter, the associations between the level of strategic innovative activity and embeddedness of firms in networks will be analyzed. Moreover, the mediating effects of exploratory and exploitative learning and the association between the last two concepts will be explored empirically. To enable these analyses, all variables involved have to be measured.

The first relevant variable is the level of strategic innovative activity, which is a compounding variable measuring the relative importance of strategic innovation targets during 1992–96. Seven separate indicators were used to construct this variable:

(1) more attention for product innovation;
(2) more attention for process innovations;
(3) shortening of time to market;
(4) quality mark-up;
(5) customization;
(6) specialization; and
(7) customer selection.

Respondents could react to a five-point Likert ranging from 'very unimportant' (1) 'very important' (5). The variable was included in the analysis on the basis of an exploratory factor analysis (Cronbach's alpha = 0.72). Higher scores on this variable signal that organizations have formulated relatively broader and more ambitious innovation targets in their innovation strategy during 1992–96.

To measure James G. March's concepts of exploratory and exploitative learning, we developed two measures. The level of exploratory learning was measured as a compound variable combining two indicators (Cronbach's alpha = 0.97): (a) the percentage of turnover invested in radical new technologies applied in existing products in 1992–96, and (b) the percentage of turnover invested in radical new products with new functions and new technologies in 1992–96. Higher values of this variable indicate higher levels of radical product innovations, thus signalling exploratory learning. The second variable, the level of exploitative learning, was measured as a compound variable of two indicators in terms of the percentage of turnover invested during 1992–96 in product innovations that are: (a) incremental improvements of existing products without functional or technological changes; (b) redesigned products with additional features or functions, with the same technology. The Cronbach's alpha of two items included is 0.96, indicating a reliable scale. Since both indicators point at the refinement and increased efficiency of existing products, they can be regarded as expressions of exploitative learning.

As far as the level of embeddedness of organizations is concerned, two compound variables were constructed – the level of external embeddedness of organizations in the value chain (customers, and suppliers of equipment and raw materials), and the level of embeddedness in the knowledge infrastructure (knowledge institutions within 20 km, and knowledge institutions outside of the region) in terms of their importance for the acquisition of knowledge and methods in seven areas: state of process technology; application of technologies; development of new or improved products; organization structure; finance; marketing; HRM. The companies were asked to indicate the relative importance of these actors in all these areas using a five-point Likert scale ranging between very unimportant to very important. Higher scores on this variable indicate that organization utilize the value chain or the knowledge infrastructure more intensively.

7.3.3. Model estimation issues

The structural relationships between the variables described in the previous section have been estimated and statistically tested for by means of the LISREL 8™ computer program (Jöreskog & Sörbom, 1989, 1993). LISREL is well suited for this purpose because it is designed for the simultaneous estimation of all unknown but constant parameters in linear structural equation models of latent variables, which are specified to be measured in factor analysis models on *a priori* specified sets of observable variables, by means of the maximum likelihood (ML) method. For reasons of brevity we do not go in detail of the technical details of our measurement model.

7.4. Results

In this section, we present the results of our analyses, which can be summarized as follows (with a statistical summary in Figure 7.2):

- Proposition *1a* was supported by our findings. Relatively higher levels of strategic innovation activity are positively associated with a stronger embeddedness in the value chain (β 0.25, p. < 0.05).
- Proposition *1b* that was about the relatively stronger effect of innovation strategy on the level of embeddedness in the value chain, as compared to the level of embeddedness in the knowledge infrastructure was indeed confirmed. The latter effect turned out to be not statistically significant.
- Findings as to propositions *2a* and *2b* about the relation of exploratory and exploitative learning suggest that higher levels of exploratory learning are associated with higher levels of exploitative learning (β 0.73, p. < 0.001).
- The effect of level of strategic innovative activity on the level of exploratory learning is not significant (proposition *3a* rejected), whereas it turns out to be statistically significant on the level of exploitative learning (proposition *3b* confirmed).
- The level of exploitative learning is statistically significantly negatively associated with the embeddedness in the value chain (proposition *4a* rejected), but this effect is not significant for the knowledge infrastructure (proposition *4b* not confirmed).

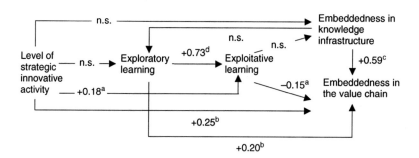

Figure 7.2. Structural coefficients in the structural equation model (n = 276)[1]

- Proposition *5a* claiming an effect of the level of embeddedness in the knowledge infrastructure on the level of exploratory learning is not statistically significant. Proposition *5b* was confirmed meaning that higher levels of exploratory learning turn out to be positively associated with higher levels of embeddedness in the value chain.
- Proposition *6* is confirmed in the sense that a higher level of embeddedness in the knowledge infrastructure is strongly associated with a higher level of embeddedness in the value chain.

7.5. Discussion and conclusions

The main conclusion is that the direct effect of levels of innovation strategy activity on external structures is stronger and broader than the indirect effects via learning. Organizations with relatively higher innovation targets turned out to have more extensive and intense external relations in the value chain, whereas this effect was absent with regard to the embeddedness in the knowledge infrastructure. Innovation strategy activity did affect significantly the level of exploitative learning, but this effect was insignificant for the level of exploratory learning. However, although more strategic innovative activity impacts significantly on the level of exploitative learning, this in turn loosened the embeddedness in the value chain. The level of exploratory learning enhanced the embeddedness in the value chain. Taken together these findings imply a very partial confirmation of the intermediary effects of learning on the embeddedness in the value chain.

Chandler's (1962) main proposition turns out to be valid also in case one specifies 'strategy' as *innovation strategy and in case of external structuring*. It turns out that Cyert *et al.*'s (1963) assumption that a search for better problem solutions is stimulated as soon as existing strategic targets are relatively outdated and no longer guarantee the achievement of organization's goals.

The recent upsurge of the information-processing perspective (Wolf & Egelhoff, 2002) stresses that specifically activities intensifying the importance of knowledge and information exchange bear on organizational distance, openness, and permeability of boundaries hence on decentralization and external ties. Even after the millennium, this implies a dramatic change for many companies, not to be underestimated in a sector that has been socialized in terms of hierarchy, profit and competition, resulting in N-learning (Boisot, 1998). N-learning is the neoclassical learning of building first mover advantages, based on protection of R&D investments by means of IPR, and trust in own competence.

Our main finding as to the mediating effect of learning is that relatively broader and more ambitious innovation strategies induce exploitative learning, but also imply a lower level of embeddedness in the value chain. Furthermore, higher levels of exploitative learning are associated with higher levels of exploratory learning – in other words, radical innovators produce incremental innovators. This indicates that contrary to March's idea there is no trade-off of exploitation and exploration, but there seems to be a logical alternating sequence of both types of learning processes.

The embeddedness-inducing effect of exploratory learning, in contrast to the embeddedness-loosening effect of exploitative learning, seems to point to a configuration of external structuring related to stages in the innovation process. The early phases of innovation that are decoupled from innovation strategies draws more heavily on external partners in the value chain, than does the later stage in which one is optimizing artefacts incrementally.

In sum, these findings as to the mediating effect of learning between strategy and structure yield interesting additional explanations for the emergence of networks. However, for a substantial part these findings are contrary to our expectations and expectations in the literature. In general, the effects in our model are moderate or even weak. Why? First, neither the data nor the measurement model has been polished. So, to a large extent it is a WYSIWYG model that can be refined and adapted in many ways. Of course this is not a decisive argument at all. From a theoretical point of view, we would be very suspicious of very strong structural effects of strategy and learning. After all, structures are the pillars on which the organizational fabric rests; they stabilize and ascertain longevity. This temporal invariance of organizational structures should not be underestimated. Besides this general notion of structural inertia – it is clear that learning efforts only have to be assimilated partially in a structural sense, because for the larger part they should precipitate in new products and processes.

The implication of our main findings is that the co-evolutionary part of our argument *a la* Miller and Friesen – although not on the basis of past performance – has to be adapted slightly. Learning efforts – that is to say, the operationalization of innovation strategies – materialize partially in a structural way as far as procedures and rules are involved, but for the larger part they yield repertoires, and to an even larger extent new product and processes. Furthermore, our findings support the existence of a sort of cumulative (Colombo & Mosconi, 1995) and self-reinforcing effect of strategy – learning and structuring at *the level of the firm*, in which exploration and exploitation seemingly have counteracting effects on external embeddedness. Exploitation is associated with weakening ties, and exploration is associated with strengthening ties.

Note

1 Goodness of fit statistics of the estimated model: Goodness of fit index (GFI) = 0.89; adjusted goodness of fit index = 0.82. The goodness of fit measures GFI and AGFI of Jöreskog and Sörbom (1989) (cf. Tanaka and Huba, 1985) do not depend on sample size explicitly and measure how much better the model fits as compared to no model at all. Both GFI and AGFI vary between 0 and 1. Levels of significance: $d = p < 0.001$, $c = p < 0.01$, $b = p < 0.05$, $a = p < 0.10$.

Bibliography

Alter, C. & Hage, J. (1993), *Organizations Working Together* (Newbury Park: Sage).

Aoki, M. (1986), 'Horizontal vs. Vertical information structure of the firm', *American Economic Review*, 76(5), pp. 971–83.

Baum, J.A.C. & McKelvey, B. (eds) (1999), *Variations in Organization Science: In Honor of Donald T. Campbell* (Thousand Oaks, CA: Sage).

Belderbos, R., Carree, M. & Lokshin, B. (2004), 'Cooperative R&D and firm performance', *Research Policy*, 33(10), pp. 1477–92.

Boisot, M. (1998), *Knowledge Assets: Securing competitive advantage in the information economy* (Oxford: Oxford University Press).

Borgatti, S.P. & Foster, P.C. (2003), 'The network paradigm in organizational research: a review and typology', *Journal of Management*, 29(6), pp. 991–1013.

Carr, C. (1993), 'Global, national and resource-based strategies: an examination of strategic choice and performance in the vehicle components industry', *Strategic Management Journal*, 14(7), pp. 551–68.

Chandler, A.D. Jr (1962), *Strategy and Structure: Chapters in the History of Industrial Enterprise* (Cambridge, MA: MIT Press).

Colombo, M.G. & Mosconi, R. (1995), 'Complementarity and cumulative learning effects in the early diffusion of multiple technologies', *Journal of Industrial Economics*, 43(1), pp. 13–48.

Cyert, R.M., March, J.G. & Clarkson, G.P.E. (1963), *A Behavioral Theory of the Firm* (Englewood Cliffs, NJ: Prentice-Hall).

Damanpour, F. & Gopalakrishnan, S. (1998), 'Theories of organizational structure and innovation adoption: the role of environmental change', *Journal of Engineering and Technology Management*, 15(1), pp. 1–24.

Dierkes, M., Antal, A.B., Child, J. & Nonaka, I. (2001), *Handbook of Organizational Learning and Knowledge* (Oxford: Oxford University Press).

Duncan, R. (1972), 'Characteristics of organizational environments and perceived environmental uncertainty', *Administrative Science Quarterly*, 17(3), pp. 313–27.

Freel, M.S. (2003), 'Sectoral patterns of small firm innovation, networking and proximity', *Research Policy*, 32(5), pp. 751–70.

Freeland, R.F. (1996), 'The myth of the M-form? Governance, consent, and organizational change', *American Journal of Sociology*, 102(2), pp. 483–526.

Gopalakrishnan, F. & Damanpour, S. (1998), 'Theories of organizational structure and innovation adoption: The role of environmental change', *Journal of Engineering and Technology Management*, 15(1), pp. 1–24.

Hage, J. (1980), *Theory of Organization* (New York: Wiley).

Hage, J. (ed.) (1998), *Innovation and Organization* (New York: Wiley).

Jöreskog, K.G. & Sörbom, D. (1989), *LISREL 7; A Guide to the Program and Applications* (Chicago: SPSS Inc.).

Jöreskog, K.G. & Sörbom, D. (1993), *New Features in LISREL 8* (Chicago: Scientific Software International).

Khandwalla, P.H. (1972), 'Environment and its impact on the organization', *International Studies of Management and Organization*, pp. 297–313.

Levinthal, D. & March, J.G. (1993), 'The myopia of learning', *Strategic Management Journal*, 14, Winter special issue, pp. 95–112.

Levitt, B. & March, J.G. (1988), 'Organizational learning', *Annual Review of Sociology*, 14, pp. 319–40.

Lundvall, B.A. (1992), *National Systems of Innovation. Towards a Theory of Innovation and Interactive Learning* (London: Pinter).

Madhavan, R., Koka, B.R. & Prescott, J.E. (1998), 'Networks in transition: How industry events (re-)shape interfirm relationships', *Strategic Management Journal*, 19, pp. 439–59.

March, J.G. (1991), 'Exploration and Exploitation in Organizational Learning', *Organization Science*, 2(1), pp. 71–87.

March, J.G. & Olsen, J.P. (1975), 'The uncertainty of the past: organizational learning under ambiguity', *European Journal of Political Research*, 3, pp. 147–71.

Meeus, M.T.H. & Oerlemans, L.A.G. (1993), *Strategic Policy in Industrial SMEs in Zuidoost-Brabant* (Eindhoven: Technische Univ. Eindhoven).

Meeus, M.T.H., Oerlemans, L.A.G. & Hage, J. (2001a), 'Sectoral patterns of interactive learning. An empirical exploration of a case in a Dutch region', *Technology Analysis and Strategic Management*, 13(3), pp. 427–51.

Meeus, M.T.H., Oerlemans, L.A.G. & Hage, J. (2001b), 'Patterns of interactive learning in a high tech region. An empirical exploration of complementary and competing perspectives', *Organization Studies*, 22(1), pp. 145–72.

Meeus, M.T.H., Oerlemans, L.A.G. & Hage, J. (2004), 'Industry – public knowledge infrastructure interaction: intra- and inter-organizational explanations of interactive learning', *Industry and Innovation*, 11(4), pp. 327–52.

Miller, D. (1999), 'Selection processes inside organizations: the self-reinforcing consequences of success' (in Baum & McKelvey).

Miller, D. & Friesen, P.H. (1977), 'Strategy making in context: ten empirical archetypes', *Journal of Management Studies*, 14, pp. 253–80.

Miller, D. & Friesen, P.H. (1982), 'Innovation in conservative and entrepreneurial firms: Two models of strategic momentum', *Strategic Management Journal*, 3, pp. 1–25.

Miller, D. & Friesen, P.H. (1984), *A Quantum View* (Englewood Cliffs, NJ: Prentice-Hall).

Nooteboom, B. (1999), 'Innovation, learning and industrial organisation', *Cambridge Journal of Economics*, 23(2), pp. 127–50.

Nooteboom, B. (2001), *Learning and Innovation in Organization and Economies* (Oxford: Oxford University Press).

Oerlemans, L.A.G. & Meeus, M.T.H. (1998), *High Performance Organizations. A comparison of firm characteristics* (The Hague: Research Commissioned by the Dutch Ministry of Economic Affairs).

Oerlemans, L.A.G. & Meeus, M.T.H. (2001), 'R&D cooperation in a transaction cost perspective', *The Review of Industrial Organization*, 18, pp. 77–90.

Pettigrew, A., Massini, S. & Numagami, T. (2000), 'Innovative forms of organising in Europe and Japan', *European Management Journal*, 18(3), pp. 259–73.

Pfeffer, J. & Salançik, G.R. (1978), *The External Control of Organizations* (New York: Harper & Row).

Poot, T. (2004), *Determinanten van kennisintensieve onderzoeks- en ontwikkelingssamenwerking* (Delft: Delft University Press).

Salançik, J., Pfeffer, G. *et al.* (1976), 'The effect of uncertainty on the use of social influence in organizational decision making', *Administrative Science Quarterly*, 21(2), pp. 227–45.

Tanaka, J.S. & Huba, G.J. (1985), 'A fit index for covariance structure models under arbitrary GLS estimation', *British Journal of Mathematical and Statistical Psychology*, 38(2), pp. 197–201.

Volberda, H. (1998), *Building the Flexible Firm* (Oxford: Oxford University Press).

Volberda, H. & Lewin, A. (2002), *Special Issue of Organization Studies on Co-evolution*.

West, J. (2000), 'Institutions, information processing, and organization structure in research and development: evidence from the semiconductor industry', *Research Policy*, 29(3), pp. 349–73.

Wolf, J. & Egelhoff, W.G. (2002), 'Research notes and commentaries. A reexamination and extension of international strategy-structure theory', *Strategic Management Journal*, 23, pp. 181–9.

8
Strategic Reflexivity as a Framework for Understanding Development in Modern Firms. *How the Environment Drives Innovation*

Jon Sundbo and Lars Fuglsang

8.1. Introduction

In this chapter, we argue that 'strategic reflexivity' can be seen as one way to conceptualize the development of modern firms. Modern firms and other organizations are often under pressure to develop or innovate in order to survive, but they depend on future markets and environments of which they do not have objective knowledge. Therefore they have to make use of uncertain development strategies within a framework of what we here call 'strategic reflexivity'. Strategic reflexivity is based on reflexive interpretations about developments in the environment (or the market) of the firm. For instance, what is normally conceived as market driven innovation (Nyström, 1990; Tidd, Bessant & Pavitt, 1997) must, within the framework of strategic reflexivity, be understood as a process in which the firm does not react directly on the basis of 'objective' market changes, but creates an interpretation of the future environment that guides their development process. This approach to strategy can also be found in Mintzberg (1998) as well as Daft and Weick's (1984) view of the firm as an interpretation system; thus it is not new. What is new in this chapter is the combination of this approach with Weick's (1995) sense-making approach and the resource-based view of the firm (e.g., Grant, 1991) in an attempt to explain innovation. This theoretical combination is particularly useful as it leads us to a broader interpretation of the concept of innovation and a new model of the innovative organization, which specifies the firm as a system of roles.

Strategic reflexivity, we argue, is a form of development activity that must be based on experience, general education and social intelligence in order to work, and it entails a risk of uncontrolled or misbehaved management styles, because of the uncertainties and dualities with which it is connected. We have earlier discussed the notion of strategic reflexivity (Sundbo & Fuglsang, 2002, 2004; and Sundbo, 2002, 2003) to explain innovation. In this chapter we develop this concept of organizational development by investigating how the notion can explain development behaviour in organizations. Our development of the notion is an attempt to conceptualize results of empirical studies. We see strategic reflexivity as an adequate description of innovation and development processes within service organizations and we base this view on comprehensive case studies undertaken by us and others (cf. Boden & Miles, 2000; Sundbo, 1998; Hauknes, 1998; SIC, 1999; Gallouj, 2002; Fuglsang, 2001; Howells, 2004). We will, however, claim that strategic reflexivity is a valid description of development activities in a growing number of organizations. It is also an approach that is relevant to the description of organizations characterized by R&D technology based innovations and entrepreneurship, which have been seen as the classic aspects of the development of the firm. In the first part of this chapter we discuss strategic reflexivity as a response to an uncertain and complex environment. In the second part we examine how strategic reflexivity can be managed and organized.

8.2. Development as the basis for theory

Our approach takes its staring point in innovation theory. However, we argue that the renewal of modern organizations is a broader process than traditionally conceptualized in innovation and entrepreneurship theory. The term innovation suggests that we are talking about expert-based technological change (even if that has been modified lately, cf., e.g., Tidd, Bessant & Pavitt, 1997). The concept of entrepreneurship has a connotation to individual struggle (even though that also has been modified, cf., e.g., Kanter, 1983; Schendel & Channon, 1990). None of these concepts sufficiently reflect the complexity, uncertainty, and interconnectedness of modern development processes. By contrast, Schumpeter's (1911 [1994]) classic concept of 'development' characterizes more clearly the renewal we wish to discuss here because it emphasizes all types of structured change. In addition to this, the notion of development indicates that there is a 'red thread' in the changes, and this fits well with the reflexive strategy approach that we wish to emphasize here.

We shall not argue for complete abandonment of the concept of innovation. Innovation can be seen as a special case of development, which is relevant to some firms and organizations. Innovation could be defined as the successful introduction and development of new products or processes that can be clearly isolated and identified and which have a certain degree of radicalism and novelty. The innovation process should be identifiable as a process *per se*, it should have the character of a specific, novelty-oriented project. Extreme novelty is not a requirement for development. The following can briefly illustrate our distinction between change, development and innovation: A house may 'change' over the years in various ways, due to the weather, for example. If the owner of the house adds a chimney and some windows, this is a 'development' of the house according to the owner's taste. The chimney and the windows may be new for this type of house, but even if they are not, they add something new to this particular house, and this may, for example, increase its value. A development can be understood as an expansion of an organization that 'adds on' to it, perhaps also subtracting something. In the case of strategic reflexivity, development is understood in relation to what fits into the environment, for instance the market. When the house owner adds the chimney and windows, this must fit into and be accounted for in relation to requirements in the environment. If, during the process of development, the owner comes up with an entirely new to the world kind of window, this is an 'innovation'. We argue that 'development' is more characteristic than 'innovation' for the growth and success of modern organizations. Development includes such phenomena as expanding market behaviour (for example, shifting to a discount supermarket chain instead of using a luxury grocer) or the introduction of a new organizational form (e.g., self-governing teams) that leads towards the expansion of the organization.

8.3. Strategic reflexivity

Strategic reflexivity characterizes a certain way in which development is organized. More precisely, it is a specific way in which the firm relates to its environment, namely as something that has to be interpreted and accounted for (cf. Mintzberg, 1994). Once it has been accounted for, the organization has to respond to it. The organization can respond by adapting to the environment, but it can also try to influence the environment, thus creating, for instance, its own market conditions. This response includes the introduction of new products and services, new market behaviour or increased productivity. The firm manages this process by an overall policy that sets some framework for the development. This policy is expressed in the strategy, which may be more or less formalized.

Since knowledge about the environment is uncertain, the organization has to adjust its interpretations continuously in order to consider whether the strategy is still the best and whether the implementation of it (which means the innovations and other concrete developments) is suitable. This can be compared to what Weick (1995) has called sense making. The notion of strategic reflexivity is composed of two concepts. One is strategy, which comes from the literature on strategy (which is enormous, see, e.g., Mintzberg, 1994; Grant, 2002). There are many definitions of strategy, but one that is generally accepted is that it is a goal-orientation of an organization's future development. This aspect is important to our understanding. The other concept is reflexivity, which comes from sociological literature (Giddens, 1984; Beck, 1992) where it has been used to describe citizens' reflection on their own lives in a societal framework in contrast to governance through tradition or authority. Reflection is obviously related to strategy in the sense that strategy comes a step after reflection. Reflection is a phenomenon related to the individual in Giddens' and Beck's theories; however, we use it as a collective phenomenon. Reflections are carried out in organizations.

8.4. The two scripts of strategic reflexivity

Our discussion takes its point of departure in the relationship between the organization and its environment. The environment can be the market or people's ideological and ethical values, their lifestyle, political ideology and ideas that may change regulations and world policy, changes in nature (pollution, climate changes and so on). The concept of strategic reflexivity is grounded in the analysis of the relation between the organization and its environment. However, our position is not that the market and societal development determine the strategy in a simple cause-effect relation (cf. the contingency theory, Lawrence & Lorsch, 1967). Strategic reflexivity is not pulled by the market, because organizations cannot directly observe the needs in the market for a specific development or innovation. The relation between the organization and the environment is, as mentioned above, basically interpretative. The relationship between the organization and the environment may be expressed as shown in the simple model in Figure 8.1.

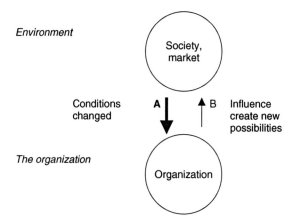

Figure 8.1. The relation between the organization and its environment

Figure 8.1 shows a standard model of the relation between an organization and its environment. We argue that this model is still important, but due to increasing complexity, the external conditions are no longer perceived by the organization as objective and given, but as interpretative and flexible. Nobody knows exactly what the conditions are, but everybody is trying to summarize them in a reflexive 'summary text' (Knorr-Cetina *et al.*, 1981). Organizations will use surveys, consultants, networks, and interviews in order to summarize the external conditions in a plausible way.

In addition to a summary text that describes the external conditions, an organization will also write a script for itself that describes its own role *vis-à-vis* the external conditions as they have been summarized. Such a script may describe the role of the organization as purely reactive. The role of the organization is in this case to adapt itself to the external conditions as they are described in the summary text (the A relation). The script may also assign a more proactive role to the organization as one that can attempt to influence the external conditions as described in the summary text (the B relation). In this case, the organization attempts to influence the perceived external development by innovating, thus making itself conspicuous in the environment (becoming itself an important actor in the summary text) and able to set the agenda of, for example, technological renewal. We have thus defined two different forms of summary text relations, the A-script, which could be called an outside-in script, and the B-script, which could be called an inside-out script (cf. Sundbo, 2001). Both of these scripts are strategic reflexive to the extent that they both reflexively rely on interpretations (summary texts and scripts) rather than perceived objective knowledge of the external conditions. The script is a general approach to the relationship with the firm's environment. It is the basis of the strategy, which is an operationalization of the script and further includes more detailed missions and goals. Hence, in these scripts there is no such thing as an objective need for a new product. Customers, for example, do not have an objective need. Their needs have to be interpreted in a summary text. The innovating firm can therefore not identify the needs in an objective way.

A need in a strategic reflexive setting is constructed in a process of interaction where the provider influences the potential customers through summary texts while simultaneously being influenced by him. This is also reflected in the fact that in services where customers are often involved in the production (cf. Grönroos, 2000), the ideas for innovations very often come from the service encounter when an employee meets a customer. A development in a strategic reflexive setting is a long process with successive elements. It is not a one-shot innovation, but more a multidimensional development and a series of different changes as stated earlier. It is a process of adding new elements to the product and perhaps of going back and changing the product. This means that the traditional single-product diffusion-curve, the S-curve, for a new innovation is not as smooth as assumed in innovation theory. It is much more complex, as is illustrated in Figure 8.2.

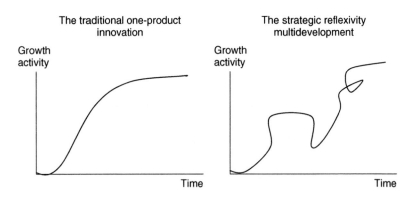

Figure 8.2.   Diffusion models for firm developments

8.5. The outside-in script

In the outside-in script, the organization attempts to adapt itself to interpretations of external conditions as presented in its summary text. This is the main form of the strategic reflexive development process. The management and other actors within the firm are led by interpreted potential changes, which are described in a summary text. A summary text is not one single text, but a body of texts, written or spoken, that frame sense making in the organization (cf. Weick, 1995). The script is both the operational basis and the legitimization of the strategy. The outside-in process is expressed by the A arrow in Figure 8.1. It is the type of development process that Michael Porter (1985, 1990) stresses in his analyses. The process contains three steps.

8.5.1. Pre-strategic reflections

The organization constructs the summary text by interpretatively investigating customers' behaviour, but also by testing hypotheses about the external conditions by launching new products. The external conditions can only be described approximately in the summary text. The organization also investigates new input possibilities, for example new technology, new scientific results and new management philosophies and tools. The organization observes in its own way the external conditions and perhaps the society in general to see what is happening. This is why organizations often are interested in futuristic social research. The purpose is to establish some goals or ideas concerning innovation and other changes that can give the organization a better position in the future. The observations may be very systematic and formal-analytical or they may be intuitive and informal. The top management may manage the observations through a special analytical or strategy department or even through some employees or middle managers. Reflections are not mechanical reflections (as in a mirror) of the external conditions, not even as a kind of 'reproduced other' (cf. Mead, 1934). As mentioned, they are an interpretation in the form of a summary text, which is made in interaction with other members of the organization. The changes in the summary text do not directly determine a specific development or strategy that may be predicted. They start some organizational processes, which can be of different kinds and all of which will result in development strategy, although this will rarely be identical to that predicted in the summary text. This can be expressed visually by presenting the internal processes in the model shown in the Figure 8.3.

Figure 8.3.   Internal processes within the organization – reflexivity

The interpretation of the summary text is a collective framework for sense making (cf. Weick, 1995). This may be shared by the whole organization. There may also be norms, values or idea systems of subcultures within the organization, which are not widely shared by other members. This is the case in the loosely coupled organization, where the summary text and the organization are only loosely attached to each other. This situation often leads to an inconsistent and vague strategy. The summary text may also be new ideas that occur in interaction processes within or outside of the organization and which breaks the hitherto dominant organizational framework. A strategy is formulated on the basis of the pre-strategic reflections about the external conditions. The strategy is based on the interpretation of the summary text. It focuses on the development of several societal agents including customers, competitors, 'trendsetters' in society, political agents and so on. The strategy expresses the belief of how the organization can maneouver. That includes an assessment of the organizations' internal resources and capabilities (cf. Teece & Pisano, 1994) (as, e.g., expressed in the popular SWOT analyses), its organizational culture and values and maybe the ideas of owner(s).

Pre-strategic reflection may rely on three factors: (1) formal methods; (2) norms, action patterns and education in society (the social heritage), and (3) creativity. The interpretation is influenced by general analytical and strategic methods (that managers and employees, for example, learn in business schools), the social and organization–cultural heritage and new ideas, diffused within society or invented within the firm. The interpretations and the summary text thus are explicitly social constructions, but they are seen to mirror 'real' external conditions. This means that they are not understood to be completely individual and free from structural constraints. On the contrary, the individuals will in their interpretative constructions follow the patterns of the social structure that are embedded in the firm's culture, values and goals, and they imagine that the strategy will be constrained by real external conditions.

8.5.2. Movement

Next, the organization will reflect upon whether or not to move and if so, when and how. The latter means that the firm may move on different factors, also in relation to interpretations of competitors' behaviour. If one manufacturer of radio equipment has made a technological innovation and invented a new medium for storing and playing music, the importance of this must be interpreted. A competitor may answer the challenge by maintaining the old technology, but investing in pop groups or others musicians that record on the old medium and establish a distribution company. Or the competitor may make political moves and convince politicians to set a standard that institutionalizes the old technology. A development of a product may give advantages, but it is also risky because success is not guaranteed. The strategic behaviour influences actors as they are described in the summary text and it leads to revisions of the summary text. The organization will make scenarios of competitors' new steps on the basis of the organizations own moves. The idea of strategic reflexivity behaviour is similar to that of game theory (e.g., Owen, 1995), but not as mathematical-cybernetic in its approach, but more interpretative. Within the framework of strategic reflexivity, human creativity is supposed to be able to change the rules of the game. Those within the organization who decide the strategy are the top management, but a larger part of the organization may be involved in the development of the strategy. This may include a group of managers or employees. Many organizations have a process where strategy is widely discussed in the organization. The initiative for a new strategy may even come from below in the organization.

The strategy shows the route that the organization should follow in the future. It sets up the framework for innovations and other developments. The strategy is not a manual that the employees and managers can use to decide on innovations and other changes (e.g., changed market behaviour, procurement of new competencies, new knowledge, the introduction of new IT, a new management philosophy) and how to carry them out (or this will at least very rarely be the case). However, it presents some general goals for the development of the firm. Each individual, team or department has to interpret for himself or herself whether concrete ideas about change are in accordance with the strategy or not. This interpretation is intertwined with the organizational hierarchy and thus middle managers and in some cases the top management are involved in deciding whether the interpretation is in accordance with the strategy.

8.5.3. Post-strategic reflection

Further, there is a permanent post-strategic reflexivity. The organization must continuously consider whether the chosen strategy is the right strategy. It is based on a construction – the strategy. The strategy may turn out to be wrong, either because it was a bad interpretation or because other actors and organizations do not relate to the summary text. Post-reflexivity also includes considerations of whether the chosen means are adequate. Are they the right innovations, the right behaviour and the right mixture of means? Post-strategic reflection often leads to cancelling ongoing innovation processes and the introduction of new innovations and sometimes to a change of the strategy. This illustrates how innovation processes and innovations as a means and choice of technology are subordinated to the strategy and reflections and that the question of which innovations and which technology is also subordinated to the strategic reflexivity.

Post-strategic reflexivity is not a rational process. Even post-strategic reflection is a trial without guarantee of success, even though it can be based on analyses. Concrete agents within the firm also undertake post-strategic reflections. This is a task for top management of course, but employees and middle managers are also involved. Positions in the organization have the task to reflect; permanent or ad hoc teams are set up to do the same. Post-strategic reflection is built into development processes such as innovation processes and middle managers will reflect as a part of their tasks. Informally reflections come from below. Employees and managers make their own observations of the summary text and the firm's organization. In successful firms these reflections will also be taken into consideration.

8.6. The inside-out script

An organization may also attempt to construct the summary text inside-out by attempting by itself to set up new 'rules of the game' to which others are supposed to relate. This is a more radical form of behaviour than the outside-in form. In the inside-out form, the organization's summary text and its interpretation of the environment are not necessarily taken for granted. Hence the organization is not interested in a general condition outside of itself, but in particular elements and particular actors that it waves into its own summary text and tries to get support for it from other actors and organizations. The organization is not attempting to mirror any external condition, but to convince others about certain developments of its own. This is an approach that is more entrepreneurial. Such a strategy will be based on an analysis of the internal resources as theoretically expressed in the theory of the resource-based firm (Penrose, 1959; Grant, 1991; Hamel & Prahalad, 1994) and the creation of an entrepreneurial spirit (cf. Drucker, 1985). The latter may break with previous scripts and strategies.

In this way, an entrepreneur may also create a radical inside-out development. This is a situation where one person from the firm creates and carries out a completely new behaviour by picking up some specific external element, such as a specific technology, service or experience and develop it into an innovation. The entrepreneur may be the managing director, but it can also be another manager or an employee. The inside-out development is the result of creativity, which can break the adaptive dependence on the external conditions. It is the result of internal processes of representation in the organization. Individuals in the organization are creative and entrepreneurial people, thus they might invent or in other ways introduce new elements or new relations between the elements. However, corporate entrepreneurship is an interactive process in which other members of the organization should be convinced about the idea. This is a more radical development because it breaks existing patterns of behaviour and meaning. This phenomenon is what has been associated with the classic, radical innovation. This type of creative, radical development – as we term it – may transform the organization through creation of new networks and new routines. Radical development may, as mentioned above, be a top-down, planned process as when a firm sets up an R&D department with a specific goal. Research may lead to representation of new ideas. The development process and the product in itself are of course also important factors, however, and within this framework the first action or reaction is the most important to understand. Radical development is illustrated in the model in Figure 8.4.

In addition to the interactive, strategic-reflexivity process that is carried out, a new element of radical innovation or entrepreneurial behaviour occurs. This may be a research result or a new idea of behaviour towards the market and the organization (illustrated by the cross in Figure 8.4). The new element will have a huge influence on the development.

The inside-out script can be planned for when a fundamental research process is started. It can also be impulsive as when a corporate

Figure 8.4.   Renewals of the internal reflection processes within the organization – radical development

entrepreneur starts a radical development. However, the process is not even in the latter case out of control, it is strategic reflexive. The top management will even in that case consider whether the development process should be accepted and if it should lead to a change in strategy. The radical new element must be accepted by the top management to be implemented (e.g., as a new product, market behaviour, organizational form and so on). The management and other parts of the organization will consider whether they should implement the new element or not. If they decide to implement it, they will next consider whether to change the strategy. In the inside-out script, the process starts with movement and all strategic reflexivity follows.

8.7. The organizational representation of the strategic reflexivity development process

8.7.1. The dual development organization

Strategic reflexivity requires a dual structure of top-down and bottom-up organizational forms, because of the double sidedness of strategy and reflexivity, decision making and scepticism (cf. Sundbo, 2001). The dual structure means that there is a formalized hierarchical process, which is not just a top-down system of orders and an informal bottom-up process of change and renewal coming from employees' and managers' reflection, creativity, entrepreneurship and interaction. These two structures are dialectic, they need each other. The formal, management-based structure needs the creativity and reflectivity of the employees to get the best innovations, the most valid reflectivity and the effort that independent entrepreneurship gives. The informal, interactive structure needs the management-based structure to decide and steer the development process and as a result the organization does not waste too many resources. Thus, the two structures are united in a dialectical relationship – they are in opposition to each other and yet they need and presuppose each other. If the opposition between two structures becomes too polarized, the firm will face a decline that will hit the employees too. Both structures may create an outside-in as well as an inside-out script. The top management will normally guide the process of outside-in strategizing, but initiatives may come from the informal, interactive structure. Radical inside-out development may come from top-managed research processes, but also from entrepreneurial activity in the informal, interactive structure.

In the dual organization, there is a top management that makes the final decision and the strategy is the guideline both for these decisions and the development. However, neither the top management nor the strategy can tell which precise renewals, including innovations, should be developed. The criterion for successful development is acceptance in the environment, including the market. As we have argued, the environment is complex and difficult to predict. Development thus depends on trial-and-reflection. The development process becomes a complex process which – although at some fundamental level it is managed – must have its own life. Thus, the strategic reflexivity development organization structure is complex. Our suggestion is that roles are the core element that can explain how this complex structure works and lives its own life. They create the development with its summary texts and scripts. The balancing of the dual structure and the outside-in and inside-out scripts is ensured by a system of roles.

8.7.2. The roles of strategic reflexivity

We argue that strategic reflexivity will give rise to particular professional roles in the organization. By roles we mean patterns of behaviour that partly determine the interaction among actors within the organization and in relation to its environment. The new roles are those that deal with reflections, the construction of the summary texts and development activities (including innovation). We can see them in a context of what we will call dramaturgy. In role theory, we can identify three views on roles: functional, interactional and dramaturgic. In the functional view (cf. Linton, 1936), roles are external norms and patterns of behaviour that the individual will appropriate. Roles are seen in relation to certain functions they fulfil in the social systems that define them. In the social-psychological view (Mead, 1934), roles are constituted in specific face-to-face contacts. Roles are established through interactions and mutual empathy among people in a practical context. In the dramaturgic view (Goffman, 1959), roles are specific to each situation, and roles are codes of conduct that are manipulated by the involved actors. An individual can step out of a role and manipulate it back stage, that is, there is a distinction between back stage where the role is created and front stage where the role is performed.

The dramaturgic role-view presumes that actors can clearly distinguish between specific social situations. Furthermore, it also presumes that actors are conscious of the different relevant roles in a situation and are able to manipulate it. Furthermore, the person must be able to change between roles, what we could call 'role gliding'. In the dramaturgic view, the manager achieves a much more dynamic position as a director in a theatre that will orchestrate the roles with reference to their meaning rather than their function. We will argue that the dramaturgic role view is typical of the strategic reflexivity organization and its attempt to construct summary texts. To construct a summary text, one has to view the organization as a theatre were people are playing roles that are not directly related to an objective reality, but which constitute interpretations or representations of external conditions. The different functions of reflection, strategy making and development including innovation also require that people in the organization play different roles to make the development optimal. In the context of the strategic reflexivity approach, the dialogue among actors, rather than the more primitive 'symbolic interaction', plays a strong role. Dialogue can underpin the construction of the summary text and the script for the organization. The roles can be created from below in a process of social framing, but also from above as a role ascribed by the management. All the time, it is clear that for the participants the roles are not objective but dramaturgic.

The dramaturgic roles may be improvised as in a jazz band (Weick, 1998). However, there is a certain fundamental pattern in the role play (as there are certain rhythms, keys and modes in the jazz that have to be followed). Some fundamental core roles may be identified. These core roles ensure the development and integration at the same time. This can be compared to the many roles involved in making a movie, from director, script writer to casting. The development requires creativity and entrepreneurial venturing, reflexive and analytical considerations and cooperation and interaction. It also requires awareness of a goal and the use of resources. Four such roles can be stated. The formulation of these four roles is based on our empirical research, primarily in the service sector (Sundbo, 2001; Fuglsang, 2001). The four fundamental roles are:

- The *entrepreneur* (initiates the summary text).
- The *analyst* (ensures the reflexivity).

- The *interactor* (ensures quality of the changes and rooting in the values and sense; a social entrepreneur cf. Fuglsang, 2001).
- The *decision maker* (ensures efficiency and rooting in strategy).

The entrepreneur's role is that of taking the first steps in the construction of a summary text. It is a role that is well known from the studies of corporate entrepreneurship (Schendel & Channon, 1990). This role is creative and it presses for change and innovation. However, the development process must be well considered, particularly in organizations working outside-in, and that secures the role of the analyst, which is the analytical, reflexive role. The analyst executes more formal analyses (such as analyses of the potential environment for a new product or the internal resources), but he also analyses whether the development process is in accordance with the organization's values and sense picture. The interactor is a role that seeks to represent changes as described in a summary text in the organization and make people relate to them. The interactor creates a common feeling of ownership of the change. Conflicts may occur in the development process, but the interactor may help in making them less severe. The interactor is a socializing role that makes people feel that they are living in a social community.

The decision maker is typically a project or department manager, but other managers or a group of managers may also play this role. The decision maker decides on new ideas – should they be developed further or stopped? The strategy is the most important framework for making these decisions and the decision maker thus is the role that secures the implementation of the strategy. Besides this, the decision maker may solve conflicts, at least by taking sides in them. The top manager may get this role of process decision maker (one who decides throughout the process) and is thus an equal actor to the other roles. All of these four roles must be present if the strategic reflexivity development system is to function optimally. Together they ensure creativity and pressure for development, strategic reflexivity, knowledge base and a maximal rooting in the market, and legitimacy in the organization. The weight of each role and the interaction between the roles define the pattern that ensures an optimal development process. Which mixture and mutual relation of the roles is most efficient depends on the situation of the organization, for example if it is in a stable phase or in a crisis that demands fast changes. Besides these roles there are also the roles of the boss and the expert.

- *The boss* is someone outside of the development who can cut through uncertainties and make the final decision even if people do not like it. The boss is outside of the development activities (e.g., in project teams) and only intervenes occasionally. Most often it is the top manager who plays the role of the boss, but it may be some other manager.

- *The expert* is a person with special knowledge that can support the analyst. The expert is one that can solve special problems (e.g., a consultant) or one that can create new prototypes such as a technical invention or a method for a service action (e.g., a researcher).

These two roles are outside of the development process; they are not necessary, but might be nice to have. Therefore they are often present in the strategic reflexivity development mode. The expert role can be bought from outside, thus it does not necessarily have to exist in the organization. The employees and managers play these six roles for a certain time and then they stop. Often they go back to what may be called their 'normal' production role, which is their daily work task. People may play several roles at the same time. In many strategic reflexivity organizations people are aware that they are playing a role temporarily, which means that they do not internalize it.

8.7.3. Innovation

The development process includes innovation. In the outside-in script, development is a series of incremental renewals. Some might be innovations as we have defined it here, for example, a new product or a new production process. Some might be small improvements of existing products or adding a new element to existing products. The latter does not need to be technical. It could, for example, be the addition of a service or experience element (cf. Pine & Gilmore, 1999) to the product in sale or after-sale. Innovation projects may be established during the development process, however, innovation is subordinated the strategic reflexivity. Whether innovations should be introduced and which innovations should be introduced, will be decided successively according to creative ideas and market-related reflections. Planned radical innovations might also occur by setting up an R&D organization or buying R&D form outside of the organization. This organization will normally have a defined task based on the strategy. However, the R&D work is continuously reflected in relation to the odds of success, the market possibilities and possible strategic changes. The R&D is subordinated the strategic reflexivity. The R&D may also be established without a specific task (basic research), but even that is subordinated strategic reflexivity. In these cases researchers playing the expert role are extremely important.

8.8. Uncertainties and risks in strategic reflexivity development

The strategic reflexivity-based development is often the most efficient way to grow and create profit or other types of success. However, it is also filled with risks and uncertainties that we discuss in this section. The strategic-reflexive process and summary texts are very uncertain because the environment is uncertain and the organizational process of creating developments is uncertain. Strategic reflexivity may lead to the top management's lack of control, which is not a good situation, neither for the management nor for the organization's survival. Or it might lead to a mismanagement that under-represents important aspects of the organization. Important inputs to the reflexive development process will then be missing. Strategic reflexive development is a balance between creativity and enthusiasm on one side (represented by the entrepreneur and the interactor roles) and reflexivity and scepticism on the other side (represented by the analyst and decision-maker roles). Too much emphasis on the creativity and enthusiasm side might lead to utopian strategies that over-stimulate the organization and thus an over-optimal use of resources. It may also lead to unproductive stress in the organization. Too much emphasis on the reflexive and sceptical side may lead to dystopian strategies that demotivate. The right balance depends on the character of the concrete organization and the situation. It becomes a difficult task for the top management to find the right balance.

To solve these problems, managers and employees must be able to make qualified reflections. Competencies and social intelligence that can analyze and reflect on the development process must be developed within the organization. It is also vital to have practical steering from the top management – not of all details, but of the overall development process. New conditions occur in the environment and the summary text and the strategy must be changed from time to time. The chosen direction of development may also show to be sub-optimal and must be adjusted, like a car wheel has to be adjusted regularly. Even though risks and uncertainties make the strategic reflexivity-based development unsure, we argue that this nevertheless is the best way for most modern firms and other organizations. An important task for them is to work to minimize risks and uncertainties as much as possible.

8.9. Conclusion

We have argued that firms and other organizations increasingly have to respond to complex environments. Therefore they have to rely on developments in which they can use different means and not only on R&D-based innovation or person-dependent entrepreneurship. Organizations become strategic reflexive in their development activities. Organizations cannot collect objective knowledge in a conventional way about a complex environment. Instead, they have to construct summary text about the external conditions based on reflections. The summary text becomes the basis for the strategy. A summary text can be scripted in two different ways: outside-in, where the organization tries approximately to mirror what they believe to be real external conditions to which the organization must adapt itself; this adaptation is expressed in the strategy and inside-out, where radical development elements occur in the organization, which leads to subsequent reflections, innovations and possibly strategic change. The development activities are carried out in a complex dual organization. The top management and the strategy are leading factors in the development activities, but they depend on creative and interpretative-reflexive processes in the organization. The interpretative activities and the radical inside-out renewals lead to new roles in the firm that take care of the strategic reflections, the summary text and the development. We have distinguished six roles, of which four are core roles in the development process and two are help functions that may be enrolled in the process if necessary. Furthermore, we have discussed how the strategic reflexivity mode creates uncertainties in an organization that can lead to under-representation, demotivation and stress. These strategic reflexivity mode problems cannot be solved in any principle way, but have to be solved through practical steering based in general education and social intelligence.

Bibliography

Beck, U. (1992), *Risk Society* (London: Sage).
Boden, M. & Miles, I. (eds) (2000), *Services and the Knowledge-based Economy* (London: Continuum).
Daft, R.L. & Weick, K.E. (1984), 'Toward a Model of Organizations as Interpetration Systems', *Academy of Management Review*, 9(2), pp. 284–95.
Drucker, P. (1985), *Innovation and Entrepreneurship* (New York: Harper & Row).
Freeman, C. & Soete, L. (1997), *The Economics of Industrial Innovation* (London: Pinter).
Fuglsang, L. (2001), 'Management Problems in Welfare Services: The Role of the 'Social Entrepreneur' in Home-help for the Elderly, the Valby Case', *Scandinavian Journal of Management*, 17(4), pp. 437–55.
Gallouj, F. (2002), *Innovation in the Service Economy* (Cheltenham: Elgar).
Giddens, A. (1984), *The Constitution of Society* (Cambridge: Polity).
Goffman, E. (1959), *The Presentation of Self in Everyday Life* (New York: Doubleday).

Grant, R. (1991), 'The Resource-Based Theory of Competitive Advantage: Implications for Strategy Formulation', *California Management Review*, spring, pp. 114–35.

Grant, R. (2002), *Contemporary Strategic Analyses* (Malden, MA: Blackwell).

Grönroos, C. (2000), *Service Management and Marketing* (Chichester: Wiley).

Hamel, G., & Prahalad, C.K. (1994), *Competing for the Future* (Boston: Harvard Business School Press).

Hauknes, J. (1998), *Services in Innovation – Innovation in Services* (SI4S final report, Oslo: STEP Group).

Howells, J. (2004), 'Innovation, Consumption and Services', *Service Industries Journal*, 24(1), pp. 19–36.

Kanter, R.M. (1983), *The Change Masters* (London: Unwin).

Knorr-Cetina, K., Aaron, V. & Cicourel, A. (eds) (1981), *Advances in Social Theory and Methodology. Toward an Integration of Micro- and Macro-sociologies* (London: Routledge).

Lawrence, P.R. & Lorsch, J.W. (1967), *Organization and Environment* (Boston: Harvard University Press).

Linton, R. (1936), *The Study of Man* (New York: Appelton Century-Crofts).

Mead, G.H. (1934), *Mind, Self and Society* (Chicago: Chicago University Press).

Mintzberg, H. (1994), *The Rise and Fall of Strategic Planning* (New York: Free Press).

Mintzberg, H., Ahlstrand, B. & Lampel, J. (1998), *Strategy Safari* (New York: Free Press).

Nyström, H. (1990), *Technological and Market Innovation* (Chichester: Wiley).

Owen, G. (1995), *Game Theory* (San Diego: Academic Press).

Penrose, E.T. (1959), *The Theory of the Growth of the Firm* (New York: Blackwell).

Pine, B.J. & Gilmore, J.H. (1999), *The Experience Economy* (Boston: Harvard Business School Press).

Porter, M. (1985), *Competitive Advantage* (New York: Free Press).

Porter, M. (1990), *The Competitive Advantage of Nations* (New York: Macmillan).

Schendel, D. & Channon, D. (eds) (1990), 'Special Issue on Corporate Entrepreneurship', *Strategic Management Journal*, 11, summer.

Schumpeter, J. (1911 [1934]), *The Theory of Economic Development* (Boston: Harvard University).

Shavina, L. (ed.) (2003), *The International Handbook on Innovation* (New York: Pergamon).

SIC (Service Development, Internationalization and Competence Development) (1999), *Danish Service Firms' Innovation Activities and use of ICT*, Report no. 2 from the project.

SIC (Service Development, Internationalisation & Competence Development), (Roskilde: Centre for Service Studies, Roskilde University) (http://www.ruc.dk/css/sic/published.html).

Sundbo, J. (1998), *The Organisation of Innovation in Services* (Copenhagen: Roskilde University Press).

Sundbo, J. (2001), *The Strategic Management of Innovation* (Cheltenham: Edward Elgar).

Sundbo, J. (2002), 'Innovation as a strategic process' (in Sundbo & Fuglsang).

Sundbo, J. (2003), 'Innovation and Strategic Reflexivity' (in Shavina).

Sundbo, J. & Fuglsang, L. (eds) (2002), *Innovation as Strategic Reflexivity* (London: Routledge).

Sundbo, J. & Fuglsang, L. (2004), *The Organizational Representation of Innovation: Three Modes* (Roskilde, manuscript).

Teece, D.J. & Pisano, G. (1994), 'The Dynamic Capability of Firms: An Introduction', *Industrial and Corporate Change*, 3(3), pp. 537–56.

Tidd, J., Bessant, J. & Pavitt, K. (1997), *Managing Innovation* (Chichester: Wiley).

Weick, K. (1995), *Sensemaking in Organizations* (Thousand Oaks, CA: Sage).

Weick, K. (1998), 'Introductory Essay – Improvization as Mindset for Organizational Analysis', *Organization Science*, 9(5), pp. 213–34.

9

Innovation as Institutional Change.
A Complexity Approach

Jaume Guia, Lluís Prats and Jordi Comas

9.1. Introduction

Over the past few decades, the literature on innovation management has focused on explaining how to be innovative in one's own organization. Even though there is a variety of prescriptions, a key question in all of the perspectives relates to how manageable the innovation process is.

Two main streams of literature can be found. First, some think of innovation as a rational, intentional, sequential process (Drucker, 1985; Crawford, 1991; Cooper & Kleinschmidt, 1991). Thinking here reflects the rational behaviour assumption of classical and neoclassical economics and falls within the paradigm of strategic choice and planning. Second, there are those who understand innovation to be a social, political and behavioural process, reflecting the position of evolutionary economics. Writers in this tradition are claiming that while it may not be possible to control and manage innovations, it is possible to design and control the contextual and organizational conditions that enhance the probability of innovation occurring (Kanter, 1988; Quinn, 1991).

Therefore, some authors claim that innovation is incremental rather than revolutionary; others claim that the strategic planning of innovation is far superior to intuitive approaches; yet others justify the superiority of soft human-centred approaches compared to strategic planning. However, the empirical validation of those claims shows inconsistent results (Wolfe, 1994). Regardless of whether innovation is thought of as a hard scientific and technological process, or a rational management process, or a soft intuitive human process, all these perspectives have in common the assumption that innovation is a phenomenon that can be subjected to human control. It is taken for granted that humans can purposefully design in advance the conditions under which innovation will occur. The chapter shows that this assumption of controllability is the distinguishing feature of mainstream thinking about innovation. Our purpose is to argue for a very different understanding of innovation drawing on complexity theories. Innovation is presented as the emergent continuity and transformation of social institutions understood as patterns of human interaction. In what follows we first describe the mainstream and complexity ways of thinking about innovation; then, we define innovation as institutional change and, finally, draw some conclusions.

9.2. Mainstream thinking

The management sciences (Taylor, 1911; Fayol, 1916 [1948]) and human relation perspectives (Mayo, 1949; Likert, 1961) focus on actions of individuals, and do so within a theory of causality in which organizations are designs chosen by individuals in pursuit of efficiency. Stability is preserved by efficient rules that govern the behaviour of the members of an organization. Change is brought about by managers when they choose to change the rules, which they should do in a way so that the designed set of rules will produce optimum outcomes. The shift to systems thinking (Burns & Stalker, 1961; Lawrence & Lorsch, 1967; Miller & Rice, 1967) moved attention from entities to interactions between them, where now those interactions are governed by a different kind of causality. The theory of causality here is one of a formative process producing movement to an already given final state (Stacey *et al.*, 2000). The systems, in systems thinking, can only do what they are designed to do, and the choice about the system and its rules is made by an observer outside the system who has the freedom to design it.

While the shift to systems thinking represents an enormous increase in the capacity to understand the complexity of real human action, it entails a dual causality. When individual agents – the workers – are thought of as parts of the system, they are governed by the rules of the system and their actions spread out the enfolded design of the system. It follows that, in their role as parts of the system, individuals are not autonomous and innovation, in the sense of the completely new, cannot arise in the system itself because its behaviour is the spreading out of what has already been enfolded in its design. However, when individual agents are conceptualized as autonomous individuals standing outside the system – the managers – designing it and setting goals, the origin of novelty is located in the reasoning of these individuals.

Thus, when dealing with human systems in systems thinking, we have freedom confined to the observer, but absent to the organizational members in the system. Two main criticisms of this approach can be found (Stacey *et al.*, 2000). The first problem is that individuals in the system are presented as deterministic, thinking machines (reason-based) and that emotion, conflict, politics and cultural aspects of organizational life are ignored. The response of systems thinkers to these criticism, has taken the form of redefining the boundaries of the system. For example, Checkland (1981) and Chekland and Schöles (1990) propose an approach to systems thinking in which account is taken, by the designer of the system, of the social rules and practices of participants in the system. However, the participating managers still stand outside of the system, now including cultural and political subsystems, which they can control.

The second problem is that the designer 'is also part of the system'. Again, to remedy this, systems thinkers widen the boundary of the system to include within it the designer (Bateson, 1973). In the first instance, all that is incorporated in the system is the designer's current mental model, and therefore some processes outside of the system so outlined are still required to change it. This new challenge can be solved again by expanding further the boundaries of the system to include now the designer's model for changing current mental models (Argyris & Schön, 1978). With this last extension, the pattern of change in mental models is also included in the system, but the choice about how to change this 'pattern of change' is still located outside of the expanded system in the form of meta-learning models (Argyris, 1990). Therefore, the problem with this type of explanation is that it rapidly runs into an infinite regress and has to be abandoned to some kind of mysticism (Shermer, 2000). None of the solutions seem, therefore, to solve these problems or criticisms in a convincing way.

9.3. Complexity thinking

In a recent review of systems thinking, Flood (1999) identifies complexity theory as another strand in systems thinking. The insights he draws on from the complexity sciences are the limits to predictability and the way in which self-organizing interactions at a local level can produce coherent global patterns of behaviour. This means that self-organizing systems produce emergent order that is unknown to the human mind. This puts into question whether long-term intended action is possible and it leads him to conclude that the most we can do is manage what is local, that is, over a small number of interactions between people and over short periods of time in the future. Seeing complexity as simply a strand of systems thinking implies a narrowing of the system to encompass only the local, known interactions, once again relegating the unknown to a position outside of the boundary where it and its impact are not open to explanation within the terms of systems thinking itself. In fact, there is as yet no single science of complexity but, rather, a number of different strands comprising what might be called the complexity sciences. The writing about complexity in human organizations usually draw on concepts to be found in one or more of these three strands, namely, chaos theory, dissipative structure theory, and the theory of complex adaptive systems. All of these model complex, turbulent systems and demonstrate the possibility of order emerging from disorder through processes of spontaneous self-organization in the absence of any blueprint.

Chaos theory (Gleick, 1988; Stewart, 1989) establishes the properties of systems that can be modelled by recursively applied nonlinear equations, just as the systems dynamics strand of systems theory does. These mathematical models display movement toward and within pre-given patterns called attractors, a mathematical description of an end state toward which a system moves. A move to a different attractor requires an objective observer outside of the system to alter a control parameter. This alteration results in a move to a new attractor, where the move itself does not depend upon the internal dynamic in any way. However, how such a system moves within the bounds of the strange attractor is determined by its own internal dynamic, which is affected by small changes. Therefore, chaos models display the unfolding of patterns in a sense already enfolded in the specification of the model. Here, like in systems thinking, causality is of a formative kind in that the nonlinear structure of the equations, the iterative process and the sensitivity to initial conditions together cause the attractors, the final state toward which, and within which, the system moves. Given that both chaos theory and systems thinking are built on the same theory of causality, it is likely to be difficult to take up the challenge to develop new ways of thinking about organizations.

By contrast, many of the mathematical models used in dissipative structure theory (Prigogine, 1997) incorporate micro-diversity and, therefore, the modelled system moves to another attractor without any intervention by an objective observer outside the system who changes a parameter. Still, an external observer designs the model of the system, but what is being discussed here is a model design that simulates an internal capacity to change spontaneously without any outside intervention. The paths available for selection are not given beforehand but emerge unpredictably in the micro interactions prevailing at a particular time.

What the designer is constructing is a model with the characteristics of difference and showing that this can cause emergent change in the absence of any external interference or control. The purpose is to demonstrate the possibility of such a process in nature, where there is no external observer in control. For its part, the theory of complex adaptive systems assumes a system with large numbers of agents, each of which behaves according to its own principles of local interaction. No individual agent determines the patterns of behaviour that the system as a whole displays, or how those patterns evolve, and neither does anything outside of the system. Here self-organization means agents interacting locally according to their own principles, or intentions, in the absence of an overall blueprint for the system. Within this strand of complexity theory some views differ very little from neo-Darwininan or adaptionist views on causality. For instance, Gell-Mann (1994) argues that novelty arises in a system when it passes through bifurcations at which the particular path it follows depends entirely upon chance and its subsequent survival depends upon competitive selection.

By contrast, Kauffman (1993) and Goodwin (1994) argue that it is interaction between the components of a system that causes the coherent pattern that inevitably, but unpredictably, emerges from that interaction when the system operates at the edge of chaos.[1] The intrinsic properties of connection, interaction and relationship cause emergent coherence in the particular conditions prevailing at the edge of chaos and that emergent coherence is radically unpredictable. Therefore, there are views that are probably reflective of the majority of complexity scientists, which do not form the basis of any significant challenge to currently dominant ways of thinking and talking about innovation. There are, however, views within the complexity sciences, probably reflective of a minority that do challenge the dominant discourse in important ways and so sustain the claim that the complexity sciences may offer a new way of thinking about innovation in organizations.

Prigrogine (1997), Kauffman (1993) and Goodwin (1994) exemplify scientists who do seem to move from formative and adaptionist causality. They point to a different type of causality, namely transformative causality (Mead, 1934; Stacey *et al.*, 2000) that challenges the notions of causality underlying the dominant discourse on innovation. In transformative causality, the major source of variety lies in the interaction between entities (not in chance or in an external observer's choices and designs). It is the number and strength of connections between entities in a network that forms the dynamic of the network, including the dynamic at the edge of chaos, where endless variety is an intrinsic possibility of the interaction itself.

Furthermore, the dynamic of the whole network is not only solely determined by its own internal connections but also by its connections with other networks. Networks of networks are in perpetual construction moving toward an unpredictable future. The dynamics of individual networks form and are formed by each other simultaneously and it produces repetitive patterns always with the potential for transformation.

9.4. Complexity and innovation management

The question now is just how those who write about complexity in human organizations are taking up the insights of the complexity sciences. Many of them select the demonstrated possibility that coherent behavioural patterns of great complexity can emerge when large numbers of agents interact with each other in a self-organizing way according to simple relational rules. The next implicit move is to assume that the managers can choose the simple rules that will yield a desired pattern of outcomes (Connor, 1998; Beinhocker, 1999; Sanders, 1998; Brown & Eisenhardt, 1998). This immediately places them in the framework of both formative and rationalist causality. The result is a causal framework that is exactly the same as that to be found in the dominant innovation management discourse. It is hardly surprising, then, that the conclusions drawn about what complexity means for innovation management have to do with being in control. In this discourse, self-organization becomes another term for empowerment or delegation. This immediate drive to reduce complexity to simplicity leads to no new insights into how organizations function. Simply reproducing the dominant discourse does not help us in talking about how people are really getting things done. When one succumbs to the powerful drive to reduce complexity to simplicity, one loses sight of what is so striking about the possibility of selforganizing interaction producing emergent coherence.

There is a second aspect to this powerful desire to reduce complexity to simplicity. Currently, ways of talking and thinking about innovation, based on the engineer's notion of control, make the implicit assumption that successful change occurs when people are persuaded to hold the same beliefs. This bypasses the essential role, with the emergence of novelty, of diversity and the conflicting constraints that relationships impose. It sidelines the fundamental transformative cause of power relations and politics in relation to human action (Pascale, 1990). The drive to simplicity eludes the fundamentally paradoxical nature of the transformative processes producing novelty. Novelty means a pattern that has never existed before, not some hidden form that already exists but has not yet been revealed. Diversity and conflicting constraints, that is, power relations, are all essential to the emergence of true novelty. This is one of the central insights coming from the complexity sciences that are simply missed when one thinks in terms of hidden order and deep structures. Creativity is intimately intertwined with destruction (Schumpeter, 1943) and this insight is concealed when harmony and sharing are placed at the centre. Those who give a central role to conflict are rare and the call is usually for strongly shared cultures and harmonious teamwork. Managers seek to remove the conflicts that arise when people differ, seeing such conflict as disruptions to orderly processes of change. It is all part of a framework of thinking, drawn from mechanical logic and systems thinking which equate equilibrium and harmony with success.

As we have seen above, the works of Prigogine (1997), Kauffman (1993) and Goodwin (1994), in focusing on a notion of transformative causality incorporating difference, challenge this perspective, suggesting that the very difference managers seek to remove is the source of spontaneous potentially creative change. Living beings in organizations need to evolve in novel ways in order to survive and if these strands of complexity sciences reveal anything about life in organizations it will mean that many of the current ways of making sense of life in organizations are completely antithetical to this need. Managers may be struggling to change their organizations in ways that ensure that they stay the same. Therefore, complexity theories within the framework of transformative causality can, as we have learned, serve as the basis to shift from system-environment thinking to a new paradigm of identity difference. In this new paradigm, an innovation develops because of the intrinsic need human beings have, individually and collectively, to express their identities and thereby their differences. Identity and difference emerge, becoming what they are through the transformative cause of self-organization, that is, relationship. Innovation emerges from the relationships of its members rather than being determined by the choices of individuals.

9.5. Institutions

Organizations are made up of two categories of institutions. The first comprises the organizational routines that determine the coordination patterns in the organization and has an ontological and epistemological character. The second includes the organizational values that give purpose and motivate individuals to engage in collective actions and has a more teleological and ethical character.

9.5.1. Routines

Routines can be defined as processes of communicative interaction in which they are continually reproduced, always with the potential for transformation. This potential lies in the possibility that small differences and variations in the reproduction of habits, will be amplified into new actions or routines. This continual interaction between individuals who are all choosing and acting in relation to each other as they go about their daily work together, both stabilizes around coherent, repetitive routines, and at the same time these routines are potentially transformed by those same interactions (Mead, 1934; Shotter, 1993). Mainstream thinking tends to identify routines with these repetitive patterns of interaction and power and then ignore the complex relational process in which such order has emerged and in which it is potentially transformed. These routines tend to be formalized, using the legitimate language of the organization. Within organizations themselves, people tend to institutionalize already emerged routines, regarding them as always having been there. This process of institutionalization reduces perceived uncertainty and so lowers anxiety (Voyer *et al.*, 1997). It follows that people in organizations become used to the stability and security of habitual routines and will feel threatened when new routines are introduced.

9.5.2. Values

Mead (1914, 1923) differentiated cult and functional values. He argued that individualizing a collective or group and treating it as if it had overriding motives or values, amounted to a process in which the collective or group constitutes a cult. The actions of members of such cults are driven by the cult's values. A cult provides a feeling of enlarged personality in which individuals participate and from which they derive their values as persons. Cult values are an idealization of the collective, which functions to divert people's attention from the ethics of their daily actions.

Idealized cult values emerge in the historical evolution of any organization and they become functional values in the everyday interactions between members of the organization.[2] As soon as cult values become functional values in real daily interaction, conflict arises and it is this conflict that must be negotiated by people in their practical interaction with each other. This means that cult values and functional values are not in any sense mutually exclusive. On the contrary, they are both paradoxically and simultaneously a part of the evolutionary process. In modern corporations, cults are maintained by the use of visions and value statements. Leaders are supposed to set out a vision, that is, an idealized future for the organization, and then empower people, that is, drive leadership down through the hierarchy. Participation becomes participation in an idealized systemic whole. The notion of participation as ordinary interaction between people and the notion of ethical and moral behaviour in our accounting to each other tends to be lost. However, as Griffin (2002) points out, the cultural identity of an organization with its values is formed by the participants in their interaction while at the same time it forms them. Therefore, its values are also continually being transformed by participants in their practice, as they practice, in the course of their ordinary, everyday interactions in which they account to each other for their actions.

9.6. Innovation as institutional change

In the context of organizational life, people are not primarily and intentionally seeking originality. Innovation does not emerge for its own sake. Even when powerful people perceive a need to think and talk in new ways for their organizations to survive, there will always be defensive responses to deal with the anxiety that uncertainty arouses (Menzies-Lyth, 1988). This tendency is understandable and inevitable, not only as a defence against anxiety but also as an attempt to sustain existing power relations. If people naturally tend to stabilize power relations, routines and values, and if they naturally tend to resist the introduction of new patterns of interaction, and if the innovation process is not the operation of formal mechanisms of control, then, how and why do they produce novelty?

As part of their tasks in organizations, people are expected to perform some clearly defined sequence of actions during which their behaviours are bound by rules, cultures or shared expectations. This is necessary for the efficient performance of daily tasks. This is the behaviour that is validated by the legitimate patterns of interactions in companies. However, while people are performing these actions, they also engage in redundantly diverse behaviour in attempts to accommodate the ambiguity and uncertainty that relates directly to the job in hand. In addition, people engage in talk with their colleagues, friends, customers and other people, about issues that do not relate to the organization or its goals and procedures (Lazega & Pattison, 1999), tell jokes about organizational leaders, gossip, disseminate rumours, engage in boycotts, and perform all types of shadow communication interactions in order to fantasize, play, contain anxiety and release frustration (Stacey, 2001). If people question what they normally do and debate alternatives to their routines and values, these activities might actually be economically productive and lead to better solutions or to the creation of new problems.

Therefore, there are many routines and values going on within the same interactive process as people continue trying to make sense of their ordinary experiences. The official institutions protected by legitimate and formal streams of communicative interaction seek to remove redundancy because it is inefficient in terms of day-to-day activities. And at the same time, shadow streams of communication, both conscious and unconscious, enable the potential for engaging in non-redundant conversations with the possibility for generating misunderstanding, the precondition for the emergence of novelty. However, when routines and values change, patterns of inclusion and exclusion change too and with them power relations are inevitably reconfigured (Lozeau *et al.*, 2002; Huzzard & Östergren, 2002). This inevitably raises anxiety in those participating, and if innovation is to continue there must be something that allows people to overcome this anxiety and avoid the collapse of the creative potential into the regular institutional patterns already in place. This, we suggest is curiosity and, most importantly, trusting those that engage in interaction that might reach a critical level of redundant diversity and its associated potential for misunderstanding (Paterson & Cary, 2002). Finally, if innovation emerges from interactions characterized by critical levels of redundant diversity, how do we account for the existence of intentional activities in R&D departments, for structured projects of new product development, and so on? Fonseca (2001) argues that such activities are the visible phases of innovation that are preceded by a long period of interactions. Structured activities take place only when new words have already become part of the official talk patterns. It is new knowledge already stabilized that enables organized and purposeful action.

Prior to this phase, Fonseca argues that there must have been communicative interaction involving speculation, imagination and fantasy. This process occurs among different people and in different locations. Since no purpose is detectable at the beginning of a particular interactive sequence from which an innovation emerges, and because such purpose itself emerges in communicative interaction, anyone within an organization might engage in this kind of talk. Speculation, imagination, and fantasy might arise anywhere: from conferences people have attended, from magazines, from analogies drawn from other social settings, from social practices. As interactions progress, some of the routines and values might recur. If this happens there then follows a period of intense negotiation of meaning. The outcome of these negotiations is that alternative explanations are increasingly ruled out. As new institutions become agreed upon, eventually some of the original contributors might withdraw as they disagree with what is stabilizing.

The acceptance of the newly stabilized routines and values might spread among groups or communities of practice. They acquire a new instrumental dimension. They are no longer just words, but instead they are part of new institutional patterns. If these new actions are supported by those who have the power to authorize the use of resources, then experiments start. The results of these experiments will form the input to new redundant interactions. As new solutions emerge, there will be further questioning of novel experiments compared to the merits of old solutions that have become routine. And if the outcome of experiments becomes a socially accepted fact, it will be incorporated as legitimate institutions or 'formal' innovations.

9.7. Conclusion

From a complexity perspective, what we perceive as innovations are temporary stabilizations of institutional patterns organizing the social experience that emerge in the process of human interaction in ordinary local situations. The process of communicative interaction, in which habitual patterns (routines and values) are continually reproduced, is at the same time the process in which even small variations in the repro-duction of habits are potentially amplified. In this way of thinking, no institution is fixed but is always potentially changing in its perpetual reproduction. Therefore, in understanding why and how an institution is, or is not, changing, attention is focused on the way people reproduce them (Shaw, 2002). Most of the time, in ordinary interactions we face some ambiguity and we sometimes have to look for the meaning of the actions taken by others. This happens because we engage in interactions using routines and values that are pertinent to our own local interac-tions and life experiences, while others use different routines and val-ues that have been developed in their own local interactions. It is because they use routines and values referring to their own life experi-ence that the potential for misunderstanding occurs.

We suggest that what is being dissolved in interactions is this misunderstanding. We argue that when the potential for misunderstanding in an interaction reaches a critical point, usually because different routines and values are interacting with each other, the potential arises for novelty to emerge. Mead (1934) sees conflict not only as unavoidable, but also as the very essence of change and evolution.

Therefore, innovation is not a function or a rational choice but a potential in all-communicative interaction. We might innovate and through these innovations we might find new balances between our joint actions and some outside conditions. Through new streams of interactions, people might build the perception that change is required. They might try to reduce changes to a minimum in order to protect their identity and their stability, and they might try new things. If these things work, they will incorporate this novel behaviour as part of their own identity, thus reaching a new stabilization, passing through a kind of transition phase to reach a new degree of order that will inevitably once again be undermined by yet further interactions. Then, the actual innovations at any moment in the evolutionary path are but mere conventions resulting from past locally based social interactions carried out for particular practical purposes. Accordingly, the evolution of innovations is the result of an emerging and ongoing flux of co-creation by the network of actors. Formal interventions are just one more voice in this process of co-creation. It might be powerful, but still only one among all. The process is, thus, self-organizing since no one can control the course of interaction patterns, no matter how powerful they are. Although they might be able to terminate them, no one can control or shape the output.

Finally, we conclude that from a complexity perspective, innovation and the consequent institutional change have a pragmatic foundation; and also that the potential for purposeful innovation design is limited.

Notes

1 At the edge of chaos, a network configures itself into closely connected clusters, separated from each other to some extent, making it difficult for perturbations to flow through it. This happens because many agents follow the same rules so that there are many chances of the same responses and patterns of response being reproduced. It is not efficient but it preserves stability in a dynamic of change. At the edge of chaos, there are threads of contact between clusters of agents so that some but not all perturbations will plunge through the network but only a few large ones will. In other works, there will be large numbers of small extinction events but only small numbers of large events. It is this property that imparts control, or stability, to the process of change at the edge of chaos.

2 For example, the cult value of a hospital might be to provide each patient with the best possible care. However, such a cult value has to be repeatedly functionalized in many unique specific situations throughout the day.

Bibliography

Argyrys, C. (1990), *Overcoming Organizational Defences: Facilitating Organizational Learning* (Needham Heights, MA: Allyn & Bacon).
Argyrys, C. & Schön, D. (1978), *Organizational Learning: A Theory of Action Perspective* (Reading, MA: Addison-Wesley).
Bateson, G. (1973), *Steps to an Ecology of Mind* (St Albans: Paladin).
Beinhocker, E.D. (1999), 'Robust Adaptive Strategies', *Sloan Management Review*, spring, pp. 95–106.
Brown, S.L. & Eisenhardt, K. (1998), *Competing on the Edge: Strategy as Structured Chaos* (Boston: Harvard Business School Press).
Burns, T. & Stalker, G.M. (1961), *The Management of Innovation* (London: Tavistock).
Checkland, P.B. (1981), *Systems Thinking, Systems Practice* (Chichester: Wiley).
Chekland P.B. & Schöles, J. (1990), *Soft Systems Methodology in Action* (Chichester: Wiley).
Connor, D.R. (1998), *Leading at the Edge of Chaos: How to Create the Nimble Organization* (New York: Wiley).
Cooper, R.G. & Kleinschmidt, E.J. (1991), 'New Products: what separates winners from losers?' (in Henry & Walker).
Crawford, C.M. (1991), *New Products Management* (Boston: Irwin, 3rd edn).
Drucker, P.F. (1985), 'The Discipline of Innovation', *Harvard Business Review*, May–June, pp. 67–72.
Fayol, H. (1916 [1948]), *Industrial and General Administration* (London: Pitman).
Flood, R.L. (1999), 'Liberating Systems Theory: Towards critical systems thinking', *Human Relations*, 36, pp. 37–66.
Fonseca, J. (2001), *Complexity and Innovation in Organizations* (London: Routledge).
Gell-Mann, M. (1994), *The Quark and the Jaguar* (New York: Freeman).
Gleick, J. (1988), *Chaos: The Making of a New Science* (London: Heinemann).
Goodwin, B. (1994), *How the Leopard Changed its Spots* (London: Weidenfeld & Nicolson).
Griffin, D. (2002), *The Emergence of Leadership: Linking Self-organization and Ethics* (London: Routledge).
Henry, J. & Walker, D. (eds) (1991), *Managing Innovation* (London: Sage).
Huzzard, T. & Östergren, K. (2002), 'When Norms Collide: Learning Under Organizational Hypocrisy', *Brithish Journal of Management*, 13(2), pp. 47–59.
Kanter, R.M. (1988), 'When a Thousand Flowers Bloom: Structural, collective and social conditions for innovation in organization', *Research in Organizational Behavior*, 10, pp. 169–211.
Kauffman, S.A. (1993), *Origins of Order: Self-Organization and Selection in Evolution* (Oxford: Oxford University Press).
Lawrence, P.R. & Lorsch, J.W. (1967), *Organization and Environment* (Boston: Harvard University Press).

Lazega, E. & Pattison, P.E. (1999), 'Multiplexity, generalized exchange and cooperation in organizations: a case study', *Social Networks*, 21, pp. 67–90.
Likert, R. (1961), *New Patterns of Management* (New York: McGraw-Hill).
Lozeau, D., Langley, A. & Denis, J.L. (2002), 'The Corruption of Managerial Techniques by Organizations', *Human Relations*, 55(5), pp. 537–64.
Mayo, E. (1949), *The Social Problems of Industrial Civilization* (London: Routledge & Kegan Paul).
Mead, G.H. (1914), 'The Psychological Basis of Internationalism', *Survey*, 23, pp. 604–7.
Mead, G.H. (1923), 'Scientific Method and the Moral Sciences', *International Journal of Ethics*, 33, pp. 229–47.
Mead, G.H. (1934), *Mind, Self and Society* (Chicago: Chicago University Press).
Menzies-Lyth, I. (1988), *Containing Anxiety in Institutions. Essays*, Vol. I (London: Free Association Books).
Miller, E.J & Rice, A.K. (1967), *Systems of Organization: The Control of Task and Sentient Boundaries* (London: Tavistock).
Mintzberg, H. & Quinn, J.B. (eds) (1991), *The Strategy Process: Concepts, Contexts and Cases* (Englewood Cliffs, NJ: Prentice-Hall, 2nd edn).
Pascale, R.T. (1990), *Managing on the Edge: How Succesful Companies Use Conflict to Stay Ahead* (London: Viking Penguin).
Paterson, J.M. & Cary, J. (2002), 'Organizational justice, change anxiety, and acceptance of downsizing: preliminary tests ofan AET-Based Model', *Motivation an Emotion*, 26, pp. 83–103.
Prigogine, I. (1997), *The End of Certainty: Time, Chaos and the New Laws of Nature* (New York: Free Press).
Quinn, J.B. (1991), 'Managing Innovation: Controlled Chaos' (in Mintzberg & Quinn).
Sanders, T.I. (1998), *Strateging Thinking and the New Science: Planning in the Midst of Chaos, Complexity and Change* (New York: Free Press).
Schumpeter, J.A. (1943), *Capitalism, Socialism and Democracy* (London: Allen & Unwin).
Shaw, P. (2002), *Changing Conversations in Organizations: A Compexity Approach to Change* (London: Routledge).
Shermer, M. (2000), *How we Believe: The Search for God in an Age of Science* (New York: W.H. Freeman).
Shotter, J. (1993), *Conversational Realities: Constructing Life Through Language* (London: Sage).
Stacey, R., Griffin, D. & Shaw, P. (2000), *Compelexity and Management: Fad or Radical Challenge to Systems Thinking?* (London: Routledge).
Stacey, R.D. (2001), *Complex Responsive Processes in Organizations: Learning and Knowledge Creation* (London: Routledge).
Stewart, I. (1989), *Does God Play Dice?* (Oxford: Blackwell).
Taylor, F. (1911), *Scientific Management* (New York: Harper).
Voyer, J.J., Gould, J.M. & Ford, D.N. (1997), 'Systemic Creation of Organizational Anxiety: An Empirical Study', *Journal of Applied Behavioral Science*, 33(4), p. 477.
Wheatley, M.J. (1992), *Leadership and the New Science: Learning about Organizations from an Orderly Universe* (San Francisco: Berrett-Koehler).
Wolfe, R.A. (1994), 'Organizational Innovation: Reveiw, Critique and Suggested Research Directions', *Journal of Management Studies*, 31(3), pp. 405–31.

10

Towards a Better Measurement of the Soft Side of Innovation. *First Results of an Experiment Aimed at Measuring Non-technological Innovation Using an Adapted Innovation Survey in the Netherlands*

Pim den Hertog, Tom Poot and Gerhard Meinen

10.1. Introduction

10.1.1. Missing out on non-technological innovation is a missed opportunity

In contrast to the role of human and physical capital inputs and 'hard' technological innovation, such as research and development expenditure, there is as of yet no clear, widely accepted conceptual framework through which non-technological innovations can be comprehensively analyzed, let alone to determine its impact on output, employment and productivity growth (van Ark *et al.*, 2003). As often observed a 'technological view' on innovation is predominant (Gallouj, 2002). This is amazing as non-technological innovation (or for that matter, service and organizational innovation or what was coined the 'soft side' of innovation – see den Hertog *et al.*, 1997) can be said to be part of (or at least not explicitly excluded) in the widely used Schumpeterian definition of innovation: 'New combinations of inputs and the creation of new ideas leading to innovations in products (and services) and processes' (Schumpeter, 1934; see Drejer, 2004, for a Schumpeterian perspective on service-specific innovation concepts). It is also a missed opportunity as non-technological innovation offers a huge potential for raising competitiveness and economic growth.

Although it is increasingly acknowledged that the soft side of innovation does matter, this recognition is relatively new and not as widespread as some would like it to be. Lundvall (2001), for example, observed that '... the Green Paper tends to underestimate the soft aspects of innovation, such as the role of human resources, competent users, demand factors, network building and organizational change' (ibid. p. 287). In discussions on the knowledge economy from the mid-1990s onwards, the focus has gradually broadened from innovation in manufacturing and 'hard' technical knowledge and research and development (R&D), to innovation in services and other types of knowledge. This opens an opportunity to investigate technological and non-technological innovation in both manufacturing and the service sector in a similar fashion, although non-technological innovation has proved harder to define and measure.[1] The issue of whether investments in the associated softer types of knowledge show similar externalities as in technical R&D is not decided.[2] In this chapter we address the question if it is possible to develop new indicators to measure the soft side of innovation in manufacturing and in the service sector.

10.1.2. Organization of this chapter

The outline of this chapter is as follows. First, we briefly review – differentiating between non-technological aspects of innovation and non-technological innovation – some of the current insights on the soft side of innovation. On this basis, we flag some of the insights that we think are needed (section 10.2). The insights are used as an input to formulate new questions in a first attempt in the Netherlands to measure the soft side of innovation in the manufacturing sector and in the service sector. In section 10.3 we briefly present the first results of an experimental set of four new questions introduced in the Dutch 2002 innovation survey (the so-called CIS3½) that can be perceived as an attempt to better measure the soft side of innovation. We do so by presenting an analysis on the new questions. This and future analyses will for the first time provide us with more detailed data on non-technological innovation for the Netherlands covering most firms (manufacturing and services) and size classes (10 employees or more) on a considerable scale. Finally, we reflect on what we have learned thus far from this experiment, make a few suggestions as to how we can learn more from this experiment and make some wider remarks on the measurement of the soft side of innovation (section 10.4).

10.2. Current and needed insights on the soft side of innovation[3]

10.2.1. An integrative approach on innovation: the 'soft-side' of innovation

A focus on an integrative approach on innovation in the manufacturing sector and the service sector needs a search for common ground, that is the 'soft-side' of innovation but still we are lacking a clear concept of innovation that goes beyond the traditional notion of technological innovation. The discussion on the soft side seems to be somewhat blurred, given that some see soft innovation as non-technological innovation (that is, a discrete innovation still), such as organizational, service, design or transactional innovations, whereas to others the soft side of innovation merely concerns the non-technological aspects in the process of innovation (that is, the process of innovation and the characteristics of the innovative firm).

10.2.2. Current insights on non-technological aspects (NTA) of innovation

Innovative success requires innovative organizations and various types of non-technological competencies. From the early 1960s, a whole list of literature has emerged that delves into the various components that shape innovative organizations and how the innovation process can be managed. Tidd *et al.* (1997, pp. 305–37) summarized this extensive innovation management literature, differentiating between such components as varied as shared vision and leadership, appropriate organization structure, the role of key individuals, effective team working, commitment to education and training, high and organization-wide participation in innovation, external focus, extensive communication, and creative climate which ultimately should help in establishing learning organizations. They emphasize that there is no fixed recipe to build innovative organizations:

> ... no single element in isolation is likely to be effective, and no single tool or technique, however fashionable, will create and sustain an innovative environment. Moreover, all tools and techniques must be adapted to the organizational, market and technological context (ibid., p. 332).[4]

Cobbenhagen *et al.* (2001) differentiate between various aspects that can be influenced by the individual company, such as vision and strategy, organization and management/leadership, culture and learning climate, idea and creativity, knowledge and information, labour and capital, and marketing and design. In general, it seems to be agreed that there still is a need to better understand these softer aspects of innovation and to improve their measurement.

10.2.3. Current insights on non-technological innovations (NTI)

Whereas, for example, in the CIS2 survey only technological product and process innovation are included, an increasing number of scholars differentiate between more types of innovation in which the technological component is absent or features less prominently. Gallouj and Weinstein (1997) differentiate between six types of innovation, that is, radical, improvement, incremental, ad hoc, recombinative, and formalization innovation. Jacobs and Waalkens (2001) mention in addition to product and process innovation, for example, transaction innovation, organizational innovation and innovation in business concepts. Van der Aa (2000), when looking at services, mentions four types of innovation, namely chain formation, new combinations, co-production by clients, and (information) technological innovation. Den Hertog (2000), also primarily looking at services innovation, differentiates between technological innovation, conceptual innovation, client-interface innovation and service-delivery innovation. Most of the research referred to here has developed under the labels of services innovation or organizational innovation.

A very important contribution to the understanding of non-technological innovations is the so-called DISKO project.[5] In fact, it is a landmark study in the innovation systems approach that marks the shift to include the soft side of innovation more explicitly in innovation study, for example organizational innovation. It is also an attempt to really gather micro-level data on organizational innovation (see Gjerding, 1996). One of the results is that companies confronted with more intense competition show a higher propensity to change and show what was phrased as organizational and functional flexibility (see, e.g., Lundvall & Kristensen, 1997). Coriat (2001) has looked into several surveys in EU countries that have dealt with organizational innovation and observes that:

> whatever the diversity of approaches and measurements, it is striking to notice that a common lesson can be drawn from the surveys: the effects of the introduction of organizational innovation are always significant, whether they be cost or quality effects, and the correlations between innovations and performances are always obvious.

The Third Community Innovation Survey (CIS3) collects information about new or significantly improved products or processes and related activities in manufacturing and service industries during 1998–2000. Contrary to CIS2, CIS3 not only deals with new and significantly improved products (goods and services) and processes, but also refers to other creative improvements that might have been undertaken by enterprises. However, this concerns only one question on 'Other important strategic and organizational changes in your enterprise'.[6] To get additional insights, Statistics Netherlands added additional questions in their innovation survey for 2000–02.

10.3. The Netherlands CIS3½ survey and its experimental questions on non-technological innovations

10.3.1. Towards an integrative-oriented approach

Non-technological innovation is as important to service as to non-service companies.[7] It is extremely important to emphasize that non-technological innovations are developed and implemented in all sectors and are not limited to manufacturing or service industries. New business concepts, marketing and distribution systems, user–producer interfaces and the like are equally important to both manufacturing and service industries. In fact service functions, found in all companies, are innovated. Moreover:

> ... many of the so called peculiarities of service innovation, involvement of multiple actors in the process of innovation, and the importance of codification of knowledge for carrying out innovation, do also apply to manufacturing (Drejer, 2004, p. 560).

Therefore an integrative approach, a similar analytical approach to innovation in manufacturing and services (see Coombs & Miles, 2000; Gallouj, 2002, p. 1), which seems to be a natural way to proceed but there are some caveats as well.

The attempts to better understand the soft side of innovation has resulted in studies in which the notion of innovation has been stretched too far, beyond the context of the notion. The act of innovation is sometimes hard to differentiate from simple organizational change or simply good entrepreneurship. In similar ways, activities that are relevant for innovation such as learning or competence building – in fact the non-technological aspects of innovation – have maybe too much been associated with non-technological innovation. Drejer (2004) in this context correctly observed that the 'problem of mingling activities that might lead to innovation with actual innovation'. Eventually the consequence of this might be 'that the innovation concept becomes detached from the original meaning as an economically successful introduction of something new, thereby being a contrast to acting within the boundaries of routine systems'. This means that in defining non-technological innovations there has to be a link between the type of innovations and the economic performance of firms.

What is missing, or what do we want to achieve?

One of the problems with which we have to deal is that the definition of innovation in the *Oslo Manual* is still technology orientated. The second edition of the *Oslo Manual* only takes into account technological process and production innovation (OECD, 1997). Organizational innovations are excluded until now, but hopefully will be in the third edition of the *Oslo Manual* (due end 2005). From the DISKO survey, it is apparent that organizational innovations are a very important part of non-technological innovations. To have a clear understanding of the innovation process, it is important to include organizational innovations in the extended survey.

From the innovation literature, it is clear that not always the firm that is implementing a technological innovation is the originator of that innovation as well (von Hippel, 1988). Many technological innovations originate from interactions between customers and or suppliers. It is interesting to investigate whether there is analogy with nontechnological innovations and the question arises if customers and or suppliers also have a similar role in achieving non-technological innovations. Like the questions about technological product and process innovations, we ask the respondents about the origin of the non-technological innovations. Another issue of importance is what the reasons or motives are to implement non-technological innovations.

10.3.2. The questions

Statistics Netherlands has embarked on the evolutionary path of adapting the innovation survey to cater better for organizational innovation. In its 2002 Innovation Survey (in CIS terms this would be equivalent to CIS3.5, that is, figures for the period 2000–02), four questions that deal explicitly with non-technological innovation were added to the 'standard' CIS set of questions and addressed to the whole sample (10,000 firms) covering both the manufacturing and service sector. These four questions deal with:

- The nature of non-technical innovation differentiating between (Q10):
  - marketing;
  - non-technical adjustments to products/services;
  - organization with respect to customers and/or suppliers;
  - internal organization.
- The way in which these non-technological innovations were brought about (developed mainly by the firm itself, in partnership with clients/suppliers or mainly developed by others) (Q11).
- The reasons for bringing about non-technological innovation (quality improvement, lower costs, future or recent market developments, introduction of new technology) (Q12).
- The dominance of either technological and non-technological innovation in the near future (Q13).

In the annex there is a (provisional) description in English of the questions involved. Question 11 is conditional on question 10: only firms ticking 'yes' on one of the answers of question 10 are asked to respond to question 11. Firms ticking 'no' on all four categories mentioned in question 10 have to skip question 11. These four questions provide an excellent opportunity to explore ways to better measure and understand organizational innovation in both the manufacturing and the service industries.

Disclaimer

It is up to now the exception rather than the rule that a national statistical institute such as CBS includes a new set of questions on non-technological innovation and extends the survey to the whole population of manufacturing firms and service firms (with 10 or more employees). We see this experiment mainly as an investment in learning from the view of CBS on how to measure non-technological innovation. It was an opportunity that occurred suddenly while constructing the set of questions for the Netherlands CIS3½ survey. We had limited time to construct the questions, which arose in a sort of negotiation process (about two weeks) and even less time to analyze the first results. Therefore the results should be treated carefully. We plan to analyze the results more in detail – using some more advanced statistical methods and relating them to the other questions.

10.3.3. Results

Response

The aim of the non-response analysis is to discover if respondents are able to deal with questions about non-technological innovation within the usual framework of a community innovation survey. Although there is empirical evidence of the relevance of non-technological innovation in general, this questionnaire provides the opportunity to look more in detail at various aspects of non-technological innovations.

The overall item non-response on the questionnaire is about 0.6 per cent of the total questionnaires returned. Non-response has been calculated as non-valid response on question 2 of the questionnaire that deals with technological developments in general, that is, to establish whether a firm is innovative or not. If a firm does not tick any question – that is, all values are missing – this is counted as part of the overall non-response (the other questions are missing as well).

The item non-response on the questions regarding non-technological innovations is higher. Question number 10 has a non-response rate of 3.8 per cent, question 12 has a rate of 5.1 per cent and question 13 a rate of 8.8 per cent of all questionnaires received. The conditional non-response rate of question 11 is the same as question 10, namely 3.4 per cent.

In general, the item non-response rate is slightly above the overall non-response rate with an increasing trend towards the end of the questionnaire. However, the item non-response of question 13 dealing with the dominance of technological versus non-technological innovation is much higher, even though there is a 'general purpose' tick box indicating 'hard to indicate'. An explanation could be the outline of the question. Question 13 distinguishes from previous questions that it has been formulated as a five-point Likert-scale question. All previous questions are simple 'yes' or 'no' tick boxes or the respondent has to fill in a number. In the next step, we discuss the relevance of the individual questions about non-technological aspects of innovation.

Relevance of question 10: nature of non-technological innovation

After a general introduction to the concept of non-technological innovation, question 10 first deals with four types of non-technological innovations that were or were not developed by the responding firm over the period 2000–02.[8] We define the relevance of question number 10 as the percentage of respondents ticking at least one sub-aspect 'yes'. The relevance of question 10 and the four sub-aspects is shown in Table 10.1.

Table 10.1. The relevance of question 10: the percentage of respondents ticking at least one sub-aspect 'yes', distinguished to sector and size

Relevance	*% of firms ticking 'yes' on at least one item*			
		Sector		
	All firms	*Manuf.*	*Services*	*Other*
Question 10 in general (all sub-questions)	31.3	38.5	30.0	22.9
Improvements regarding:				
Marketing	16.8	18.6	17.4	11.2
Non-technological aspects of products/services	13.6	18.9	12.7	7.0
Organization with respect to customers and/or suppliers	14.3	16.5	14.1	10.4
Internal organization	22.2	27.2	21.2	16.5
		Size		
	All firms	*10–50*	*50–200*	*200 or more*
Question 10 in general (all sub-questions)	31.3	18.2	32.2	50.5
Improvements regarding:				
Marketing	16.8	9.5	17.2	28.6
Non-technological aspects	13.6	8.4	13.4	24.7
Organization with respect to customers and/or suppliers	14.3	8.0	14.4	25.5
Internal organization	22.2	12.1	22.6	39.0

Source: CIS3½ (2002), Statistics Netherlands.

Table 10.1 reports that, in general, 31.3 per cent of all firms are involved in one or more aspects of non-technological improvements. Improvements of the internal organization are mentioned the most (22.2 per cent) and non-technological improvements of products and/or service the least (13.6 per cent). It is striking that firms in the service sector reported fewer instances of improvements compared to manufacturing firms. Improvements of non-technological aspects of products/ services are of less importance to the service sector compared to the 18.9 per cent of manufacturing firms. Also, manufacturing firms reported more organizational improvements – 16.5 per cent against 14.1 per cent in the service sector. The same applies to improvements of the internal organization, 27.2 per cent in the manufacturing sector against

21.2 per cent in the service sector. This finding is consistent with Gjerding (1996), who suggests that a different perspective on organizational change might be an explanation. The sector 'others' consists of the remaining sectors of agriculture, mining, gas, water and electricity supply and construction, and are of less importance.

Table 10.1 shows a strong size effect. On average, 31.3 per cent of all firms report some kind of improvement, but only 18.2 per cent of smaller firms have dealt with improvements, compared to 50.5 per cent of larger firms with 200 or more employees.

Relevance of question 11: motives for realizing non-technological innovation

Question 11 in a way is a rather classical innovation survey question that asks non-technological innovative firms to rate the importance of a selection of five – or basically even four – motives. These motives differentiate between the importances of quality, cost, the degree to which the market is leading in becoming non-technologically innovative and the degree to which non-technological innovation is triggered by technological innovation. Although the latter is interesting of course, it can also quite easily be seen as a technologist view on innovation as technology is still seen as triggering the act of innovation and leaving not much room for autonomous non-technological innovation. Still, we think the results are worth having a look at. In later analyses we plan to compare the scores on this question with motives mentioned for realizing technological innovations.

Table 10.2 shows that two motives stand out – quality improvements, 53.7 per cent of all firms with non-technological improvements report this as a very important motive, followed by cost reduction (52.8 per cent). The former motive is more important to the service sector and the latter to manufacturing firms. Interestingly, to anticipate future changes or to react to current changes is of modest importance. New technology as a reason to improve on non-technological aspects of innovation is considered of minor importance. There are no striking differences between the sectors. The same applies to size.

Relevance of question 12: the prevalence of knowledge management

Question 12 has a somewhat different character as it not directly deals with non-technological innovation, but also starts from the knowledge perspective that is relevant to both technological and non-technological innovation. In the literature, knowledge management is considered as an important aspect or issue dealt with by the innovative firm (see, e.g, Tidd *et al.*, 1997).

Table 10.2. Motives for non-technological improvements rated to the level of importance, distinguished to sector and size, as a percentage of firms reporting non-technological improvements (question 10)

Motives non-technological innovations (Q11)	All firms	Sector		
		Manuf.	Services	Other
Quality improvement				
Unimportant, n/a	8.6	10.6	6.8	11.4
Important	37.7	39.5	34.9	47.8
Very important	53.7	49.9	58.3	40.7
Cost reduction				
Unimportant, n/a	9.6	8.3	10.5	9.0
Important	37.5	33.1	39.9	39.6
Very important	52.8	58.6	49.6	51.4
Anticipate future changes				
Unimportant, n/a	14.9	15.1	14.4	17.1
Important	42.9	45.2	42.6	37.3
Very important	42.2	39.7	43.0	45.7
React to current changes of supply and demand				
Unimportant, n/a	18.9	20.5	17.7	19.6
Important	47.2	46.0	48.4	44.7
Very important	34.0	33.5	33.9	35.7
New technology as reason for non-technological improvements				
Unimportant, n/a	62.6	58.3	64.4	66.8
Important	29.0	31.9	27.4	28.3
Very important	8.4	9.9	8.2	5.0

	All firms	Size		
		10–50	50–200	200 or more
Quality improvement				
Unimportant, n/a	8.6	9.1	8.3	9.2
Important	37.7	34.3	38.2	38.4
Very important	53.7	56.6	53.5	52.5
Cost reduction				
Unimportant, n/a	9.6	8.3	10.5	9.0
Important	37.5	33.1	39.9	39.6
Very important	52.8	58.6	49.6	51.4
Anticipate future changes				
Unimportant, n/a	14.9	15.1	14.4	17.1
Important	42.9	45.2	42.6	37.3
Very important	42.2	39.7	43.0	45.7

Continued

Table 10.2.   Continued

Motives non-technological innovations (Q11)	All firms	Size		
		10–50	50–200	200 or more
React to current changes of supply and demand				
Unimportant, n/a	18.9	20.5	17.7	19.6
Importantly	47.2	46.0	48.4	44.7
Very important	34.0	33.5	33.9	35.7
New technology as reason for non-technological improvements				
Unimportant, n/a	62.6	58.3	64.4	66.8
Importantly	29.0	31.9	27.4	28.3
Very important	8.4	9.9	8.2	5.0

Source: CIS3½ (2002), Statistics Netherlands.

Contrary to expectations, Table 10.3 reveals a very low level of commitment towards knowledge management. The majority of firms have no intention to implement knowledge management on the strategic level. The scores on other aspects of knowledge management reflect the same lack of commitment. Differences across sectors are small. However the importance of knowledge management is increasing with firm size.

An explanation could be that, especially in small firms, knowledge management is a bit of overkill. It is safe to assume that inter-personnel contact is decreasing with size, or to put it differently, only larger firms need some kind of knowledge management to diffuse the knowledge throughout the whole company. Still, the majority of large firms have no intention or just plan to implement knowledge management. This is a negative interpretation of the results. A positive interpretation would be that knowledge management, although it has received a great deal of attention in the (management) literature, in practice it is still in its infancy. For future development we could expect a rising awareness of the importance of knowledge management and hence rising scores on this type of questions.

Relevance of question 13: technological versus non-technological innovation

The final question deals with the dominance of technological aspects of innovation against non-technological aspects. This type of question turns out to be very demanding. Table 10.4 shows that almost one half

Table 10.3. Scores on question 12: commitment to knowledge management as a percentage of all firms

Knowledge management (Q12)	All firms	Sector		
		Manuf.	services	other
Strategy applying knowledge management				
No, no intention	58.6	56.8	58.0	64.4
No, but planned for 2003–04	19.4	22.7	18.3	17.5
Yes	22.0	20.4	23.6	18.0
Responsibility assigned to a specific person or department				
No, no intention	57.9	55.9	57.7	63.1
No, but planned for 2003–04	11.6	13.0	11.1	10.9
Yes	30.5	31.1	31.2	26.0
Indicators to measure the success of knowledge management				
No, no intension	70.7	69.8	70.2	74.4
No, but planned for 2003–04	21.3	23.0	21.0	18.9
Yes	8.1	7.2	8.9	6.6

	All firms	Size		
		10–50	50–200	200 or more
Strategy applying knowledge management				
No, no intention	58.6	74.5	57.3	36.2
No, but planned for 2003–04	19.4	12.3	20.5	26.8
Yes	22.0	13.2	22.2	36.9
Responsibility assigned to a specific person or department				
No, no intention	57.9	71.6	56.7	39.8
No, but planned for 2003–04	11.6	6.4	12.4	16.6
Yes	30.5	22.0	30.9	43.6
Indicators to measure the success of knowledge management				
No, no intention	70.7	83.1	69.3	56.1
No, but planned for 2003–04	21.3	11.9	22.3	32.2
Yes	8.1	5.0	8.4	11.8

Source: CIS3½ (2002), Statistics Netherlands.

of all respondents have difficulty to tell whether technological or non-technological innovation dominates. One explanation could be that this question is about future development. Another explanation could be the lack of a proper introduction of the question or the fact that the question is not explained well enough. Due to the constraints on the

Table 10.4. The relevance of questions regarding non-technological innovations, distinguished to sector and size

	% of firms ticking 'yes' on at least one item			
			Sector	
	All firms	*Manuf.*	*Services*	*Other*
Difficult to tell	48.4	38.9	50.5	58.8
Score on Likert scale	51.6	61.1	49.5	41.2
			Size	
	All firms	*10–50*	*50–200*	*200 or more*
Difficult to tell	48.4	63.1	46.9	30.6
Score on Likert scale	51.6	36.9	53.1	69.4

lengths of the questionnaire there was little room available for a more
extensive explanation (examples). Last, the question implicitly assumes
that dominance has its impact on the firm level. From the literature we
know that many issues of the innovation process are more relevant and
possibly better measured at the project level. It might be the case that
dominance is very much related to project-specific properties.

Slightly more than one half of the responding firms filled out the
five-point Likert scale. Table 10.4 shows that in manufacturing
non-technological innovations seem to prevail, while in the service
sector technological and non-technological innovations are of equal
importance. Looking at the firm size we see that the larger the firm the
more important non-technological innovations are. This comes as no
surprise; larger firms probably will benefit more from, for instance, organizational innovations, than will smaller firms.

The distribution of the scores on the Likert scale is also a point of interest. Figure 10.1 shows the average score on the five-point Likert scale of
all firms. To economize on space we only present a histogram of the score
of all firms. The detailed figures do not reveal a sector or size effect. It is
not surprising that the majority of the respondents show equal results for
the dominance of technological and non-technological. Still, 21 per cent
of the respondents indicate that non-technological aspects of innovation
dominate the innovation process by a long Margin.

A final remark about the scores on the questions reviewed; until now
we took into consideration all firms, distinguished by sector and size.
The size effect seems to be of more importance than a sector effect that

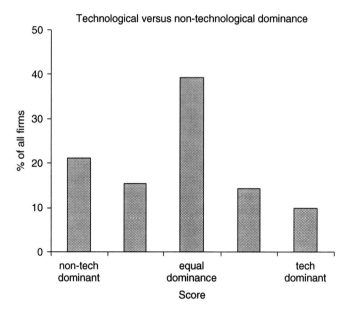

Figure 10.1.   Scores on the five-point Likert scale of all firms
Source: CIS3½ (2002), Statistics Netherlands.

is a very broad distinction between manufacturing firms and service firms. Also, there are no differences in relevance between innovating and non-innovating firms (not presented here). Finally, the scores on the sub-question do not reveal many differences between innovating and non-innovating firms (results not shown here).

10.4. What have we learned thus far and some options for future analysis?

10.4.1. What have we learned from this experiment so far?

It is important to realize that the questionnaire is a first attempt by Statistics Netherlands to introduce more detailed questions on non-technological innovations within the framework of an innovation survey. The main purpose of this questionnaire was to gain information about the relevance of non-technological innovations in general and on some detailed aspects of non-technological innovation. A second goal was to experiment with different types of questions and to test whether manufacturing firms and the service sector were both able to respond to these questions.

As stated in the introduction of this chapter, it is very compelling to have a very broad definition of non-technological innovations at the expense of clarity and blurring the contribution of non-technological innovations to the prosperity of the firm. Are we looking at real innovative efforts or plain and ordinary adjustments an entrepreneur has to make every day in order to stay competitive? At the present level of analysis we cannot tell.

Did we succeed? Yes, and no. The scores reveal that both manufacturing and the service sector are dealing with non-technological innovation, although not in equal ways. The response to question 13 seems to indicate that non-technological innovations are perceived differently within the sectors, considering the relatively high scores on non-technological in manufacturing. Probably the same applies to other aspects of innovation. Does that imply that we need a different approach and that we have to distinguish between manufacturing and services, that is, the demarcation approach? It is too early to come up with a definitive answer. Our impression is that with more emphasis on specific examples, a meaningful comparison is indeed possible. Interesting results are the scores on knowledge management. Contrary to expectations, knowledge management appears to be of less importance. Future measurements will shed some light on the question, are we on the brink of the emergence of knowledge management or is it a hype: much ado about nothing that is a common practice? The issue of technological versus non-technological dominance, although of great importance, appears to be too complicated an issue to ask in a relatively simple way.

Another set of lessons relate to the actual wording and position of questions on non-technological innovation. The definition of non-technological innovation is a residual and maybe too much phrased in examples where a proper explanation of what is an innovation, what is regular organizational maintenance or even simply good entrepreneurship without innovation is much needed. Yet there is no certainty (if ever) of how responding firm's interpreted non-technological innovation. Furthermore, putting a few questions on non-technological innovation as a sort of appendix at the end of a survey might result in some distortions because only the committed respondents will take the time to understand the differences between technological and non-technological innovation (the rising trend of non-response towards the end of the questionnaire). Question 12 now seems to be the odd one out as it should not be exclusively part of the questions dealing with non-technological innovation. Question 13 probably is biased towards the viewpoint of an innovation researcher and probably less relevant from a firm's perspective and is in need of reformulation.

10.4.2. Some options for further analysis

We very much agree with Drejer (2004), who remarks that 'the acknowledgement of services as important – and in some cases peculiar – economic activities is thus not entirely new. But empirical studies of the development of services through innovation surveys are a relatively new phenomenon'. We see this experiment as a step into this direction. We are very much aware that a lot of work needs to be done before we can 'catch' non-technological innovation in standardized innovation surveys that allow for international comparisons and can be used to inform innovation policy making. In this context, this experiment is only one small building block. More experiments and analytical work on this and other experiments are needed.[9] However, notwithstanding the limitations of this experiment, we see some possibilities for further learning from this experiment, such as:

- Perform more advanced statistical (regressions) and econometric analyses (estimate models) using the four questions introduced in this chapter.
- More systematically relate questions 10–13 to questions dealing with technological innovation. Are motives for firms investing in both technological and non-technological innovation for example comparable or not?
- Perform more detailed sectoral analyses to determine if any sectoral patterns regarding non-technological innovations can be identified and the degree to which different categories of (groups of) industries emerge sharing certain characteristics.
- More systematically differentiate between firms that are neither technological nor non-technological innovative: (1) only technological innovators; (2) only non-technological innovators; (3) and firms that are involved in both technological and non-technological innovation.

10.4.3. Some wider remarks on measuring the soft side of innovation

On a somewhat less practical level of working we stumble into a lot of issues related to measuring non-technological innovation with which the innovation studies community will have to deal in the years to come. Examples of these types of issues are:

- The fact that a tidying up of overlapping concepts and typologies of service, organizational and non-technological innovation is much needed.
- As part of the much-needed act of tidying up as mentioned above, it should be strived after not to name every single act of regular organizational improvement, fine entrepreneurship or every single act that is not an act of innovation. Put differently, we need a definition of innovation that – as Drejer (2004) in our view correctly observes – does justice to the criterion that an innovation should add economic value in the end and not be identical to change *per se*. Starting with systematically differentiating between non-technological aspects of innovation (and hence of innovative firms) and discrete non-technological innovations would be an option here.
- As mentioned by Tether and Miles (2001), attempts should be made to further contextualize the innovative activities undertaken by the enterprise, especially the competitive position *vis-à-vis* its principal competitors that are missing (what is the competitive context?) and that it is not clear what the enterprise's strategic intent is.[10]

Currently, we do not really measure the level of innovativeness of a firm. Taken on a three-year period, a firm that manages to put 100 innovative products and or services on the market is treated in the same manner as a firm that manages to get in the same period one innovation onto the market. An output indicator for measuring the level of (relative) innovation activity is much needed.

Regular production statistics and national accounts do not always cover service industries or are not detailed enough, and as a result analyses in which innovation data are combined with regular statistics troublesome. In a way, the history of neglect still requires an investment in bringing service sector statistics up to date with mainly those of manufacturing industries.

The idea that technological and non-technological innovations can be surveyed separately needs possibly to be abolished in the first place. Eventually, we will be mostly in need of – using the categorization as mentioned by Coombs and Miles (2000) – a synthesis approach in which we no longer differentiate between the increasingly artificial division between technological and non-technological innovation. Maybe we are simply in need of a more unified innovation theory that is sufficiently flexible to cover both technological and non-technological innovation, but present them more on a continuum than as discrete phenomena.

Notes

1 Currently the drafting process of the 3rd edition of the *Oslo Manual* on proposed guidelines for collecting and interpreting innovation data is underway. Organizational and marketing innovation will get a more prominent role in addition to the traditional emphasis on technological innovation.

2 For discussions about different attempts to measure innovation in the service sector, see Coombs and Miles (2000), Delaunay and Gadrey (1992), Djellal and Gallouj (2001), Gadrey and Gallouj (2002), Gallouj (2002), Tether and Miles (2001).

3 This section is largely based on chapter 5 of den Hertog, Oskam, Smith and Segers (2003).

4 See also Sundbo and Gallouj (2000) on various aspects of the organization of innovation within the firm.

5 Danish abbreviation for a three-year project (1996–99) to increase the knowledge on the Danish Innovation System.

6 Enterprises are asked whether they are engaged in any of the following activities in 1998–2000:
   – Strategy: implementation of new or significantly changed corporate strategies.
   – Management: implementation of advanced management techniques within your enterprise.
   – Organization: implementation of new or significantly changed organizational structures.
   – Marketing: changing significantly your enterprise's marketing concepts/ strategies.
   – Aesthetic change (or other subjective changes): significant changes in the aesthetic appearance or design or other subjective changes in at least one of your products.

7 As observed in a series of interviews with 20 entrepreneurs by Langendorff (1997).

8 The highly interesting follow-up question for firms that report a certain type of non-technological innovation was developed focuses on the degree to which the innovation was developed mainly in-house, in partnership with clients/suppliers or mainly by others still needs to be analyzed. The complete dataset to perform was these kind of analyses only available early 2005.

9 Additional information will become available. In 2005 the CIS4 questionnaire will be launched by EU member states. This survey not only contains a question on organizational and marketing innovation, but also on effects of organizational innovations.

10 What is especially important to know better is on what the firm is actually competing, a cost-based strategy will require different levels and forms of innovation compared to a high quality (customized) strategy in which there possibly is more room and need to innovate.

Bibliography

Archibugi, D. & Lundvall, B.-A. (eds) (2001), *The Globalizing Learning Economy* (Oxford: Oxford University Press).

Cobbenhagen, J., van der Meer, H. & Mulder, S. (2001), *Niet technologische aspecten van innovatie* (Enschede: van der Meer & van Tilburg).

Coombs, R. & Miles, I. (2000), 'Innovation, measurement and services: the new problematic' (in Mectalfe & Miles).

Coriat, B. (2001), 'Organizational Innovation in European Firms: A Critical Overview of Survey Evidence' (in Archibugi & Lundvall).

Delaunay, J.C. & Gadrey, J. (1992), *Services in Economic Thought: Three Centuries of Debate* (Dordrecht: Kluwer Academic).

den Hertog, P. (2000), 'Knowledge Intensive Business Services as Co-producers of Innovation', *International Journal of Innovation Management*, 4 (4), pp. 491–528.

den Hertog, P., Bilderbeek, R. & Maltha, S. (1997), 'Intangibles. The soft side of innovation', *Futures*, 29(1), pp. 33–45.

den Hertog, P., Broersma, L. & van Ark, B. (2003), 'On the Soft Side of Innovation. Services Innovation and its Policy Implications', *de Economist*, 151(4), pp. 433–52.

den Hertog, P., Oskam, E., Smith, K. & Segers J. (2003), 'Innovation research and innovation policy. Usual Suspects, Hidden Treasures, Unmet Wants and Black Boxes', *Innovation Research. EZ-onderzoeksreeks* (Den Haag: Ministerie van Economische Zaken no. 2).

Djellal, F. & Gallouj, F. (2001), 'Innovation Surveys for Service Industries: A Review', *Innovation and Enterprise Creation: Statistics and Indicators* (Luxembourg: European Commission, EUR 17038), pp. 70–76.

Drejer, I. (2004), 'Identifying innovation in surveys of services: a Schumpeterian perspective', *Research Policy*, 33, pp. 551–62.

Gadrey, J. & Gallouj, F. (eds) (2002), *Productivity, Innovation and Knowledge in Services* (Cheltenham/Northampton: Edward Elgar).

Gallouj, F. (2002), *Innovation in the Service Economy: The new wealth of nations* (Cheltenham/Northampton: Edward Elgar).

Gallouj, F. & Weinstein, O. (1997), 'Innovation in Services', *Research Policy*, 26, pp. 537–56.

Gjerding, A.N. (1996), 'Organisational innovation in the Danish private business sector' (Aalborg: DRUID working paper no. 96–16).

Jacobs, D. & Waalkens, J. (2001), *Innovatie. Vernieuwingen in de innovatiefunctie van ondernemingen* (Deventer: Kluwer).

Langendorff, T. (1997), *De kunst van het innoveren. 20 ondernemers aan het woord* (The Hague: SDU).

Lundvall, B.A. (2001), 'Innovation Policy in the Globalising Learning Economy' (in Archibugi & Lundvall).

Lundvall, B.A. & Kristensen, F.S. (1997), 'Organisational change, innovation and human resource development as a response to increased competition' (Aalborg: DRUID working paper no. 97–16).

Metcalfe, J.S. & Miles, I. (eds) (2000), *Innovation Systems in the Service Economy. Measurement and Case Study Analysis* (Boston: Kluwer Academic).

OECD (1997), *Science, Technology and Industry* (Paris: OECD).

Schumpeter, J.A. (1934), *The Theory of Economic Development* (Cambridge, MA: Harvard University Press).

Sundbo, J. & Gallouj, F. (2000), 'Innovation as a Loosely Coupled System in Services' (in Metcalfe & Miles).

Tether, B. & Miles, I. (2001), 'Surveying Innovation in Services – Measurement and Policy Interpretation Issues', *Innovation and Enterprise Creation: Statistics and Indicators* (Luxembourg: European Commission, EUR 17038), pp. 77–87.

Tidd, J., Bessant, J. & Pavitt, K. (1997), *Managing Innovation. Integrating Technological, Market and Organisational Change* (Chichester: Wiley).

van Ark, B., Broersma, L. & den Hertog, P. (2003), *Services Innovation, Performance and Policy: A Review* (Den Haag: Ministerie van Economische Zaken: Rijksuniversiteit Groningen/Utrecht, Dialogic. EZ-onderzoeksreeks no. 4).

van der Aa, W. (2000), *Organisatorische innovaties en groeistrategieën van dienstverlenende bedrijven* (Rotterdam: EUR).

von Hippel, E. (1988), *The Sources of Innovation* (New York and Oxford: Oxford University Press).

Annex 1

Table 10.5. Part II of the Netherlands CIS3½ survey dealing with non-technological innovations

---

PARTII:NON-TECHNOLOGICALINNOVATIONS
Besides technological innovation other, NON-technological innovations, e.g in the area of organisation, can occur. Also think of developing completely new marketing concepts or developing other, non-technically oriented competences in your enterprise.

10. Non-technological innovation

a. Marketing
During 2000-2002, did your enterprise introduce significantlys improvement in marketing?

Concerns significantly new marketing concepts or strategies, like a clearly different approach of customers, opening up new markets and/or strenghtening of business image

Yes — such innovations were developed:
- mainly by your own enterprise
- in partnership with clients/suppliers
- mainly by others

No

b. Non-technical improvements of producs/services
During 2000-2002, did your enterprise make essential, NON-technological improvements to your products/services?

Think of e.g. packages (in abroad sense), colour, design and/or taste/smell of products/services; also indicated as product differentiation

Yes — such innovations were developed:
- mainly by your own enterprise
- in partnership with clients/suppliers
- mainly by others

No

c. Organisation with respect to customers and/or suppliers
During 2000-2002, did your enterprise introduce radical changes in the way of contacting customers and suppliers?

Significant changes in the relation/business process with your customer and/or suppliers.Takes place e.g. if your enterprise changes its distribution channels or if delivery by suppliers changes fundamentally

Yes — such innovations were developed:
- mainly by your own enterprise
- in partnership with clients/suppliers
- mainly by others

No

d. Internalorganisation
During 2000-2002, did your enterprise introduce significant changes in the internal organisational structure of your enterprise?

This concerns significant changes in the internal organisation of your enterprise e.g as a consequence of a new company strategy, market orientation and/or the buying/selling of parts of the enterprise group

Yes — such innovations were developed:
- mainly by your own enterprise
- in partnership with clients/suppliers
- mainly by others

No

If 4 times No has been ticked, go to queston 12

Continued

Table 10.5. Continued

11. Motives non-technological innovations

How important are the motives mentioned below for realising the NON-technological innovations as reported in question 10?

	Very important	Important	In significantly important/n.a.
Quality improvement Aiming at e.g. better after sales service, new forms of service improving the image of products/services, and/or other, NON-technical improvements of those products, etc.	☐	☐	☐
Cost reduction Aiming at lower costs, efficiency improvements, higher productivity	☐	☐	☐
Market changes a. Anticipate *future* changes on supply or sales markets. Think of changing preferences of customers or changes in operational management of suppliers	☐	☐	☐
b. Reacton *recent* changes on supply or sales market. Think of changing preferences of customers or changes in operational management of suppliers	☐	☐	☐
New technology The introduction of *technological* Innovation (whether developed by others or not) gave rise to **also** aspire **NON**-technological innovations	☐	☐	☐

12. Knowledge management

Knowledge management (KM) is aimed at making knowledge available for a relatively small group of people *accessible* for **larger** groups of people with in an organisation

For this purpose it is necessary that knowledge is stored systematically e.g in databases and that it is made available for others through *easy* accessible media (e.g. intranet or extranet)

	Yes	No (but planned for for 2003–2004)	No (and also no intention)
At the end of 2002, did your enterprise have a clear policy or strategy with regard to applying knowledge management?	☐	☐	☐
Has the responsibility for this KM policy appropriated to a person or department?	☐	☐	☐
At the end of 2002, did your enterprise have at it's disposal indicators to measure the success of the advantages of KM?	☐	☐	☐

13. Final question

Innovation in enterprises can be the consequence of (new) technology. It is also possible that completely different non-technological (e.g.market oriented) a spects or considerations were dominant; see previous page.

Innovations can also be a combination of both types. Technological and non-technological a spects in that case simultaneously play a role.

Please indicate (by ticking one box on the scale of 1 to 5) *which type* of innovation will be **most** important for your enterprise in the next two years

Technological aspects area dominant	Both spect are equally important	Non-technological a spects dominant	Difficult to specify
☐ 1	☐ 2 ☐ 3 ☐ 4	☐ 5	☐

Filled in by:

Name

Phone (optional)

E-mail enterprise (optional)

Part IV: Economics of Innovation

Introduction
Information, Knowledge and Appropriability

Jerome Davis

Appropriability

The three chapters in this part each in its own way sheds new or different light on information, knowledge and the appropriability puzzle, and their implications for the management of innovation. By 'information' in this context is meant knowledge of relevant details (in this case, details pertaining to the innovation). By knowledge is meant 'a set of understandings used to make decisions or take actions vital to the company'. In terms of the management of innovations, knowledge can be defined as 'that intellectual capital, which may be used as a strategic factor' (see e.g., the definitions in Wikipedia,[1] 2004).

The appropriability puzzle, simply put, deals with the public good nature of information. Once an information about a technical or service innovation is publicly available, it is argued, this information can costlessly be appropriated by parties other than the innovator; these then can replicate the innovation concerned without incurring any of the non-recoverable research and development (R&D) costs of the innovator. This replicating ability then becomes a disincentive for innovators, who as a response do not innovate. And society as a whole is made worse off. Thus, the 'privatizing' of public good nature of new information becomes a major strategic goal of innovative management, a so-called 'appropriability strategy'. Appropriability strategies are surprisingly diverse, but the major strategies are those of patenting, use of trademarks, copyright, lead-time, secrecy, and preemption (publishing in the public domain) with different firms in different industries using different strategic mixes.

There are essentially three insights that these chapters bring to the appropriability strategy puzzle: the distinguishing of knowledge from information and the impact that this has on appropriability strategies; the use of prizes as alternatives to the use of intellectual property rights to secure appropriability; and appropriability strategy as a function of firm size.

Imperfect appropriability

Cristiano Antonelli's chapter, the most ambitious of the three, essentially weds the transactions cost theory of the firm with the resource-based perspective of management literature. Here the problems of appropriability can be seen in a firm's decision as to how to appropriate rents from technical knowledge. Focusing on modularized production processes in particular, Antonelli utilizes the transaction cost insights of Coase, Williamson, and others (Coase, 1937; Williamson, 1996; Geroski, 1995). Firms can realize rents from innovation from either selling the innovation on the market or retaining it within the firm. In the latter alternative, technological knowledge is perceived as 'a good which can either be sold as such in the markets for technology or used as an internal intermediary input' (Antonelli, 2005, p. 180). In either case, whether sold on the market or retained in the firm, transaction costs from the suppliers' side, a spectrum of knowledge costs consuming firm resources (such as the costs of marketing, product or service customization, and customer service) render any form of appropriability imperfect.

While traditional appropriability instruments – patents, copyrights, trademarks – are acknowledged to the degree that they allow the market system to work, such property rights are not seen as universally essential to firm management of innovation. For those innovations where firm knowledge (and the transaction costs necessary for third party replication) may not guarantee appropriability, the firm can internalize those aspects that are easily copied by competitors by integrating the innovation in a larger modular form so that appropriability by competitors becomes too costly to contemplate. Thus vertical integration of innovation within the firm becomes an alternative to the sale of innovation on the market. Either way, the innovation is sold on the market or kept within the firm. Finally, by implication, the strategic supplier manipulation of knowledge transaction costs, while rendering supplier appropriability imperfect can also render any possible appropriability by third parties imperfect as well.

Prizes as an alternative to instruments of appropriability

The second contribution, that of the incentive use of prizes as an alternative to existing intellectual property rights mechanisms as a tool of technology strategy is largely rooted in the welfare economics view of appropriability. Here, social welfare costs of patents as instruments of appropriability are seen to be significant. In addition to the transaction costs incurred by patent application, litigation, and by the creation of often unnecessary 'patent thickets', there are the welfare costs incurred by the resulting monopoly position of the patent holder, and the welfare costs incurred by the possible non-development of the patented innovation.[2] Finally, there is welfare economic costs created by a diversion of R&D and innovatory efforts into those products or services which are clearly patentable, to the detriment of other, perhaps more societal beneficial, products or services. It is the realization of the societal costs of this diversion of activity that has led economists to renewed interest in the role of prizes in innovation, the topic of the co-authored chapter by Lee and Jerome Davis.

There already exists a considerable literature in this field (see, e.g., Galini & Scotchmer, 2002), most of it of fairly recent date, and written from a welfare economic perspective, where the costs of implementing a prize system are defined as the opportunity costs of abjuring patents and the automaticity of their 'rewards', here the rents which market monopoly advantage confer. Note is also made of the transaction costs of creating, administering and, given a successful winner, making the award inherent in a prize system. (Yet this is seldom seen in terms of its alternative, the transaction costs of a patent system that are also significant.) Rather than contribute to the theoretical literature here, Davis and Davis examine three well documented cases of innovative activity where prizes have played a significant role, all having to do with human flight – motorized flight, human powered flight, and the commercial development of space travel. They find, despite difficulties, particularly in the area of contest design, that (1) prizes have led to innovative activity that might otherwise not have been forthcoming; (2) prizes have interacted in a positive manner with other incentive systems such as patents (often hastening the innovation of patentable products); and (3) prizes may potentially have significant positive indirect spillover effects for the sponsors and/or competitors, particularly if these can use a prize system either to enhance their reputations in related activities or to develop subsidiary products that have a commercial value.

Appropriability strategies as a function of firm size

In contrast to the other two chapters that are either theoretical in orientation (Antonelli) or are based on case studies (Davis and Davis), Lee Davis's second contribution is an interview enquiry. She addresses the question of whether firm patenting strategies can be a function of firm size. An imbalance has long existed between investigating patenting in large firms and researching patenting patterns in smaller firms. Recently, this imbalance has been corrected somewhat (see Audretsch, 2002; Lefebvre & Lefebvre, 1993; Lindman, 2002). Yet little attention has been paid to how small firms use patents strategically, and how these strategies differ from large firm patent strategies. As previous studies in this field have indicated that the value of patents (and consequently firm patent strategies) varies between industries, Davis's contribution compares patent strategies for big and small firm in three industries: telecommunications, software, and biotechnology. As the nature of large sized firm patent strategies in these sectors is well documented, Davis uses the conclusions of this literature as a basis of comparison with the results of her interview enquiry. For each sector, she investigates small firms' general approach to patents, what they see as the main advantages of patents, what problems have arisen, and the role patents play in their larger business strategies. To this end, the chapter presents the results of an interview survey of patent experts in 34 small Danish firms. Of interest in this context is Davis's conclusion that smaller firms' patent experts' perceptions largely reflect those of patent experts in larger firms in the same industry, but that due to a lack of resources, a series of patent strategic options (blocking patents, suits for patent infringement, and the like) render the appropriability strategies of the larger firms too costly for small firms to imitate.

Notes

1 Wikipedia. 'Information' and 'knowledge', Wikipedia, at <http://en.wikipeda/org/wiki> (8 Sept. 2004).
2 It should be noted in this context, that these costs of patenting are counterbalanced to some extent by their social value as signaling devices which can prevent duplication of innovator effort.

Bibliography

Antonelli, C. (2005), 'The Governance of technological knowledge. To Use or Sell', in J. Sundbo, G. Serin, A. Galina and J. Davis (eds), *Contemporary Innovation Management* (London: Palgrave-Macmillan), p. 209.

Audretsch, D.B. (2002), 'The dynamic role of small firms: evidence from the U.S.', *Small Business Economics*, 18(1–3), Feb.–May, pp. 14–40.

Coase, R.H. (1937), 'The nature of the firm', *Economica*, 4, pp. 385–405.

Galini, N. & Scotchmer, S. (2002), 'Intellectual property: when is it the best incentive system?' *Economic Working Paper Series at WUSTL*, Law and Economics Series 0201001.

Geroski, P. (1995), 'Markets for technology' (in Stoneman).

Lefebvre, L.A. & Lefebvre, E. (1993), 'Competitive positioning and innovative efforts in SMEs', *Small Business Economics*, 5 (4), pp. 297–306.

Lindman, M.T. (2002), 'Open or closed strategy in developing new products? A case study of industrial NPD in SMEs', *European Journal of Innovation Management*, 5(4), pp. 224–36.

Stoneman, P. (ed.) (1995), *Handbook of the Economics of Innovation and New Technology* (Oxford: Blackwell).

Williiamson, O.E. (1996), *The Mechanisms of Governance* (New York: Oxford University Press).

11
The Governance of Technological Knowledge. *To Use or Sell*[1]
Cristiano Antonelli

11.1. Introduction

The grafting of the recent advances of the theory of the firm into the economics of knowledge seems a promising field of investigation and cross-fertilization. The result can be relevant both for the economics of knowledge and for the theory of the firm itself.

Economics of governance has benefited from the resource-based theory of the firm so as to include the analysis of such processes as the accumulation of competence and knowledge and the introduction and selection of technological and organizational innovations as well as the assessment of their effects on the design of the portfolio of activities that are arranged to be respectively included within the firm and assigned to transactions in the market place (Williamson, 1996; Penrose, 1959). The dynamics of the firm is shaped by the dynamic interdependence among the accumulation of localized knowledge and competence, respectively, in coordination, transaction and production. The characteristics of the process of accumulation of competence, of the generation of technological knowledge and of the introduction of technological and organizational innovations, are key factors to understanding the firm. Parallel to knowledge, competence is a central ingredient. Competence is defined in terms of problem-solving capabilities and makes it possible for the firm not only to know-how, but also to know-where, to know-when, and to know what to produce, to sell, and to buy. Competence and knowledge apply to the full set of activities: production activities, transaction activities and coordination activities.

The fabric of the economics of governance, however, can be extended to include in its fabric the broader array of issues related to the alternative means of exploitation of technological knowledge.

The attention of governance economics has been traditionally concentrated upon the 'make or buy' alternative. More and more attention is now being paid to the symmetric and yet complementary issue of the 'use or sell' alternative. The 'use or sell' alternative requires the assessment of the relative costs of using the markets to sell a product with respect to the costs of using that product in a further stage and to eventually sell it, embodied in a more elaborated product. The inclusion/exclusion choice concerns whether to sell the output at a given stage of the production process or to use it to make another product. The firm is seen here as an intermediary between production stages coordinated by the market place (Spulber, 1999).

The 'use or sell' trade-off applies to a wide range of industries where the general production process is broken down into production units characterized by high levels of specialization and technical indivisibility. The selective internalization of modules highlights the choice between the direct sale of the goods of a given module into the intermediary markets or the use of its products to feeding further sequential manufacturing modules. On a similar ground, the extensive growth of the service economy and the decline of the manufacturing industry at large, seems characterized by the intensive externalization of knowledge-intensive business services. Again, firms decide whether to sell their knowledge as a service or embody it into goods, through internalized manufacturing activities.

The 'use or sell' choice seems most relevant from the viewpoint of the integration of the transaction costs economics and the resource-based theory of the firm into the broader context of the economics of governance in general. This approach becomes extremely fertile, with regard to its analytical and normative implications, when attention is paid to technological knowledge, as a good, which can be either sold as such in the markets for technology or used as an intermediary internal input.

11.2. Supply side transaction costs

Modularity is swarming into economics and the economy. The architecture of the production process is more and more articulated in an array of modules of quasi-indivisible production units. Modularity is the result of the intensive and systematic breaking down of complex production processes into self-contained production units where technical indivisibility is reduced to minimum levels (Baldwin & Clark, 2000).

The governance of the transactions between modules is more and more complex. Modules can be included within corporations or excluded, according to the economics of governance as dictated by the assessment of the costs of using both the inputs and products markets with respect to the costs of internal coordination. The coordination of the supply and the demand for the products of the modules can be either left to the market place or can be provided by means of bureau-cratic organization within the firm.

This process is well documented in many industries. In the automo-bile industry as well as in most engineering industries, the traditional vertical integration has been supplanted by a variety of interdependent players that contribute the general production process with specialized services and products. The general production process leading to auto-mobiles, as well as appliances and machinery, has been broken down into a variety of complementary modules of specialized units, which sell and buy in the market place their components and their products. The inclusion and exclusion of these units might take place at different stages of the general production process and this is frequently re-assessed (Bonazzi & Antonelli, 2003).

Traditional industries, such as textiles, garments and fashion industries generally, have a long-standing tradition of modularized production processes. The evidence shows that the inclusion and exclusion of the modules in these industries is no longer organized along the sequential lines of the general production process but rather according to system-atic and selective evaluation of the incentives to buy or make and to make or sell, applied to each stage of the production process and each intermediary product. The design of the structure of each company gets closer and closer to a flexible jigsaw where each element enters and exits the company. The correspondence between the structure of the corpora-tion and the layout of the general production process leading to the final products purchased by households is more and more fuzzy.

The communications industry provides excellent evidence on these processes: six layers of specialized activity can be identified: equipment and software, networks, connectivity, navigation and middleware, applications, and contents packaging. The actual specialization of firms into each layer depends upon a variety of factors. The levels of transac-tion costs in each market differ widely as well as barriers to entry and levels of mark-ups. Sunk costs characterize each firm in different ways. The dynamics of the institutional factors affecting the definition of property rights, such as the forms and levels of mandatory inter-connection and the evolution of *de-facto* and *de-jure* standards, plays a major role. The boundaries of the firms with respect to the layers vary according to their own specific and idiosyncratic characteristics. In the communications industries, a great variety of firms can be found with respect to the mix of layers into which they are active. Fully vertically integrated firms coexist next to others, fully specialized in just one layer. Many firms select specific combinations of layers and they systematically operate in the intermediary markets either as sellers and/or buyers.

In this context the characteristics of intermediary markets play a key role. The product of each module is sold and bought in markets that are far away from the final consumers. In intermediary markets customers are firms. The same firms are also sellers. Often the same firm is at the same time a customer and a supplier. Because of modularity and inclusion/exclusion practices, intermediary markets are more and more populated with an increasing number of players on both the demand and the supply side. The relative efficiency of intermediary markets, both from an informational viewpoint and a competitive viewpoint, plays now a key role in the design of the portfolio of activities that are retained within the companies. The firm considers whether to make or buy a specific component or stage of the production process, and also whether to sell the products of each module in the intermediary markets or to use the output of the same module as an intermediary input for the following production process and eventually deliver the product to the final markets where households are the customers (Teubal, Yinnon & Zuscovitch, 1991).

Such transaction activities, however, must be considered not only on the demand side, as in the 'make or buy' tradition, but also on the supply side. Transaction costs on the supply side include an array of resource-consuming activities. The actual sale of a product requires appropriate levels of marketing, advertising, credit assessment, and post-sale assistance. Customization and versioning costs can be assigned to transaction costs on the supply side when monopolistic competition prevails and the entry in a market requires that dedicated investments be made in order to identify and implement a niche of loyal customers.

Markets differ widely in terms of the quality of information available on the products and the dispersion of prices, and the characteristics of users and customers. The distribution of information among vendors as well as among customers has varying levels of asymmetry. Markets differ widely also in terms of their conditions of competition. Market power can be found with varying levels of intensity, either on the supply or on the demand side. These differences matter when a firm is considering whether to sell a product or use it as an intermediary input for the production of another downstream good.

When transaction costs on the demand side are high, coordination costs are lower, and the market price for the product is higher than the internal production costs, the firm decides to make a component instead of buying it. Upward integration in the general production process takes place. A new module is added to the portfolio of activities retained within the boundaries of the firm and the coordination between the production of the upstream module and the production process of the downstream module is provided internally by bureaucratic structures. The firm is not a customer in the market for that intermediary input. The firm instead enters the market for that input, on the demand side, when it chooses to buy. Here, third parties provide the supply of the product and the coordination takes place externally in the market.

Symmetrically, in the 'use or sell' approach, the firm needs to assess whether or not to enter the market for each component or intermediary product or to use each product as a component of a downstream product. The role of transaction costs on the supply side becomes evident. When the cost of using the product markets is high and in any case higher than the cost of using the markets for downstream products, the firm has a clear incentive to integrate downstream and enter the market in next stage of the production process.

More specifically, it is clear that the firm confronts the costs of using the market upstream, with the costs of using downstream markets, after discounting the costs of the internal coordination between the two stages of the production process, and the direct manufacturing costs of the second stage of the production process. In other words, it is clear that the firm has an incentive to integrate downstream when the net revenue of the sale in the upstream markets is lower than that stemming from the entry in the downstream markets. The case is interesting when such difference is determined primarily by lower transaction costs.

It is now clear that the firm can decide whether to selectively integrate and diversify downward, as well as upward. The firm can also make the choice to sell and eventually to buy again at a later stage of the production process. Here the firm selects the stages of complex and interdependent production processes, which can be internalized, and the stages to externalize, but retains control of the overall production process articulated in sequential steps. The market and the organization become interdependent. The firm can be at the same time a vendor of a product and a buyer at a later stage of the same chain of complementary and interdependent modules. The firm can buy back the full amount of the goods produced with its own original inputs or only a part. The boundaries between the firm and the markets become more and more flexible and subject to continual redefinition.

The choice between make or sell and make or buy, moreover, is most frequently partial, rather than exclusive. Firms decide whether to sell in the intermediary markets varying shares of the production of upstream production modules. They rarely swing from the sale of the full output to its full inclusion. By the same token, firms rely upon intermediary markets for the provision of varying shares of the intermediary inputs that are necessary for subsequent production stages: some production is retained within the boundaries of the firm.

In this broader economics of governance context, transaction costs are defined as the costs of using the markets on both the supply side and the demand side. The firm uses the markets not only to sell its products, but also to buy the intermediary inputs to manufacture its products. In the governance economics context of analysis a new area of analysis emerges, one where the governance choice concerns also the markets for outputs, rather than the sole markets for inputs. The firm in fact considers not only the possibility to make or buy a specific component or stage of the production process, but also whether to sell its products in the intermediary markets or to the final ones.

The firm considers not only the possibility to make or buy a specific component or stage of the production process, but also whether to sell its products in the intermediary markets or to the final markets. Needless to say, the stages of the intermediary markets where to sell are also a matter of choice and assessment. The firm can decide whether to integrate and diversify downward, as well as upward. In this context, the firm can also make the choice to sell and eventually to buy again at a later stage of the production process. Here the firm selects the stages of complex and interdependent production processes, which can be internalized, and the stages to externalize, but retains control of the overall production process articulated in sequential steps. The market and the organization become interdependent. The firm can be at the same time the vendor of a product and the buyer at a later stage. The firm can buy back the full amount of the goods produced with its own original inputs or only a part. The boundaries between the firm and the markets become more and more flexible and subject to continual redefinition. The firm is more and more a system integrator, able to combine the subsystems that are included and those that are delivered by third parties (Antonelli, 2003; Bonazzi & Antonelli, 2003).

11.3. A new knowledge trade-off: to use or to sell

11.3.1. The rationale

The analysis developed so far has important applications to understanding the conduct of the innovative firm and more broadly the economics of knowledge governance. The stock of proprietary technological knowledge accumulated within each firm and the competence built by means of learning processes and formal research and development activities can be considered an output *per se*, rather than exclusively and necessarily an input for the subsequent production of goods and services in the markets for technological knowledge.

In this context the analysis of the factors affecting the choice between to sell or to make use of the knowledge as input, makes sense. Specifically firms implement not only knowledge exploration strategies, but also knowledge exploitation strategies. This means that firms need to assess not only whether to produce internally all the knowledge that is necessary for the introduction of new technology or purchase it in the markets for external knowledge, but also whether to sell the knowledge in the markets for knowledge or to use it to make other products.

The use of the market place to exchange technological knowledge is more and more common. Technological knowledge can be fully generated internally or partly purchased in the markets for knowledge: external knowledge can be an intermediary input for the production of other knowledge.

Markets for technological knowledge are spreading in the economic systems. The use of the market place to exchange technological knowledge is more and more common. Technological knowledge can be sold with varying levels of embodiment into other goods and services. Technological knowledge can be sold as an intangible good, more or less associated with other services, such as the assistance of the vendors to the customers. Technological knowledge can be sold as a service – knowledge-intensive business service. Technological knowledge can be sold as incorporated in weightless products such as software. Technological knowledge can be sold embodied at an early stage of a broader production process, or embodied in products that are manufactured at other stages farther down in the general production process within the same procedures or across different processes leading to the products actually purchased by the final consumer: the household (Arora, Fosfuri & Gambardella, 2001; Guilhon, 2001).

The case of numerical control provides the full range of cases. The technology of numerical control can be sold as a patent or a license. It can be sold embodied in software, in the numerical control itself or, finally, it can be embodied in a machine tool with numerical control. The machine tool in turn can be sold as such or it can be used as a capital good in the production of cars and trucks. The engineering industries and specifically the packaging and textile machinery industry, provide similar evidence. Each of these industries differs widely in terms of transaction costs on the supply side.

The chemical industry is characterized by similar trends with the identification of companies specialized in the supply of the design for chemical plants, as well as by companies that coordinate internally the competence in the design and the delivery of the plants. Finally, important companies in the chemical industries operate the full range of activities from the design of the plants, to their construction to the use for the delivery of chemical products to the markets.

The analysis of the 'make use or sell' trade-off applied to knowledge as a product *per se* makes it clear that the knowledge exploitation strategies of the firm will be influenced, for given levels of relative revenues in either markets, by the relative levels of transaction costs on the supply side in the upstream markets for knowledge as a product *per se*, compared with the costs of coordinating internally the application of the knowledge to the production of a new good, the costs of the sheer production and the costs of using the downstream markets to sell the products.

11.3.2. Knowledge transaction costs

The governance approach elaborated by Ronald Coase and Oliver Williamson can be successfully applied to the analysis of knowledge generation and dissemination. The characteristics of knowledge and the details of its generation and dissemination process can be appreciated from the view point of the economics of governance especially when the basic ingredients of the resource-based theory of the firm are taken into account and properly integrated into a single interpretative frame (Coase, 1937; Williamson, 1996; Penrose, 1959; Foss, 1997).

The integration of the transaction costs approach with the resource-based theory of the firm shows that firms select their boundaries by means of the inclusion and exclusion of specific activities, including knowledge generation, exploitation and exploration activities, according to the characteristics of technological knowledge and to the related levels of knowledge transaction costs. Following the resource-based theory of the firm, the corporation is a resource pool designed and managed so as to implement the opportunities for the accumulation of both new technological and organizational knowledge. The rates of technological and organizational learning influence each other in shaping the dynamics of the firm and the evolving composition of the collection of activities that are retained within its boundaries and ultimately its growth (Chandler, 1990; Teece, 2000).

Knowledge transactions and interaction costs can be identified and defined in terms of the costs of all the activities that are necessary to exchange knowledge among independent parties. Two important distinctions must be introduced here. The first is the between-knowledge transaction costs on the demand side and knowledge transaction costs on the supply side (Antonelli, 2003).

Knowledge transaction costs on the supply side define all of the costs that agents bear to use the markets for knowledge as a product *per se*. Knowledge transaction costs on the supply side consist primarily of all the activities that are necessary to ensure that, while attempting to exploit proprietary knowledge, it does not leak out and thus deprive the legitimate holder of part of, if not the whole, revenue. Knowledge transaction costs on the supply side can also be quantified by the sum of the costs of the activities that are carried on to prevent disclosure and to secure the possession of proprietary knowledge plus the missing portions of revenue stemming from unintentional disclosure and the following leakage. Next to the problems determined by imperfect appropriability, the costs of using the markets for knowledge include more traditional activities such as marketing, advertising, technical assistance and in general all of the activities that are necessary to identify prospective customers and to strike appropriate contracts with them. The provision of technical assistance to the users of technological knowledge is at the same time a cause of considerable cost and an effective mechanism to prevent uncontrolled leakage and the opportunistic behaviour of users. Technical assistance is the base on which to implement pricing strategies that take into account the effective amount of economic benefits stemming from the downstream use of the knowledge.

Knowledge transaction costs on the demand side define all of the costs associated with the exploration activities in the markets for separate areas of knowledge such as search, screening, processing, and contracting. Knowledge exploration strategies take into account knowledge transaction costs on the demand side in the context of the choice between 'make' internal knowledge or 'buy' external. As it is well known, the assessment of the actual quality of the knowledge can be difficult when the vendor bears the risks of opportunistic behaviour and dangerous disclosure. A close interaction takes place between knowledge transaction costs on the demand side and knowledge transaction costs on the supply side.

The second distinction is between static knowledge transaction costs and dynamic knowledge transaction costs. Static transaction costs are defined by the costs of using the markets to trade knowledge at each point in time and with no understanding of the stream of long-term consequences engendered by the use of the markets. Dynamic transaction and coordination costs are defined in terms of opportunity costs of the governance of the stock of knowledge with respect to the stream of generation of new knowledge. Inclusion now yields the opportunity to appropriate the eventual benefits stemming from the accumulation of knowledge in terms of higher opportunities for the introduction of additional units of knowledge. Exclusion and transaction instead yields new costs in terms of the missing opportunities to benefit from the cumulative learning processes associated with the production process itself.

Dynamic knowledge transaction costs are relevant both on the demand side and the supply side. On the demand side, search and screening costs include the resources to evaluate the scope for incremental advance on the supply side; dynamic knowledge transaction costs arise mainly because of the high risks of opportunistic behaviour of the customers with respect to derivative knowledge. When derivative knowledge matters, the vendor of the knowledge bears the risks of nonappropriation of the results of the scope of implementation of the knowledge, which has been sold. Uncontrolled appropriation of the flow of revenue associated to use of the stock of proprietary knowledge, by means of small incremental research costs, can take place with evident damages for the vendor. The working of the markets for knowledge is greatly favoured by the extent to which patents and copyrights can be enforced in the market place and licensing is an effective tool to trade specific items of knowledge and competence. The enforcement of the markets for patents is a primary condition for the reduction of knowledge transaction costs and hence the creation of markets for knowledge. The role of the judicial system in this context is extremely important (Geroski, 1995).

When the markets for knowledge are available, the selection of knowledge activities that firms retain within their boundaries is much wider. The exploration for external sources of knowledge and knowledge outsourcing becomes common practice. Firms can rely on external providers for specific items of complementary knowledge. Knowledge outsourcing on the demand side matches the supply of specialized knowledge intensive business service firms. Universities and other public research centres can complement their top-down research activities finalized to the production of scientific knowledge with the provision of elements of technological knowledge to business firms. The exploitation of the knowledge generated as well can take a variety of forms. Firms can use it to produce a new product or sell it as a product *per se*.

The governance of technological knowledge is deeply affected by the comparative assessment of the costs of making, buying and selling each component of the knowledge that is required. With low coordination costs and high transaction costs in upstream markets, the firm has a clear incentive to produce internally all of the necessary knowledge. Conversely, with low coordination costs and high transaction costs in downstream markets, the firm has a strong incentive to use the knowledge and apply it to manufacturing products and eventually sell them. Coordination costs apply to both the specific activities that are required to generate new knowledge and to the production processes that are necessary in order to use the knowledge generated. When transaction costs are low and coordination costs are high, the firm has a strong incentive to act as a knowledge intensive business service provider. It will acquire the knowledge in the markets for knowledge, add its specific competence, and sell it as a separate piece of knowledge, a product *per se*.

In the context of analysis of the governance of knowledge a new area of analysis emerges, one where the governance choice concerns also the markets for outputs, rather than the sole markets for inputs. The failure of markets as the appropriate governance mechanisms for the organization of the generation and dissemination of knowledge does not necessarily lead to undersupply but rather pushes the knowledge-creating firm to use it as an intermediary input for the sequential production of economic goods. Downstream vertical integration is the remedy to the problems raised by the non-appropriability and low tradability of knowledge as an economic good.

Poor appropriabilty of proprietary technological knowledge can be considered a specific cause of knowledge transaction costs on the supply side. When knowledge appropriability is reduced to nil, firms will integrate downstream. Conversely, when knowledge appropriability is high, firms will specialize in the production of knowledge and will rely on the market place as an appropriate mechanism for its economic exploitation. With imperfect knowledge appropriability, firms will select the markets where proprietary knowledge can be sold. In other contexts, firms will exploit their proprietary knowledge by means of vertical integration.

This result is important as it contrasts the traditional argument about the failure of markets, as a coordination system, in the allocation of resources to the production of knowledge because of the lack of incentives stemming from low appropriability and the related 'knowledge as a public good' tradition of analysis. The generation of appropriate quantities of knowledge can be stimulated by the opportunities in the markets for the products that are manufactured and delivered by means of the technological knowledge they embody.

The analysis developed so far has important applications for understanding the conduct of the innovative firm when the stock of technological knowledge accumulated within each firm and the competence built by means of learning processes and formal research and development activities is considered an output *per se*, rather than an input for the subsequent production of goods and services in the markets for technological knowledge. The choice between make or buy is integrated by the choice between sell or make. Specifically, firms assess both whether to produce internally all of the knowledge that is necessary for the introduction of new technology or purchase it in the external knowledge markets, and whether to sell the knowledge in the knowledge markets or to use it to make other products.

11.3.3. A simple model

At any time, the firm needs to assess whether to sell the stock of proprietary knowledge or to use it as an intermediary input for sequential stages. The levels of profitability attained with inclusion are compared with the profitability stemming from exclusion. The inclusion of a sequential step into the complex production process that takes place within the boundaries of the firm and hence the choice to make instead of selling, depends upon three classes of factors – the quality of the markets from an informational and competitive viewpoint, the relative efficiency of the internal stage with respect to that performed by third parties, and the implications for the process of accumulation of technological knowledge. Upon this basis a simple model can be compiled.

The revenue function is defined as the revenue obtained by the firm by the sale of its products. Two revenue functions (R) can be identified respectively for the proprietary knowledge K and the product Z,[2] which embodies the proprietary knowledge. The revenue functions for the proprietary knowledge K (RK) and Z respectively (RZ) are equal to the standard product of prices and quantities (PK QK) and (PZ QZ):

$$RK = PK \ QK \tag{1}$$

$$RZ = PZ \ QZ \tag{2}$$

Equations (1) and (2) provide the basic ingredients to build a map of isorevenues. Their slope is measured by the ratio of the unit revenue of the proprietary knowledge PK sold as a product with respect to the unit revenue of the good Z (PZ/PK). The map of isorevenues in turn provides the constraint to the to make or to sell decision making.

The firm will decide whether to sell directly the proprietary knowledge K or to use it as an intermediary input for the sequential production of the good Z, also according to the comprehensive production costs.

The firm is represented as the set of activities that are necessary to produce and deliver the proprietary knowledge K and the product Z. It includes the strict manufacturing process as well as the organizational activities necessary to coordinate the internal exchanges between the research and the production functions and to use the downstream markets. In the case of the specialized production of proprietary knowledge, no coordination activity is necessary. Here all of the production is contained within with the single module specialized in research activities. The activities that are necessary to use the market to sell the proprietary knowledge K must be considered.

The organizational inputs that are necessary to use the markets on the supply and the demand side and to coordinate the exchanges between modules within the firm, are the product of well-identified activities with inputs, outputs and specific levels of efficiency. This confirms that the firm is a set of activities that which goes beyond the production functions of the modules. Formally, we have then the activities that are necessary to use the markets for knowledge on the supply side (TRSK), the activities that are necessary to use the markets for the product Z on the supply side (TRSZ), and the activities that are necessary to coordinate internally the applications of the proprietary knowledge K to the production of the good Z. Hence:

$$TRSK = a(I) \, H(QK) \tag{3}$$

Here the dedicated supply transaction activities necessary for the sale of the proprietary knowledge (K) are the result of appropriate inputs (I) and specific efficiency levels (a) with a fixed coefficient H.

$$TRSZ = b(I) \, W(QZ) \tag{4}$$

where the dedicated transaction inputs necessary for the sale of the quantities of the product Z (QZ) are the result of appropriate inputs (I) and specific efficiency levels (b) with a fixed coefficient W.

$$CO = c(I) \, T(QK) \tag{5}$$

where the dedicated inputs necessary for the coordination of the production of proprietary knowledge K and the product Z are the result of appropriate inputs (I) and specific efficiency levels (b) with a fixed coefficient T.

The production and sale of the proprietary knowledge K requires the combination of research and development activities and transaction cost activities on the supply side to operate in the markets for knowledge. Formally, we have:

$$K = (R\&D + TRSK) \tag{6}$$

where R&D measures the unit of inputs specialized in research and development activities, and TRSK measures the units of inputs that are necessary to use the market to sell the proprietary knowledge K as a good *per se*.

In the case of the product Z, the resources that are necessary to perform the coordination between the modules K and Z are taken into account together with the inputs into the production function of the module Z and the resources that are necessary to use the markets on the supply side. Formally:

$$Z = (R\&D + PRO + TRSZ + CO) \tag{7}$$

where PRO measures the units of inputs that are necessary to manufacture the good Z, TRSZ the units of inputs that are necessary to use downstream markets for the product Z, and CO measures the activities that are necessary to coordinate internally the exchanges between the module R&D and the module Z.

The total cost equation is determined by the unit costs of all the inputs:

$$TC = r(R\&D) + e(PRO) + f(I) \tag{8}$$

where, usually, r is the unit costs of R&D activities (R&D), e is the unit manufacturing costs of the product Z, and f is the unit cost of organizational resources (I).

The combination of the two sets of activities yields the transformation curve:

$$K = f(Z) \tag{9}$$

According to standard optimization procedures, the equilibrium conditions are easily found where the slope of the isorevenue equals the slope of the transformation curve:

$$f'(Z) = PZ/PK \qquad (10)$$

In Figure 11.1, the shape of the transformation curve reflects the relative convenience of the supply conditions in the two alternative markets. The slope of the isorevenue reflects the relative prices of the two products in their respective markets. The equilibrium point found in the tangency of the relevant isorevenue and transformation curve identifies the best mix of make-use and sells for the profit-maximizing firm.

The decision whether to sell or to make use of the proprietary knowledge is now framed into an analytical context where many variables matter – the relative prices of the goods delivered to the market place, the relative efficiency of production in the modules, the relative efficiency of the two transaction activities on the output markets, the efficiency of the internal coordination activities. Let us consider them in turn.

The effects of transaction costs on the supply side are now fully accounted for. It is clear that when transaction costs on the supply side in the upstream markets are too high, firms prefer to make and use rather than to sell. Conversely, efficient and transparent upstream markets favour specialization. When the markets for intermediary products do not exist, transaction costs are very high both on the supply side and

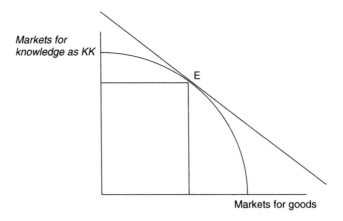

Figure 11.1.   The frontier of possible markets

on the demand side. The prices of the proprietary knowledge PK can incorporate a relevant portion of transaction costs on the supply side. Prices are too low, well below marginal costs, when, for instance, appropriability is low and uncontrolled leakage takes place beyond all possible efforts of vendors to retain some control of the knowledge. The case for loss of profits (*lucrum cessans*) due to imperfect inappropriability can be registered on this side of the equation as well, when it occurs even after the holders of proprietary knowledge have taken all possible measures and relative transaction costs on the supply side have been registered on the cost side.

The degree of relative competitiveness of upstream and downstream markets matters. If in upstream markets barriers to entry are high and large mark-ups prevail, while the downstream product market is closer to perfect competition, the firm operating the module R&D has a strong incentive to sell rather than to make. Conversely, if higher price–cost margins are found in downstream markets it will not sell, but rather make.

When upstream activity is shaped by technologies that cannot be easily copied, the sale of products both upstream and downstream can affect the competitive conditions of the markets. Here the firm will choose whether to be a monopolist upstream or downstream according to the differences in the revenue and price elasticity of the demand. The rates of imitative entry downstream can play a role in non-myopic decision making. The equilibrium conditions can easily identify the convenience for the firm to either sell or use to manufacture and sell downstream products. This result is consistent with much empirical evidence and confirms the heuristic strength of the analytical framework elaborated.

The efficiency of the internal coordination of the production of the modules K and Z has a direct bearing on the make use or sell trade-off. Firms may be forced to sell proprietary knowledge simply because internal coordination is too expensive. This in turn may depend on the size of the firm. The slope of the curve of coordination costs may become steeper and steeper with the general size of the firm. Large firms may be obliged by coordination costs to be very selective with respect to the make-use option and sell their proprietary knowledge or simply let it 'spill into the air', while smaller firm may prefer, *coeteris paribus*, to make use of their proprietary knowledge and integrate downstream.

Production costs exert similar effects, *coeteris paribus* the conditions of the markets from the viewpoint of their informational efficiency, and firms are induced to make use or sell by the slope of production costs, and specifically by the levels of their production costs with respect to those of downstream competitors. Entry in downstream markets may be foreclosed by sharp differences in production costs that favour downstream incumbents. The sale of proprietary knowledge remains the single opportunity to exploit it.

11.4. Implications for knowledge exploitation strategies

The implications of the analysis on knowledge transaction costs on the supply side and vertical integration, as a remedy to imperfect knowledge appropriability, are most important for understanding knowledge exploitation strategies.

When an individual generates new technological knowledge, downstream vertical integration takes the form of entrepreneurship. Individual inventors face the clear alternative of either selling their proprietary knowledge as a product *per se* or using it as an intermediary input. To do so, however, the inventor needs to create a new firm. The entry of new firms, hence, can be seen as the direct consequence of a flow of new technological knowledge modules, which cannot be sold as products *per se*. Actually, the creation of a corporation can be the indirect form of the trade of the technological knowledge. An incumbent corporation might eventually acquire the new company. The inventor in this case sells the property rights rather than the intellectual property rights to the company. Here there is a direct relationship between patents and shares, and the markets for knowledge and the financial markets.

When the inventor is an incumbent corporation, already existing and active at least in a given product market, knowledge exploitation strategies lead to the growth of the firm. The application of the technological knowledge to the current activities of the firm is expected to have positive effects in terms of performance and ultimately profitability. In turn, the growth can be internal or external. Takeovers, mergers and acquisitions can be seen as the direct consequence of the internal use of new technological knowledge by the firm. The acquisition of new firms makes it possible to extend the scope of application of the new knowledge and hence the range of its exploitation. Such growth can take place within the same product market or in adjacent markets. When technological knowledge applies to products that differ from the current products, diversification, vertical integration and multinational growth can be seen as remedies to the imperfect appropriability of proprietary technological knowledge. Vertical integration, for an incumbent, can be both downward and upward: the new proprietary knowledge can be used both as an input for the internal production of a new product or for the direct internal production of an intermediary input, previously purchased in the market for components. The coherence in growth strategies can be found with respect to the characteristics of new technological knowledge rather than with respect to the portfolio of current activities and the characteristics of the stock of tangible capital.

Strategies of internal exploitation, by means of downstream and upstream vertical integration and horizontal diversification, and strategies of external exploitation by means of the sale of the technological knowledge as a product in the markets for knowledge, can coexist, especially when some barriers to mobility across markets can be found. The sale of technological knowledge can coexist with the direct exploitation when geographic distance matters, when the new knowledge applies to different products, and when barriers to international trade are found. Coexistence can be diachronic in that firms sell their technological knowledge but retain the right to implement it and to use the derivative knowledge. In this case the firm sells the proprietary knowledge that already exists but does not sell the rights to take advantage of the stream of new knowledge. Mixed strategies of direct and indirect exploitation take place within the boundaries provided by property rights. Low cost for knowledge transaction on the supply side can be found within global corporations where the internal markets are made stable by proprietary ties among affiliates that are at least partially owned by a central holding. In such cases, central laboratories can sell knowledge to divisions and affiliates when appropriability is lower and use external markets for knowledge with higher levels of natural appropriability.

The trade in technological knowledge markets is also frequent within technological districts where trust is enforced by high risks of retaliation and localization exposes firms to reciprocity. In such circumstances, firms may specialize in the production of knowledge and in its trade as a product *per se* with strong benefits in terms of specialization and access to technological knowledge.

The incorporation of new knowledge into a new company that operates in downstream markets can provide the incumbent with the opportunity to reduce internal coordination costs, and yet to retain the control of the proprietary knowledge. Moreover, the equity can be partly sold in the stock exchange, and eventually become a spin-off, or it can be used as tool for establishing alliances and joint ventures. Once more, the incorporation of the proprietary knowledge into a new company provides opportunities for mixed exploitation strategies.

In sum, the application of this analysis to the economics of knowledge is fruitful. The market place provides the opportunity for firms to sell their technological knowledge in the form of patents, licenses and services, or embodied in products. The sale of technological knowledge can substitute its use as input into both the downstream and upstream production of new goods or new processes. The sale of disembodied knowledge, however, can complement the sale of knowledge. Substitution takes place when the profits stemming from a disembodied sale are larger than those provided by an embodied sale. This can take place when the costs of internal coordination are larger than transaction costs in the markets for knowledge, or when competition is stronger in downstream markets rather than in upstream markets. Complementarity between the sale in the markets for knowledge and its internal exploitation takes place when knowledge customers operate in different markets from product customers (Baumol, 2002).

Ex-ante standardization in this context emerges as a powerful knowledge exploitation mechanism. Firms that command proprietary knowledge can impose the standards of the manufacturing process and the design of the modules that are likely to contribute the final product. Standards matter in this context as the codes of technological platforms that define the interfaces between modules and the role of each specific player. Standards are defined before the actual implementation of the manufacturing process. *Ex-ante* standards precede and complement patents as appropriation mechanisms. Standards make it possible to select the downstream applications that are retained within the boundaries of the corporations and the markets into which proprietary knowledge can be sold as a product *per se*.

11.5. Conclusion

Transaction costs economics has paved the way to understanding the firm as a bundle of activities, which coexist when the costs of internal coordination are lower than the costs of using the markets. The analysis, so far, has mainly focused the costs of using the markets on the demand side. Upward integration has been regarded as the consequence of high costs of transactions in the markets for complementary products and intermediary inputs at large.

The spreading of modularization has highlighted the key role of the costs of using supply-side markets. The relative levels of transaction costs in the usage of the markets on the supply side become a relevant factor in assessing the choice of the firm between the sale of the products of upstream modules or their integration into the operation of downward modules as intermediary inputs. When the firm decides to use the products of a module as an intermediary product for the following module, the exchange takes place in the internal market, coordinated by means of bureaucratic procedures. The firm is no longer a vendor. The firm instead is a vendor of the product of a module when the relative transaction costs on the supply side are lower upstream. The application of this analytical framework is especially fertile in the economics of knowledge.

The economics of knowledge has long been shaped by the seminal contributions of Kenneth Arrow about the public good character of technological knowledge (Arrow, 1962). In this approach technological knowledge is regarded as a public good for the high levels of non-appropriability and hence non-tradability. Following our approach, however, even the public good nature of technological knowledge does not necessarily lead to under-supply but rather pushes the knowledge-creating firm to use it as an intermediary input for the sequential production of other economic goods. Vertical integration into downstream activities is an important alternative that the possessor of technological knowledge can assess, in order to exploit its economic rents. The incentives to the generation of appropriate quantities of knowledge can be found in the markets for the products that are manufactured and delivered by means of the technological knowledge they embody. This analysis contrasts the traditional argument, according to which the market supply of technological knowledge is deemed to under-supply because of its public good nature.

When knowledge cannot be sold as a good, there are still opportunities for its exploitation in the markets for the products that can make use of it as an intermediary input. The strategies for knowledge exploitation include downstream vertical integration into the production of goods that incorporate the new knowledge and yet deliver it to the market place. It is clear that all factors increasing the absolute and relative tradeability of technological knowledge have positive effects for two reasons. First, better knowledge tradeability leads to more effective incentive alignment and hence a better allocation of resources to generate new knowledge. Second, better knowledge tradeability favours better divisions of labour and specialization, hence higher efficiency. When and if the exploitation of technological knowledge as an intermediary input and its embodiment in downstream products is not the cause of limitations to its dissemination, the plurality of markets, rather than the single market place, can provide viable mechanisms of an efficient generation of technological knowledge. Even with low levels of natural appropriability in fact, appropriate levels of incentives and divisions of labour are provided by the opportunity to exploit the proprietary knowledge embodied in downstream products.

From a welfare viewpoint the knowledge trade-off is at work again, although in a new context. The levels of fungibility of new knowledge and the timing and the costs of the reverse engineering, play a key role. Reverse engineering is the activity that is necessary to extract the basic knowledge from the downstream products into which it has been embodied. Reverse engineering costs and times are the main source of barriers to imitation and hence the main factor of appropriability for inventors. At the same time, however, with high costs of reverse engineering and long delays, the social costs of the embodiment of new knowledge in terms of impediment to other purposes, increases. The wider the scope of application, the higher the levels of fungibility, and the larger are the social costs.

Notes

1   This chapter, based on a 2004 conference paper, benefited by the preliminary comments of Jerome Davis, Lee Davis, Jon Sundbo, Göran Serin and Andrea Gallina and others, and which are acknowledged.
2   Specifically we need to assume that H is a module of technological knowledge with high levels of fungeability: it can be aplplied to a variety of different products which are sold in different markets and Z is a vector of different products with high levels of separability. Geographic distance and hence transportation costs can provide separability, as well as national boundaries and hence custom's duties. Barriers to mobility across product markets and high research costs impede the easy application of the same knowledge to different products.

Bibliography

Antonelli, C. (2003), *The Economics of Innovation, New Technologies and Structural Change* (London: Routledge).

Arora, A., Fosfuri, A. & Gambardella, A. (2001), *Markets for Technology* (Cambridge, MA: MIT Press).

Arrow, K.J. (1962), 'Economic Welfare and the Allocation of Resources for Invention' (in Nelson).

Baldwin, C.Y. & Clark, K. (2000), *Design Rules: The power of modularity* (Cambridge, MA: MIT Press).

Baumol, W.J. (2002), *The Free-market Innovation Machine. Analyzing the growth miracle of capitalism* (Princeton: Princeton University Press).

Bonazzi, G. & Antonelli, C. (2003), 'To make or to sell?: The case of in-house outsourcing at FIAT-Auto', *Organization Studies*, 24, pp. 575–94.

Chandler, A.D. (1990), *Scale and Scope: The dynamics of industrial capitalism* (Cambridge, MA: Belknap Press).

Coase, R.H. (1937), 'The nature of the firm', *Economica*, 4, pp. 386–405.

Cowan, R., David, P. & Foray, D. (2000), 'The explicit economics of knowledge codification and tacitness', *Industrial and Corporate Change*, 9, pp. 211–53.

Dasgupta, P. & David, P. (1987), 'Information Disclosure and the Economics of Science and Technology' (in Feiwel).

Feiwel, G. (ed.) (1987), *Arrow and the Ascent of Modern Economic Theory* (London: Macmillan).

Foss, N. (1997), *Resources Firms and Strategies: A Reader in the Resource-based Perspective* (Oxford: Oxford University Press).

Geroski, P. (1995), 'Markets for technology' (in Stoneman).

Guilhon, B. (ed.) (2001), *Technology and Markets for Knowledge. Knowledge creation, diffusion and exchange within a growing economy* (Boston: Kluwer Academics).

Nelson, R.R. (ed.) (1962), *The Rate and Direction of Inventive Activity: Economic and social factors* (Princeton: Princeton University Press for NBER).

Penrose, E.T. (1959), *The Theory of the Growth of the Firm* (Oxford: Blackwell).

Spulber, D. (1999), *Market Microstructures: Intermediaries and the theory of the firm* (Cambridge: Cambridge University Press).

Stoneman, P. (ed.) (1995), *Handbook of the Economics of Innovation and New Technology* (Oxford: Oxford University Press).

Teece, D.J. (2000), *Managing Intellectual Capital* (Oxford: Oxford University Press).

Teubal, M., Yinnon, T. & Zuscovitch, E. (1991), 'Networks and market creation', *Research Policy*, 20, pp. 381–92.

Williamson, O.E. (1996), *The Mechanisms of Governance* (New York: Oxford University Press).

12

Prizes as Incentives. *Reflections on a Century of Aviation Contests*

Lee Davis and Jerome Davis

12.1. Introduction

The dream of 'space tourism' has long been confined to the imaginations of science fiction writers. But in 1996, former aerospace engineer Peter Diamandis announced the $10 million 'X-Prize', to jump-start the development of a new generation of launch vehicles to carry ordinary people into space. In late October 2004, test pilot Mike Melville successfully flew the *SpaceShipOne* more than one hundred kilometres into the upper atmosphere, briefly experiencing weightlessness, before returning to earth. In early November, another test pilot, Commander Brian Binnie repeated the trip, and won the prize. A new era of sub-orbital passenger flight had begun (Bigelow, 2004; Davis & Davis, 2004).

Prizes have played a prominent role in stimulating innovative activity over the past few centuries, leading to the invention of the chronometer and synthetic chemical alkali in the 18th century, food canning in the 19th century, and energy-efficient refrigerators in the 20th century. But more prizes have been offered for achievements in aviation in the past century – by newspapers, business interests, individuals, and governments – than in any other technical area (National Academy of Sciences, 2000), where they contributed to the development of the first motor-powered airplanes, lightweight human-powered aircraft, and now, reusable space vehicles.

With prizes (and unlike patents), the promise of a cash reward provides the incentive to invest in research and development (R&D). Prizes can focus innovative efforts on important societal problems where answers are not obvious, and where incentive effects do not rely on a proprietary approach to knowledge. Yet prizes also impose costs. Rewards may be arbitrary. It is difficult to set the appropriate size of the reward, and/or to pick the most qualified contestant. Finally, there may be an inefficient duplication of innovative resources. In the economics literature, prizes have been the focus of increasing interest (e.g., Polanvyi, 1943; Wright, 1983; de Laat, 1996; Llobet, Hopenhayn & Mitchell, 2000; Chiesa & Denicolo, 1999; Gallini & Scotchmer, 2002; Shavell & van Ypersele, 2001). Other work has investigated prize system design (e.g., Kremer, 2000; Kremer & Zwane, 2002; Masters, 2003). This chapter builds on and extends the findings of this and related work, complemented by empirical data on the role of prizes in the aviation industry.

Section 12.2 starts with a discussion of the incentive effects of prizes, in comparison with those of two alternative incentive systems: patents and contracts. We then explore the issue of contest design. Section 12.3 presents the three case studies. Section 12.4 asks: what were the incentive effects of prizes? Section 12.5 summarizes the conclusions and implications of the analysis.

12.2. Prizes as incentives to R&D

12.2.1. The comparative incentive effects of prizes

The use of prizes as incentives to invention and innovation represents an attempt to address the market failures associated with R&D. Knowledge goods differ from physical goods in that they have some of the characteristics of public goods (Nelson, 1959; Arrow, 1962). Information does not diminish with use. But once a new idea is disclosed, it is difficult to prevent others from using it as they wish, creating a disincentive to undertake the costs and risks of investing in new knowledge. There are several types of incentive systems, each addressing this problem in a different way. Their distinctive features are summarized in Figure 12.1.

The most well-known incentive system is the patent system, which gives inventors the legal right to exclude others from making, selling or using their new product or process for a limited period (normally 20 years), in return for disclosing the invention. To be patented, an invention must fulfil specific criteria: novelty, non-obviousness, industrial utility. But patent examiners pass no judgement as to whether the invention itself is socially beneficial, or the applicant is best suited to develop it. The inventor identifies the relevant market, bears the R&D costs and risks, and controls the timing of development. Only if the invention succeeds on the market place (or the rights are licensed out) will the inventor realize any profits from its investments in R&D.

	Prize	Patent	Contract
Market identification	Prize-giver	Innovator	Contract-giver
Costs and risks	Innovator's costs may be covered by prize, innovator bears *ex ante* risks	Both borne by innovator	Shared between innovator and contract-giver
Control of timing	Prize-giver	Innovator	Contract-giver
'Commercial test'	Not *ex ante*	Yes	No
Main incentive effect	Encourages innovation in uncertain technologies by promise of reward	Encourages innovation in uncertain technologies by prospect of monopoly rents	Encourages innovation in uncertain technologies by prospect of guaranteed market
Benefits	Encourages innovation in both appropriable and non-appropriable technologies Focuses innovative efforts on solutions to societally important problems Creat awareness of different types of solutions Spillovers	Encourages innovation in appropriable technologies Focuses innovative efforts on novel, non-obvious, industrially useful inventions Details of invention published in patent Strong legal basis for knowledge sharing	Encourages innovation in both appropriable and non-appropriable technologies Focuses innovative activity on particular types of innovations that are needed but otherwise would not be forthcoming under the market Spillovers No duplication of resources
Costs	Prize-giver's information in determining who should win the prize may not be accurate Constructed competition, Rewards may be arbitrary Duplication of resources Possible delays in inventive activity Invention might have been made anyway	Patent officials' information for determining patentability may not be accurate Possible monopoly abuses Patent races Avoids duplication of resources, but patentee not necessarily the best to carry out innovation	Costs of administration (specifying the conditions of the contract, choosing among the submitted bids) Bearing the costs and risks of developing the good Vulnerability to political lobbying The possibility of 'hold-up'

Figure 12.1. Comparative incentive effects of patents, contracts, subsidies and prizes

The patent system provides not only a valuable incentive to R&D, but also the legal basis for licensing. It also ensures the disclosure of new research findings, since 18 months after the application has been submitted, the patent is published, so that others can read it and learn from it. Otherwise, the knowledge might be kept secret. But patents also have costs, including monopoly distortions, and the problem of over-investment in R&D (where firms compete to be the first to patent the product, and where the loser cannot necessarily realize the benefits of its R&D investments elsewhere in society). To these can be added the costs of transferring patent rights. Moreover, the firm that gets the patent might not be the best to implement the innovation. Ways have been developed to mitigate these costs, including the anti-trust system, which guards against monopoly abuses in the patent system.

A second incentive system is the development contract, which can be offered either by a government agency or by a private firm. An example is the development of a new railroad car. The contractor specifies the problem to be solved, along with the constraints in the project (in this case, the size and shape of the car, or the fact that it must be able to run on the existing track system), and invites private companies to submit bids. The contractor chooses the most cost-effective bid, and the winning firm develops the innovation. The two parties share the costs and risks of development, and the winning firm is guaranteed a market in the good once it is completed.

The main benefits of a contractual system are to focus innovative activity on needed innovations that would otherwise not be forthcoming under the market system, and spillovers (the US space programme, for example, has stimulated innovation in novel materials, such as heat-resistant surfaces, that have founded new uses in the private sector). The problem of duplication of resources is reduced, since only one firm gets the contract. But there are costs, including the costs of administering the system, and the possibility of cost overruns and delays, not least due to the mutual dependence of contractor and contractee. This problem of 'hold-up' due to asset high specificity has been well explored in the literature (e.g., Williamson, 1983). Contracts may be awarded not for their intrinsic merits, but as a result of political lobbying. Different contractual remedies exist to correct some of these problems, including dual sourcing (where the contract is two-staged: in the first, two firms are selected, on the basis of their initial bids, to developing the product, after which a winner is chosen to continue as the sole contractee), and incentive clauses within the contract to reduce the possibility of hold-up.

Prizes resemble these two incentive systems, but also differ. The prize-giver identifies the need, and defines the terms of the contest.

The contestants bear the initial R&D costs and risks. If a contestant wins, he/she can use these funds to cover his/her costs. If not, there is no reimbursement. Contestants compete to win the prize. There is no commercial test, since the prize is awarded before the good is marketed. It is up to the winner (and losers) to commercially develop their inventions. Unlike the patent system, the prize can be awarded for non-novel inventions which might not be eligible for patent protection but which can still contribute to solving important problems.

The prize system can generate unconventional inventions, which might not emerge through a contractual arrangement, where the contractor defines not only the problem, but also the nature of the solution. Prizes create awareness of different types of solutions. Like contracts, prizes yield spillover benefits. But there are also costs to the prize system. Due to problems of information asymmetry, the prize-giver's information in determining who should win the prize may not be accurate. Prizes represent a 'constructed' form of competition. As with contracts, the decision as to who should win can be arbitrary, and subject to political lobbying. In contrast to development contracts, there may be considerable duplication of resources. If two contestants come up with the same solution, their resources might well have put to better use elsewhere. Prize deadlines may cause delays in the introduction of important products. Finally, the invention might have been made anyway, with no need to reward the inventor. Section 12.2.2, below, describes ways in which these problems can be addressed (for further details, see Davis & Davis, 2004).

12.2.2. The problem of contest design

Prizes can be designed in different manners, depending on the nature of the problem to be solved and the reasons for the prize. Several key issues must be confronted and resolved:

The contest can be open or closed: Who should be eligible to compete? The contest can open to the employees of a single firm but not competing firms, or to the members of a given industrial association, and so forth. While for reasons of economics, these contests should be as open as possible, for reasons of appropriability, it might be necessary to restrict eligibility – and access to using the solutions.

'First past the post' versus 'best on simultaneous submission':   Possibly, it should be the first inventor to solve the problem that takes the prize. Alternatively, a deadline might be specified for submissions; these would be evaluated by a panel to determine the best entry.

Determining the size of the award: How can the right value be established *ex ante?* If the amount were too low, firms would not be willing to undertake the necessary R&D. If too high, this would exacerbate the problems of favouritism and, in particular, resource duplication.

Prizes can be based on absolute or relative criteria: The terms of the contract defining the nature of the contest may exclude relational achievement: 'XX dollars to the first heavier than air manpowered aircraft which can fly across the English Channel'. Conversely, prizes can be awarded on the basis of relative criteria: 'XX dollars to the first heavier than air manpowered craft which exceeds the current distance record either on the ground or over water, etc'. Another mode of introducing relative criteria is to give lesser awards for solutions which are not ideal, but still valuable, while retaining a grand prize for the 'perfect solution'. A related problem concerns defining what is preferable. A solution might fulfill the prize criteria but imply other problems. For example, a potential winner might be technically superior but pollutes more.

Prizes can be awarded on the basis of a design or idea, or on the basis of performance: To stimulate innovation and product development, a performance basis may be preferred, giving freer play to unconventional solutions. Precise specification of performance criteria can also reduce the uncertainties felt by contestants. But would this remove from consideration highly unconventional solutions whose commercial potential is not immediately obvious?

Prizes awarded for novelty versus prizes awarded for non-novel achievement: An important benefit of prizes lies in their signaling function, enabling rewards for ideas that are not patentable but still have considerable economic value, such as a unique combination of known technologies.

Prizes can be awarded as isolated ends or as ends within a greater motivational context: Participants in an intra-firm contest may be motivated as much by how winning might further their careers as by the cash value of the award. Similarly, prizes might be more effective if seen in the context of pre-bidding contractual rounds, where the prospect of winning the procurement contract is equal to or greater than the monetary amount.

12.3. Three aviation contests

12.3.1. Motorized flight

The beginning of the 20th century witnessed a surge of interest in motorized flight, with no lack of wealthy businessmen to support it. For example, wealthy petroleum magnate and aviation enthusiast Henri

Deutsch de La Meurthe sponsored the Deutsch prize of 50,000 francs, for the first person to fly around the Eiffel Tower within a half hour (this was won by the Brazilian Santos Dumont in 1901). In 1904, Ernest Archdeacon, a prominent Parisian lawyer and founder of the Aero-Club de France, established a series of prizes, starting with a silver trophy – the *Coupe d'Aviation Ernest Archdeacon* – for the first person to fly a motor-powered airplane 25 metres. The Aero-Club de France put up a prize of 1,500 francs for the first aviator to fly 100 metres. Archdeacon Deutsch de la Meurthe also announced the 50,000 franc *Grand Prix d'Aviation* to reward the first to fly a one-kilometre circle. The London *Daily Mail* offered a £1,000 prize to the first to fly across the English Channel. Many adventurers competed to win these prizes.

But the first pilots actually to fly an airplane – Wilbur and Orville Wright, on 17 December 1903, at Kitty Hawk, North Carolina – were not among them. At first, the news of the Wright brothers' feat did not attract much attention. This apparently suited the brothers, who had always been quite secretive, fearing that others would copy their invention. During the next five years, they refused to enter any contests or demonstrate their invention publicly, focusing on patenting it both at home and abroad, improving it, and negotiating with interested military and/or civilian parties for its further development. In 1906, their US patent application was finally approved. They licensed out the patent rights to companies in France and Germany to manufacture and sell their aircraft. The US Army signed a $25,000 contract with the Wright brothers in 1909.

Meanwhile, in the United States, different entrepreneurs became involved in airplane manufacture, including motorcycle manufacturer Glenn Curtiss, and Alexander Graham Bell, inventor of the telephone. One of their first projects was to build a small glider patterned after the Wright design, based in part on information provided by the Wrights. When Curtiss won a prize with a later aircraft (a contest in which the Wrights had again declined to compete), the brothers reminded Curtiss they had freely shared information with his company. Curtiss could use the patented control system for experimentation, they added, but not the patented features of their machines for exhibitions or for commercial gain. Apparently undeterred, Curtiss further developed his airplane, achieving worldwide fame in 1909 by winning the Gordon Bennett Cup Race and the *Prix de la Vitesse*. His company continued to grow.

After 1908, the Wright brothers became involved in patent lawsuits both in the United States and Europe. In the United States, they sued

Curtiss for using a stabilizing device, the aileron, on his plane, which they insisted was their own patented invention. In France, they sued the flier Henri Farman for patent infringement. In 1912, the brothers suffered a major defeat when a German court ruled that their patent should only be recognized in terms of how it involved the coupling of the rudder and wing warping in simultaneous movement (separate wing warping was judged to be common knowledge), eventually leading the Wrights to give up their presence in Germany.

Further prizes contributed to the development of the international airline industry. In 1919, the London *Daily Mail* offered a prize of £10,000 (worth roughly £300,000 today) to reward the first person to fly non-stop across the Atlantic Ocean. The Australian government offered a similar prize for the first flight from England to Australia, the longest flight ever made. Both were won later that year. The $25,000 Orteig Prize, offered by New York hotel owner Raymond Orteig was for the first non-stop flight between New York and Paris by a pilot flying alone. The response was remarkable. Nine aviator teams spent some $400,000 of their own money to compete. The prize was finally claimed by Charles Lindbergh in 1927. (For further details, see Ackman, 2003, at <www.charleslindbergh.com>, <www.militarymuseum.org>, <www.libraries.wright.edu>, <www.nasm.si.edu/wrightbrothers>, <www.first-to-fly.com>, <www.centennialofflight.gov>).

12.3.2. Human-powered flight

In the mid-20th century, aviation enthusiasts applied their imaginations to another area: human-powered flight. A few small prizes were offered in Germany, Italy and the USSR in the 1930s for achieving this goal, but were never claimed (Carlson, 1997). Two decades later, the English Manpowered Aircraft Group began experimenting on human-powered flight as a hobby. Among the group's members was the head of a company owned by British industrialist Henry Kremer. In 1959, as MacCready recounts the story, during a three-Martini lunch, the man told Kremer that the group's efforts were not progressing very rapidly. So he offered a £50,000 award for the first human-powered aircraft that could fly around a mile-long, figure eight course. The result was a burst of research into human-powered flight (see the 'Paul D. MacCready PhD Interview', at <www.achievement.org>).

After 18 years, the prize was won by an American, Paul MacCready. Observing the flight patterns of hawks and vultures, he had noticed that as a wing grew larger, it required less aerodynamic lift to keep it aloft. A plane capable of winning the Kremer prize, he realized, did not have to be elegant like a sailplane, or even satisfy the structural-safety margin for a regular hang glider (since it only had to fly once). His entry, the 70 pound bicycle-powered *Gossamer Condor*, built of simple light-weight materials (such as Mylar, piano wire, aluminum tubing, and tape), with a 30-metre wingspan, did not even look like a plane. In 1977, it became the first human-powered vehicle to achieve sustained, maneouverable flight.

Kremer then announced a second prize of £100,000 for the first human-powered aircraft to cross the English Channel. To this end, MacCready and his team did not design a new plane, but reshaped the *Condor* to fly on about one-third less power. To finance this venture, MacCready approached the DuPont Company, whose materials they were using – particularly the Mylar skin that covered the plane, and Kevlar (which is by weight five times stronger than steel). In 1979, the *Gossamer Albatross*, piloted by bicycle racer Bryan Allen, successfully made the crossing in 2 hours and 49 minutes at (<www.wikipedia.org>).[1]

Two other participants in this process should be noted here. First, DuPont played a major role in sponsoring MacCready's endeavours. Two leading DuPont products, Mylar and Kevlar, were used for the *Gossamer Albatross*, due to their strength and lightness. But neither was developed specifically in relation to the Kremer prize (Mylar was introduced in 1952, Kevlar in 1971). Both synthetics were trademarked and heavily patented, and are still in wide use today. Kevlar, for example, generates hundreds of millions of dollars of annual sales for the company worldwide at (<www.dupont.com>). So why did DuPont sponsor MacCready's wild scheme? During the flight of the *Gossamer Albatross*, the company's name was featured prominently on the body of the plane. Television exposure generated a stream of favourable publicity.

Also involved was the US space agency NASA. MacCready built a back-up plane for *Gossamer Albatross*, which NASA tested in 1980 as a part of its Langley/Dryden flight research programme. This included tests of the first ever controlled human-powered indoor flights ever made, carried out inside the Houston Astrodome.

12.3.3. Space flight

The $10,000,000 X-prize was announced in 1996 to stimulate the development of reasonably priced, reusable manned rockets capable of taking tourists into space. It would be awarded to the first private company to fly a vehicle 100 kilometres into space and back again, carrying a payload equal to the weight of two passengers – and then repeat the performance within two weeks at (<www.xprize.org>). The name of the prize was later changed to the Ansari X prize, reflecting an injection of further capital into the project.

Twenty-six teams from around the world joined the competition. The entries reflected a plethora of different approaches to solving the problem, thereby underlining a major benefit of the prize system. The *Condox-X*, for example, was designed with a large wing to allow the plane to ascend and descend gently. While it was never constructed due to lack of funding, the team hoped to further develop it to compete in a future contest. A second entry, the *Advent*, powered by a methane-fuelled rocket engine, was being tested in a Texas rice farmer's field, but had to be launched by water for safety reasons. A Romanian team proposed *The Orizont*, which contained an engine, fuelled by hydrogen peroxide. The daVinci Project, based in Ontario, Canada, developed a rocket, *Wild Fire*, fuelled by a combination of liquid oxygen and kerosene, which would be floated into the sky by a piloted, reusable helium balloon (this project, too, was later discontinued). In some of these projects, personnel was composed of engineering students or retired engineers. The Canadian project was built entirely by volunteers, who numbered as many as 500 people (Byko, 2004).

The winning entry, *SpaceShipOne*, was designed by aviation innovator Burt Ratan, working for Scaled Composites, a commercial enterprise. The company was backed by multimillionaire Paul Allen, one of the co-founders of Microsoft, reportedly to the tune of $25 million (Bigelow, 2004). But the company had never built a supersonic plane. In the end, the company chose a two-stage launch system. The rocket would be carried up by a manned jet aircraft, and be released at a height of about 15 kilometres, after which its rocket would fire, propelling the ship vertically into space. The engine used a combination of solid fuel (rubber) that reacted with a liquid oxidizer, nitrous oxide, a technology that dated back to the 1960s (Byco, 2004).

The successful flight of *SpaceShipOne* led to predictions that space tourism could be reality within the next few years. According to press reports, for example, Richard Branson, the founder of Virgin Atlantic Airways, planned to provide regular flights into sub-orbital space, possibly as early as in 2007 (Clash, 2004; Schodolski, 2004). A new corporation, Virgin Galactic, was established to construct the *VSS Enterprise*, a scaled-up version of *SpaceShipOne*, capable of carrying five to nine passengers willing to pay at least $200,000 per ticket. Seven thousand people have already signed up for a Virgin Galactic flight. Another company, SpaceDev, reportedly planned to launch the *Dream Chaser*, ultimately to transport passengers all the way to the International Space

Station. Further efforts were devoted to developing planes that could speed over long distances, such as a half-hour coast-to-coast flight in the United States (Dornheim, 2004a; Schodolski, 2004).

12.4. How important were prizes in stimulating innovation in the aviation industry?

What were the Wright brothers' incentives to invent? The major prizes for flying motorized craft, as noted above, were announced *after* their successful 1903 flight. Initially, the brothers sought to protect their invention through secrecy and patenting, and by negotiating for a military contract. They also appear to have been motivated by the sheer love of invention. Only when potential buyers insisted on public demonstrations did they agree to do so.

With regard to the development of the commercial airline industry, the 1914 outbreak of World War I played a colossal role. Stimulated by government contracts and demands for new aircraft, vast improvements were made in techniques for design and construction. After the war, a large number of aircraft became available at very low prices. Stunt pilots bought them up and entertained the public, maintaining public interest in civilian aviation. In Europe, the first commercial airplane routes were served by wartime pilots flying decommissioned warplanes.

During the 1920s, governments also provided large subsidies to establish national airlines such as the predecessors of British Airways, Air France, and KLM. In the United States, the introduction of airmail service required the establishment of a nationwide airport system. In 1925, the US government began to subsidize private carriers to deliver the mail (and in some cases to carry passengers as well). Among these solo fliers was Charles Lindbergh. The four major US airlines, Pan Am, American Airlines, TWA, and Delta, were founded between 1928 and 1931.

Given the importance of patents, government contracts, and subsidies in the innovation of the airplane, what role did prizes play? Clearly, they contributed to these developments. Thus even if the Wright brothers refused to participate in competitions, they still kept a wary eye out as to what was happening in Europe (and actually did participate in several contests, winning the Michelin Cup in 1908). Lindbergh's successful 1927 flight caught the public imagination, further stimulating the growth of the international commercial airline industry. Later, he carried out survey flights for the development of passenger and airmail routes, and thus at least indirectly contributing to the commercial establishment of the US airline industry.

Like the pioneers of motorized flight, Paul MacCready loved to fly. He had built model planes in his youth, trained as a navy pilot, taken a PhD in aeronautical engineering, and won several hand glider competitions. But 'the sole reason that I got into' competing for the Kremer Prize, by his own account, was financial. He had guaranteed a bank loan for a relative's business, and when it failed, he incurred a $100,000 debt. In 1976, MacCready realized that the Kremer prize, in which he had earlier shown no interest, was just about equal to the debt he owed at (<www.achievement.org>).

After winning the prize, MacCready continued to experiment with aircraft and environmentally friendly technologies. By studying energy storage in batteries charged by the pilot's pedalling, his team learned how to make more efficient use of very limited battery power. This contributed to the development of the electric car.[2] Data from the *Gossamer Albatross* contributed to several high-altitude projects in the United States, such as the Pathfinder. Both the Department of Defense (seeking to develop a remote-controlled craft that could stay aloft for long periods), and NASA (seeking to create an airborne platform to observe the atmosphere), utilized his designs. There was also a small market for Microlite aircraft (tiny two-seater motorized gliders), which built on MacCready's technology.

Finally, what were the incentives to develop passenger space travel? Unlike the other two cases, space travel had, from the beginning, been the province of government agencies. The US space programme was stimulated by the successful orbiting of the Soviet satellite *Sputnik* in 1959. The US government resolved to catch up with the Soviet Union, sending the first American, Alan Shepard, into space in 1961, and landing a man on the Moon in 1969. New goals were then set, motivated again mainly by the political pressures of the Cold War. Many successes were achieved, particularly in the form of pictures transmitted back to earth by craft such as the Hubble telescope. But the NASA programme has been continuously plagued by cost overruns, and together with spectacular failures such as where the entire crew were killed, have forced NASA to scale down and rethink its approach. NASA could also not be expected to devote resources to projects that sent paying passengers into sub-orbital space.

This directly set the stage for Peter Diamandis, founder and chairman of the non-profit X-Prize Foundation. An aspiring astronaut himself, but long frustrated by NASA's bureaucracy, resistance to change and cost overruns (Bigelow, 2004; Byko, 2004), he decided to harness the forces of private enterprise. The designer of the winning entry, Burt Rutan, was 17-years-old when Shepard reached sub-orbital space, inspiring a boyhood dream that lasted throughout his life. *Time Magazine* named it the 'Coolest Invention of 2004' (Taylor, 2004).

The success of the X-Prize has not only stimulated intense activity in the innovation of technologies for space tourism, but also prompted government agencies to establish similar prizes, as a complement to the existing government programs. NASA, for example, plans to offer the Centennial Challenges prizes to stimulate competition for the development of new technologies to solve specified problems, such as a way to gather samples from near-earth asteroids, or the creation of space radiation shields (Byko, 2004; Skeen, 2004).

Prizes can be exercised in such a way as to strengthen existing projects. For example, the Pentagon seems to have realized that prizes can be an effective way to tease forth new, unconventional ideas. The Defense Advanced Research Agency (DARPA) has announced a $2 million prize for the developer of an autonomous robotic vehicle to travel 142 miles across the Mojave Desert, a technology that can supplement the Pentagon's existing projects. Since the Pentagon also funds technology projects directly by way of government contracts, this idea may prove especially appealing to would-be inventors. So far, 31 teams have entered the contest. But there were problems in implementing this prize. Other federal agencies insisted that DARPA conduct environmental studies of the proposed desert route, for example to determine whether it threatened any endangered species. Entrants also found it difficult to get liability insurance to cover their unmanned vehicles.

The same logic can be applied to the private sector. A hotel owner, Robert Bigelow, who hopes to build the world's first habitat in space, has announced a $50 million prize to reward the first American team to launch a five-passenger craft into space, and repeat the feat within 60 days. The winner will also receive the option to provide service to his planned space hotel (Bigelow, 2004; Schodolski, 2004).

Even US states are getting into the act. Following the success of this prize, the X-Prize Foundation announced it would establish an annual event, the X-Prize Cup and Public Spaceflight Exposition, co-sponsored by the state of New Mexico, featuring not only space vehicle contests, but also interactive exhibits of new technology. New Mexico is hoping to become for space tourism what North Carolina, the home of Kitty Hawk, is for motorized flight. In bidding for the X-Prize Cup, it beat out bids from California and Florida (Dornheim, 2004b).

12.5. Concluding remarks

This chapter has investigated how prizes might function as incentives to R&D, the associated benefits and costs, and the problem of contest design. To illustrate our arguments, we investigate the incentive effects of prizes in three contests in the aviation industry over the past one hundred years: motorized flight, human-powered flight, and space flight. In each instance, prizes contributed to the innovation process. But other forms of incentives were important as well, including patents and development contracts, as well as government subsidies, or simply the love of invention. In all three cases, the prime movers were fascinated with flying, along with their backers. Other motivations came into play as well. With regard to motorized flight, for example, sponsor motivations included a desire to spur innovation and reap the reputational advantages (and profit-making opportunities) of being associated with dramatic flying feats.

Prizes can also stimulate innovations in areas outside the aviation industry. Paul MacCready, for example, designed several solar-powered craft, not to win prizes, but to publicize the power of solar energy.[3] The X-Prize, for example, seems to have galvanized interest in contests, which include prizes for the first four-passenger vehicle that can reach 200 miles per gallon of petrol, for a nanoscale machine for assembling molecules, and for vaccines or drugs to treat malaria, tuberculosis, and other diseases (Bigelow, 2004).

We found that the incentive effects of prizes in the aviation industry have been mixed. With regard to motorized flying, for example, it is difficult to judge how much innovation can ultimately be ascribed to prizes. To what extent, for example, would Glenn Curtiss have gone ahead and invested in his airplane business, even if he had not won a prize? Might not the European contestants (and their backers) in the first decade of the 20th century, even without the opportunity to win a prize, have been goaded into action by the Wright brothers' commercial foray into European markets? Alternatively, if the Europeans had concentrated on patenting their technologies rather than winning prizes, might they not have gained a stronger head start? Finally, there can be little doubt that the advent of World War I, along with heavy government support in the establishment of their national carriers in the 1920s, provided the major stimuli to innovative activity in airplane technology – developments which would never had occurred with prizes alone.

With regard to human-powered flight, prizes not only 'kick-started' MacCready's business career, they also inspired numerous innovative activities in related technologies, with various spin-off benefits, as mentioned above. While human-powered flight never spawned a big new industry, it did lead to the development of commercially viable niche markets, not least the electric car. The role of DuPont in the process should also noted. For example, when MacCready later approached DuPont to financially back the invention of a solar-powered plane, the company agreed. In 1983, DuPont itself sponsored a prize for the first human-powered vehicle that could break 65 mph. This was claimed three years later, and itself had a 'spin-off' effect: the winner now manufactures bicycles called Easy Racer Recumbents in California. DuPont has additionally sponsored a prize for human-powered watercraft. Thus in this case, while the prize money was important in stimulating the development of a particular bicycle-powered plane, other interests, such as NASA and DuPont, were important in promoting the wider and further use of the technology.

With regard to the X-Prize, since no government funding was involved, private companies were forced to design entries that not only met the technical demands, but also would appeal to budget-conscious consumers. The X-Prize not only led to the development of the first reusable passenger rocket, it also seems to have kick-started a new industry: space tourism. The price tag of $200,000, as mentioned above, may seem a lot, but it is substantially less than the $20 million American businessman Dennis Tito paied in 2001 to hitch a ride aboard the Russian *Soyuz* ship, which docked with the International Space Station. And following the laws of supply and demand, this price tag is expected to come down. The X-Prize also stimulated a spate of inventive activities in related areas, inspired government agencies to set their own prizes, and even brought individual states into the fray. Thus the incentive effects of the X-Prize arguably built on the imperfections of the earlier government incentive system, but had very strong direct effects on innovation. Clearly, however, only the future can tell if these plans are realized in practice.

Notes

1   During the ensuing years, Kremer and the Royal Aeronautical Society sponsored several prizes. One, offered in 1979 and worth £10,000, was specifically targeted to reward the first non-US citizen to fly the figure-of-eight course (won in 1984 by Gunter Rochelt). Mainly, these prizes aimed at rewarding new speed records, and inducing the development of smaller, more manoeverable, more practical craft, to give the sport wider appeal.

2   In 1981, his *Solar Challenger* flew 163 miles from Paris to Canterbury, England, reaching an altitude of 11,000 feet. MacCready's Bionic Bat (short for battery)

was awarded another Kremer Prize for human-powered air speed. MacCready's high-performance solar-powered *Sunraycer*, a lightweight aerodynamic vehicle using techniques of airplane composite construction, won a race across Australia in 1987. In 1990, a co-operation with General Motors produced the Impact, a battery-powered electric car that could accelerate from zero to 60 mph in eight seconds. Other prizes were offered for innovation in human-powered transport. In August 2000, MacCready's solar powered aircraft Helios, built by his company AeroVironment, reached an altitude of 96,000 feet, breaking the high altitude record for an airplane at (<www.achievement.org>).

Bibliography

Arrow, K. (1962), 'Economic Welfare and the Allocation of Resources for innovation', in R. Nelson (ed.), *The Rate and Direction of Inventive Activity: Economic and Social Factors* (Princeton, NJ: NBER/Princeton University Press).

Bigelow, B. (2004), 'Grand prizes', *The San Diego Union-Tribune*, 21 Nov.

Byko, M. (2004), 'SpaceShipOne, the Ansari X prize, and the materials of the civilian space race', *JOM* (Journal of Metals), 56(11), Nov., pp. 24–8.

Carlson, S. (1997), 'The Lure of Icarus', *Scientific American*, Available at <www.unb.ca/web/transpo/mynet/1097carlson.html>, Oct.

Chiesa, G. & Denicolo, V. (1999), 'Patents Prizes and Optimal Innovation Policy' mimeo, University of Bologna, paper presented to the XII World Congress of the International Economics Association, available at <www.aaep.org.ar/12worldcongress/congress/papers/pdf_99/chiesa_denicolo.pdf>, Aug.

Clash, J.M. (2004), 'Fly me to the moon', *Forbes*, 174(10), 14 Nov., p. 218.

Cohen, W.M., Nelson, R.R. & Walsh, J.P. (2000), *Protecting Their Intellectual Assets: Appropriability Conditions and Why US Manufacturing Firms Patent (or Not)* (Cambridge, Ma: NBER; Working Paper No. 7552).

Davis, L. & Davis, J. (2004), 'How effective are prizes as incentives to innovation? Evidence from three 20th century contest' (paper presented to the innovation conference at Roskilde University, *Management of innovation – are we looking at the 'right things'?*), 4–5 June.

Davis, L.N. (2004), 'Intellectual property rights, strategy and policy', *Economics of Innovation and New Technology*, 13(6–7), pp. 1–17.

De Laat, E.A.A. (1996), 'Patents or prizes: Monopolistic R&D and asymmetric information', *International Journal of Industrial Organization*, 15, pp. 369–90.

Dornheim, M.A. (2004a), 'Trials of SS1', *Aviation Week & Space Technology*, 161(15), 18 Oct., p. 36.

Dornheim, M.A. (2004b), 'SpaceShipWon', *Aviation Week & Space Technology*, 161(14), 11 Oct., p. 34.

Gallini, N. & Scotchmer, S. (2002), 'Intellectual Property: When Is It The Best Incentive System?', *Economics Working Paper*, Archives at WUSTL, Law & Economics Series 0201001.

Horrobin, D.F. (1986), 'Glittering prizes for research support', *Nature*, 324, p. 221.

International Institute for Energy Conservation (IIEC) (2004), *Super Efficient Refrigerator Program, Profile Number 106*, Washington, DC, available at <http://sol.crest.org/efficiency/irt/106.pdf>, 16 Jan.).

Katz, M.L. & Ordover, J.A. (1990), 'R&D Cooperation and Competition', *Brookings Papers: Microeconomics*, pp. 137–203.

Klette, T., Moen, J. & Grilliches, Z. (2000), 'Do subsidies to commercial R&D reduce market failures? Microeconomic evaluation studies', *Research Policy*, 29, pp. 471–95.

Kremer, M. (1998), 'Patent Buy-outs: A Mechanism for Encouraging Innovation', *Quarterly Journal of Economics*, 113, pp. 1137–67.

Kremer, M. (2000), 'Creating Markets for New Vaccines. Part II: Design Issues', *NBER Working Paper* No. 7717 (Cambridge, MA: NBER).

Kremer, M. & Zwane, A.P. (2002), *Encouraging Technical Progress in Tropical Agriculture* (Cambridge, MA and Berkeley, CA: Harvard University/NBER/ Brookings Institution and University of California, Department of Agriculture and Resource Economics, available at <http://are.berkeley.edu/course/envres_ seminar/zwane.pdf>, 5 Aug.).

Llobet, G., Hopenhayn, H. & Mitchell, M. (2000), 'Rewarding Sequential Innovators: Prizes, Patents and Buyouts' (Federal Reserve Bank of Minneapolis, Research Department Staff Report 273, July).

Masters, W.A. (2003), 'Research prizes: a mechanism for innovation in African agriculture', paper presented to the 7th International ICABR Conference on Public Goods and Public Policy for Agricultural Biotechnology in Ravello, Italy, 29 June, available at <www.agecon.purdue.edu/staff/masters>.

National Academy of Sciences (2000), Concerning Federally Sponsored Inducement Prizes in Engineering & Science, available at <www.nap.edu/ books/NI000221/html/1.html>.

Nelson, R. (1959), 'The Simple Economics of Basic Scientific Research,' *Journal of Political Economy*, 67(3), pp. 297–306.

Polanvyi, M. (1943), 'Patent reform', *Review of Economic Studies*, 11(1), pp. 61–76.

Schodolski, V.J. (2004), 'Success of private spacecraft suggests future of space tourism is looking up', *Knight Ridder Tribune Business News*, 1 Nov.

Shavell, S. & van Ypersele, T. (2001), 'Rewards Versus Intellectual Property Rights', *Journal of Law and Economics*, part 1, 44(2), pp. 525–47.

Skeen, J. (2004), 'NASA seeks a new pool of talent', *Knight Ridder Tribune Business News*, 29 Nov.

Taylor, C. (2004), 'The sky's the limit', *Time*, issue 22, 29 Nov., pp. 64–7.

Williamson, O. (1983), 'Credible commitments: using hostages to support exchange', *American Economic Review*, 72(3), pp. 519–40.

Wright, B.D. (1983), 'The economics of invention incentives: patents, prizes, and research contracts', *American Economic Review*, 73, pp. 691–707.

Websites

Academy of Achievement. Interview with Paul MacCready, 12 January 1991, available at <http://www.achievement.org/autodoc/page/mac0int-1>, accessed 21 Jan. 2004.

Ackman, Dan (2003), 'How the world discovered the Wright brothers', available at <http://www.forbes.com/work/entrepreneurs/2003/11/18/cx_da_1118wrights. html>, accessed 16 Jan. 2004.

'Charles Lindbergh: An American aviator', available at <http://www.charles lindbergh.com/history/paris.asp>, accessed 15 Jan. 2004.

Denger, M.J., 'California Aviation History. Domingues International Air Meet', available at <http://www.militarymuseum.org/Dominguez.html>, accessed 16 Jan. 2004.

DuPont Corporation home page, <www.dupont.com>.

'Paul D. MacCready, Ph.D, Interview', available at <www.achievement.org>, accessed 2 Dec. 2004.

Penn, C. (1993), 'Super-efficient refrigerator finalists', *Home Energy Magazine Online* March–April, available at <http://homeenergy.org/archive/hem.dis.anl.gov/eehem/93/930305.html>, accessed 19 Jan. 2004.

The Prize Patrol, 'Wright Bros. Aeroplane Co.', available at <http://www.first-to-fly.com/History/Wright%20Story/prizepatrol.htm>, accessed 15 Jan. 2004.

Smithsonian Institution, National Air and Space Museum, 'The Wright Brothers: The Invention of the aerial age', available at <http://www.nasm.si.edu/wright-brothers/age>, accessed 14 Jan. 2004.

Syon, Guillaume de (2001), 'Faded memories: the Wright brothers and Germany, 1909–1913', Symposium Papers, Following the Footsteps of the Wright Brothers (Dayton, OH: Wayne State University), available at <http://www.libraries.wright.edu/special/symposium/deSyon.html>, accessed 14 Jan. 2004.

US Centennial of Flight Commission, various sites, available at <http://www.centennialofflight.gov/essay/Wright_Bros/Patent_Battles/WR12.htm>, accessed 14 Jan. 2004.

Wikipedia. 'Gossamer Albatross', available at <http://en.wikipedia.org/wiki/Gossamer_Albatross>, accessed 19 Jan. 2004.

'X Prize' (2004), available at <www.x-prize.com>, accessed 26 Jan. 2004.

13
Patent Policies of Small Danish Firms in Three Industries

Lee Davis

13.1. Introduction

Empirical surveys of the economic effects of patents have uncovered striking industry differences in patent effectiveness and importance (e.g., Cohen *et al.*, 2000; Harabi, 1995; Bertin & Wyatt, 1988; Levin *et al.*, 1987). Other studies have focused specifically on the role of patents in high-tech sectors. In telecommunications, for example, firms typically cross-license their inventions, using patents as a kind of bargaining tool or trading currency to secure appropriability (e.g., Grindley & Teece, 1997; Hall & Ham, 1999). The software industry is interesting because the nature of digital technology renders appropriability difficult (e.g., Conner & Rumelt, 1991; Davis, 2002; Shapiro & Varian, 1999). Initially, copyrights were used to protect software innovations; only since the 1980s has it been possible to patent them. In pharmaceuticals, chemicals, and biotechnology, by contrast, patents are widely recognized as both important and effective in securing appropriability (e.g., Arora, 1997; Liebeskind *et al.*, 1996; Merges & Nelson, 1994).

Yet this research mainly reports on findings from surveys of large firms, primarily American firms and/or multinational enterprises. While occasional reference is made to the patenting policies of small firms, they are never systematically analyzed. Other scholars have investigated the innovative strategies of small firms more generally, and how they differ from large firms (e.g., Audretsch, 2002; Lefebvre & Lefebvre, 1993; Lindman, 2002). Yet little attention has been paid to how small firms use patents strategically.

To elucidate these issues, we interviewed patent experts in 34 small Danish firms in three sectors: telecommunications, software, and biotechnology. For each sector, we investigated their attitudes towards patents, why they apply for patents (and why not), and how they attempt to leverage patents strategically. We wished to determine whether there was industry differences as regards how small firms use patents. In the following, section 13.2 briefly surveys the relevant literature, and section 13.3 presents the empirical data collected for analysis in this chapter. Section 13.4 investigates the role of patents in the three industries. The conclusions are in section 13.5.

13.2. Theoretical background

Economic analysis of the patent system has mainly explored the implication of patents for social welfare (e.g., Arrow, 1962; Besen & Raskind, 1991; Kitch, 1977; Nelson, 1959; Scotchmer, 1991). Other scholars have analyzed the strategic role of patents at the level of the individual firm (Rivette & Kline, 2000a/b; Sakakibara, 2001) or sector (e.g., Bessen & Hunt, 2003; Hall & Ham, 1999), along with empirical surveys of the comparative importance of patents as a strategy of appropriability (e.g., Bertin & Wyatt, 1988; Cohen *et al.*, 2000; Harabi, 1995; Kingston, 2001; Levin *et al.*, 1987). Based on these studies, it is possible to identify distinct patterns in patent effectiveness and importance in different sectors. In particular, empirical surveys of firm choices of appropriability strategies have emphasized the importance of patent protection for pharmaceuticals. In other sectors, patents have generally been found to be less effective than alternative appropriation mechanisms such as secrecy, lead-time, and complementary assets. As mentioned earlier, however, these analyses typically focus on large firms, and with the exception of Harabi (1995), mainly US firms.

Other contributors have examined the reasons why firms apply for patents – and why not (e.g., Arundel, 2001; Bertin & Wyatt, 1988; Cohen *et al.*, 2000; Glazier, 1995; Harabi, 1995; Kingston, 2001; Levin *et al.*, 1987; Mansfield *et al.*, 1981; Oppenlaender, 1977; Pooley & Bratic, 1999; see also Davis, 2005, for a systematization and further discussion of these motivations). The classic reason to take out patents is to prevent competitors from imitating the innovator's new products and processes. A variation of this motivation is to use patents more aggressively to block rivals in their development activities. Patents may serve as the legal basis for license agreements, either to earn royalties or to obtain a strong patent portfolio to strengthen the firm's position in license negotiations. Patents can signal that the technology is protected, or strengthen the firm's negotiation position in connection with a possible patent dispute (a company may use its own patent holdings to threaten, or defend against a suit brought by another firm, forcing that firm to settle, and preventing a court case). Finally, the patent provides a means to indicate value, notably to attract capital from external investors. Otherwise it may be difficult to measure the value of a company whose primary assets are intangible.

But there can be good reasons *not* to apply for a patent. The product or process may not fulfil the criteria of patentability (to be patented, the invention must be novel, industrially useful, and non-obvious). The costs of applying for and maintaining the patent may be too high. Because patented inventions must also be published, the firm may be concerned about revealing too much information in the patent application. Competitors may actively use this information to 'invent around' the original invention. Problems can arise in relation to detecting and pursuing infringers. Further, the firm might believe that the technology is developing so rapidly that patents are irrelevant. Finally, other means to appropriate the rents from research and development (R&D) investments may be preferred. Again, it should be stressed, these findings are primarily based on surveys of large firms.

As mentioned earlier, this chapter focuses on the strategic use of patents in three industries: telecommunications, software, and biotechnology. *Telecommunications* refers to the long-distance communication of information by text, sound, images or data, or some combination, via cables or other electromagnetic systems that connect a transmitter and one or more receivers. *Software* may be generally defined as a set of computer programs and associated procedures and documents supporting the operation of a data-processing system. *Biotechnology* is concerned with the use of molecular technologies to develop new products and processes for use in the production of pharmaceuticals, food, diagnostic tools, and other goods.

Telecommunications are an example of a "cumulative systems" technology, where development cannot proceed unless firms give each other access to their innovations. Several studies have investigated the strategic use of patents in telecommunications (e.g., Bekkers *et al.*, 2002; Grindley & Teece, 1997; Hall & Ham, 1999). Typically, firms patent their inventions and then cross-license them to each other. The purpose of patents is thus not so much to exclude others as to control and facilitate the terms of access.[1] As a general rule, a firm's patent portfolio is worth most when it contains patents of high quality which other firms find important to their own operations.

In the Cohen *et al.* (2000) study of why US manufacturing firms take out patents (and why not), of the ten firms that received the most patents in 1998, nine worked in the area of electronics. Respondents noted that the main purpose of these patents was to keep from being blocked, or to build up a strong patent portfolio to strengthen their position in cross-licensing negotiations. The use of patents to force access was especially important for large firms. Only sparse attention was paid, in these studies, to the patent strategies of small firms. One intriguing insight, from Grindley and Teece (1997), is that small firms in niche markets can potentially leverage their patents strategically just as effectively as large firms – as long as others regard their patents as valuable.

The software industry differs from other industries in its origins and 'spirit'. Most of the early programmers, both in academics and corporate laboratories, gave others free access to their codes and modifications. Computer scientists and engineers have often opposed the movement towards more proprietary software. Firms seeking to profit from investments in R&D in software face numerous challenges. Unprotected digital information goods can be copied at virtually zero marginal costs, and the copies are of the same quality as the original (Shapiro & Varian, 1999).

According to von Krogh and von Hippel (2003), there are two main ways to appropriate profits from 'packaged' software products. One is to use licensing arrangements based on copyright law (see, e.g., Dam, 1995; Granstrand, 1999). Such a license usually sets restrictions on the number of computers on which the software can run, the number of software users, and backup terms. The second is to try to keep the source code secret.[2] Because of the relative weakness of copyright law, which protects only the expression of the idea, not the invention itself, large software firms have pressed for an extension of patent protection to cover more and more aspects of software technology. It is currently easier to obtain patent protection for software innovations in the United States than it is in Europe, due to different definitions of what is patentable. While software programs are used in a variety of industries (see, e.g., Bessen & Hunt, 2003; Kaiser & Roende, 2004), our survey was limited to the patenting behaviour of firms within the software industry *per se*.

In biotechnology, patents play a central role in product development (Liebeskind *et al.*, 1996). To sustain competitive advantage, small new biotech firms (NBFs) must engage in continuous innovation that generates patentable products, which can be sold to a larger firm. The product development process is characterized by a high degree of uncertainty. The new product or process may not be as technologically valuable as originally expected. Rival inventions may render the firm's own inventions, and possibly even whole research programme, obsolete.

New biotech firms may find it necessary to "race" to be the first to patent a new idea for a drug, but since the patenting process is expensive, they may not be able to recover these costs. But due to the high mobility of scientists, patents can play an important role in providing firms with the legal basis on which to protect the knowledge they generate.

In this chapter, interest is retricted to pharmaceutical-related biotechnology. The drug development process is not only immensely costly and risky, but profits from successful drugs must also cover the development costs of all the other candidates for new drugs that failed, due to problems of cost-effectiveness, safety or efficacy. The drug companies are also under pressure from generic producers, who sell copies of off-patent drugs at a price that does not have to reflect the initial costs and risks of innovation. For these reasons, pharmaceutical companies will only consider the commercial development of products with strong patent protection, ensuring not only that the innovator has carved out a well-defined, defensible position on the market, but also that it will not be subject to a future infringement suit.

13.3. Empirical data

To participate in the survey, firms had to satisfy four criteria: they had to employ less than 250 people, be located in the greater Copenhagen area (postal areas 1000–4000), possessed the industry code for one of the three industries investigated, and engaged R&D. To identify relevant firms, we consulted the database built by the Danish Business World's Information Bureau (*Købmandstandens Oplysningsbureau*). After listing the firms that fulfilled the first three criteria, we accessed their home pages, in order to include only those that stated that they performed R&D. The result was a population of 93 firms: 22 in telecommunications, 35 in software, and 36 in biotechnology.

We wrote letters to each of these firms, describing the purpose of the study and the questions we wished to ask, and followed up by telephone calls. In the end, 34 firms agreed to be part of our investigation, giving a response rate of 36.6 per cent. Of these, seven were in telecommunications (31.8 per cent of the firms we contacted), nine were in software (25.7 per cent), and 18 in biotechnology (50 per cent). We asked to speak with the firm's chief executive officer or the person in charge of patenting. It was up to the firm itself to specify whom our informant would be. The interviews took place between spring 2002 and spring 2003.

The questions were semi-structured. First, we asked our respondents a series of general questions about their use and view of patents, and how patents fit into their larger business strategy. We then requested them to indicate, on a standardized questionnaire form, how they would rate different possible reasons why they took out patents, and why not, on a scale of one to five. In the interviews, we provided extra time for our informants to go into depth, as we sought to capture the complexities of the factors that underlay firm choices.

13.4. Results of the empirical study

13.4.1. Telecommunications

Generally, our telecommunications respondents were well informed about the advantages and disadvantages of patents, and found them a useful strategic tool. They primarily applied for patents to strengthen their position in connection with license negotiations, to protect against imitation, block competitors, and as strategic signals. In some cases, there was strong disagreement about the benefit of a particular approach. Half of our seven telecommunications respondents, for example, found patents highly important to block competitors in their development activities: the others disagreed, noting that this was highly difficult for small firms to do in practice. A number of respondents stressed that a main benefit of patenting that was not included in our questionnaire was to ensure that others did not block them. 'You can't be a player without patents', exclaimed one, 'even if there is nothing really worth protecting!'.

Some of our informants, like their larger counterparts, described in the literature (see section 13.2), actively cross-licensed their patents. While they could not 'blanket' a technological area with patents in the same way as large firms, some respondents still seemed able to leverage their niche market patents successfully enough to engage in cross-licensing negotiations with the larger players. But others said they were too small to do this. One said that there were so few firms in the market they served that the result of cross-licensing among them was the creation of entry barriers so high that no new firms could come in.

Several noted that there were so many patents in their area, which often overlapped with each other, and in certain cases covered already known technologies, that cross-licensing did not even seem necessary. They reasoned that only where the patent covered a technology with a large market would an infringement lead to a lawsuit. Clearly, this is a risky strategy, since a lawsuit might well be ruinous, but apparently they 'gambled' (like larger firms they said they had heard about) that the risk was worth bearing.

Patents were important as signals for several reasons. 'There's lot of psychology involved here!' as one expressed it. Applying for a patent put others on notice to 'stay away' from the area. But this respondent also noted that if they became aware of another firm's patent application in an area into which they were considering going, this would also make them choose another direction. Patents could be valuable indicators of value to customers and investors – 'so they can be sure we can produce what we promised'. A fourth emphasized that they really needed to have the prospect of large sales before they would consider patenting, since patenting was very expensive.

According to the literature, the most important methods to secure appropriability in this industry are not patents, but secrecy, lead time, and manufacturing or design capabilities (e.g., Cohen *et al.*, 2000; Hall & Ham, 1999). Many respondents stressed the advantages of keeping the invention secret, which avoided the costs of applying for and enforcing patents. As one respondent put it: 'If we have customers or press visiting, we usually "clean up" for several hours beforehand'. These firms recognized there was a risk that their employees might disclose the proprietary information – but as one remarked, there was a greater risk that competitors would copy it. Some respondents, however, did not use secrecy. One argued that it was important for them to get input from customers, rendering secrecy impractical.

Even though the technology was changing rapidly, this was not seen as a reason not to patent. The firm could not just change production methods overnight. Nor were the costs of the application procedure seen as a reason not to patent. Most motivations not to patent specifically concerned process inventions. In particular, it was almost impossible to prove that a competitor was imitating a process patent. One respondent stated that they knew a rival firm had patented something they themselves had used for years – but could not prove it. Eventually they were able to demonstrate that the information had been published somewhere else, rendering the rival firm's patent invalid.

While our respondents generally found patents important, they also realized that certain patent strategies were not available to them, given their limited resources. The major reasons not to patent, apart from the opportunity to use secrecy, included concerns that competitors would invent around their patents, and the costs of detecting infringements, particularly for process patents.

Again, attitudes could vary widely. Three of the telecommunications respondents, for example, felt that difficulties of pursuing patent infringers were of critical importance. The remaining four felt it was not at all a problem. Among those that were unconcerned, one noted that they were not particularly worried about ending up in a lawsuit, since the area in which they worked was so complex that infringement 'was almost inevitable'! Another exclaimed fatalistically, 'We can't afford to sue a large corporation, it would be all their lawyers against our one lawyer'.

13.4.2. Software

In our survey of small Danish software firms, respondents had little that was positive to say about patents. Unlike larger firms in this industry, most did not even consider using patents. Some were ideologically opposed to patents, feeling that they harmed innovation more than they promoted it. Some simply felt the costs did not justify the benefits. As a group, they seemed basically unaware of the strategic opportunities embodied in the patent system, or the risks they ran in not ensuring patent protection. We did not get the same sense that this was a calculated risk, as with our telecommunications respondents, but that it was grounded more in their negative view of patents more generally. One respondent admitted that he did not know what it cost to apply for a patent, although he guessed it would be expensive – whatever the case, he did not care!

Some only agreed to see us if we accepted, from the start, that they viewed patents as completely irrelevant for their needs. Many emphasized that the patent application procedure was long, difficult and expensive, draining resources (time and money and employees) from more important purposes. In stark contrast to our respondents in telecommunications (and, biotechnology), seven of the nine firms we interviewed did not take out patents. Three never considered doing so, and four chose not to do so. Only two firms found patents a valuable accessory to business strategy. The first used patents occasionally, but was more focused on price, time, and problems with detecting infringements. Only the second had a well-developed patent strategy.

The main reasons they applied for patents were for strategic signalling, and to prevent imitation. But most qualified their remarks. Patents were valuable as signals, noted our respondent with the well-developed patent policy, but in relation to customers, potential partners and investors – not competitors. Another doubted that this signalling function would even work; other firms would find a way around the patent. Rarely did software firms use blocking patents, either because they felt they would not work, or on moral grounds. Many asserted that while patents might in theory help to prevent imitation, infringements would be so difficult to prove as to make it not worth the effort.

Two main reasons not to take out patents were emphasized. The first concerned the nature of the technology. Many respondents asserted their inventions were not new or different enough from existing technologies to fulfil the criteria of patentability. As one put it, the concept they used was relatively easy to develop, and thus others could do so, too. Another said that their technology was very specialized, and that others would not be able to imitate it anyway, rendering patent protection superfluous. Most opined as well that the technology was developing so rapidly that patents were irrelevant. The most important factor for success in this industry, they stressed, was to be on the forefront of technological developments, bringing new products quickly to market, and flexibly responding to consumer needs.

The second common set of complaints concerned the costs of applying for and enforcing patent rights. The patent application process was typically seen as expensive, long, and overly bureaucratic. It was difficult (if not impossible) to find out whether or not a patent was being infringed. Problems of pursuing patent infringers, one claimed, 'scares us away' from patenting. A second pointed out that at the moment, their competitors were not using patents. If this changed, the firm would consider patenting as well.

Most of our software respondents also used some form of secrecy, either alone or in combination with patents. Typically they tried to keep the source codes secret, protected by encryption and related measures. This was preferable to patenting, which required the publication of the details of the invention. But our informants also recognized that it was not always possible to ensure that the code would not be broken.

The most prevalent form of intellectual property used in this industry was copyrights. One of our respondents insisted that while they never had problems with other firms' patents, they did run into license rights, when they wanted to use or incorporate some of the copyrighted programming covered, and to download it from the Internet. In addition, both lead time and continuous product development to keep ahead of competitors were deemed important and effective alternative appropriation mechanisms. In particular, our respondents stressed the importance of the need to deliver a good product to customers, and to cultivate strong, lasting customer relationships, tailoring their products to customer needs. Some also mentioned the value of trademarks, particularly as a guarantee of quality, and in marketing. In addition, providing reliable service was paramount, and service contracts were seen as a key alternative means of earning rents.

13.4.3. Biotechnology

In our survey of biotech firms, there was uniform agreement that patents represented the only effective means of protection, and were essential to their innovative activities. All functioned as specialized suppliers to the large pharmaceutical firms, with the result that they had no choice but to patent. Unlike our respondents in telecommunications and software, these firms typically did not feel that small size affected their incentives to take out patents. On the contrary, our respondents indicated not only a considerable knowledge of patents, but also an extensive experience in leveraging patents strategically.

For these firms, patents played a key and effective role in preventing imitation. While some of our respondents leveraged their patent holdings to block competitors in their development activities, others found the practice reprehensible. Patents were also important to provide the legal basis for cooperation and increased the likelihood of cooperation. Most agreed that license royalties were a vital source of long-term income (although some stated that it was not a prime reason to take out patents, but more a luxury or a side benefit). Many stressed the importance of building up a strong patent portfolio to strengthen their position in license negotiations. And while 'strategic' cross-licensing is normally associated with the electronics industry, some of our respondents also gave examples of this. One described how patents could 'cross-lock' each other. If a firm needed access to another firm's patent, it could agree to cooperate, or they could simply mutually freeze out each other!

The signalling role of patents was frequently emphasized, not only to warn off potential competitors, but also (similarly to respondents in the other two industries) to attract the interest of customers and potential business partners. To a certain degree, the patent could also be used to 'scare off' competitors. Our respondents declared that applying for a patent showed that the firm was seriously committed to a particular line of research. It was a way to get one's name in the databases, where others searched to find out who was doing what. This could alert other firms who might be interested in cooperating. Applying for a patent, in fact, could be just as good a signal as receiving one (not least for marketing purposes). Finally, virtually all of our biotech firms emphasized the importance of patents as a means to obtain finance. Investors, partners, and customers had to be confident that the company would not suddenly have to stop producing the good, because another firm held the patent rights.

In contrast to our software firms, biotech respondents essentially dismissed the potential disadvantages of patenting. A common remark was that whatever the disadvantage, this was not a reason not to patent! Unlike software firms, again, most of our biotech respondents seemed confident that most of their inventions were, in fact, patentable. There were some exceptions. One noted that they might make incremental improvements, as when scaling up the technology that was not patentable. These were preserved instead as know-how, to be passed on to the firm that bought or licensed the rights to the invention. Many of the potential costs of patenting experienced later in the development process, like renewal fees, pursuing infringers, possible litigation, and the like, were not a concern to them, as by then they would have sold or licensed the rights to a larger firm.

Our questions about infringements elicited some intriguing responses. There seemed to be basic agreement that since it was relatively easy to describe the invention in the patent, it was also relatively easy to detect infringers – at least for products. Some insisted problems of detecting infringements kept them from patenting processes, while others insisted that this was not a reason not to patent. But basically, our biotech firms did not seem much worried about infringements. As one expressed it, by then it would be in the hands of a larger firm, and 'this is a game for the big boys'. Another said the decision to pursue infringers depended on the importance of the patent. A third contended that since people in the sector knew each other, word would probably get around if someone were infringing another's patent. But another noted that even if you knew who was doing it, it could be hard to prove it.

Our respondents generally agreed that firms did respect each other's patents. Several noted that lawsuits were not only costly, they were also bad for your reputation. One declared that when they realized their own patent had been infringed, they contacted the infringer and negotiated a license agreement, enabling royalty payments to be made. Another described how one advantage of presenting research to another firm was that they were less likely to try and steal it. If a big pharmaceuticals company cheats a small firm, it would get around and hurt their reputation. Companies respected each other's patents mainly because they did not want to risk lawsuits and accusations of infringements.

Finally, and again in contrast to firms in the two other industries, our respondents did not believe that alternative strategies of appropriability were particularly useful. Perhaps these strategies could serve as complements to patents – but never as replacements. Several respondents mentioned the value of trademarks, as part of their 'branding' strategy, to signal reputation. Lead time was not practical for inventions with long development times, subjected to extensive testing and government approval. Complementary sales and marketing capabilities did not matter since by the time the product was marketed, it had been taken over (or at least supported by) a larger firm.

Similarly, they did not view secrecy as a generally feasible means to appropriate rents. In clinical tests, and during the government approval process, they noted, details about both the product and the processes used had to be revealed anyway. Some details of the processes used might be kept secret. Yet this was risky, because if competitors learned about the secret, they could take out their own patent, blocking the first firm from further developing it.

13.5. Concluding remarks

In surveying how small Danish firms use and view patents in three high-tech sectors, distinct industry differences emerged. Our telecommunications firms often protected their inventions by a combination of patents, secrecy, and tacit knowledge related to the production process. Most of our software firms, operating in narrowly defined niches, mainly allocated their resources to building close customer relations, preferring to appropriate rents by providing upgrades and better service (along with keeping the source code secret). Our biotech informants found patents essential to prevent imitation and create value. They were consistently more pro-active in their use of patents than software firms, several of whom declared that patents were completely irrelevant to their needs. Respondents in telecommunications adopted the most 'neutral' view, appreciating the benefits of patents while acknowledging the problems.

Several reasons may be advanced to explain these differences in small firms' approaches to patents. One concerns the nature of the technology. Some inventions, particularly in pharmaceuticals, chemicals, and relatively simple objects, can be precisely described in the patent application, showing how the invention fulfils the criteria of patentability, while others cannot. This clearly enhances the use of patents in biotechnology, but not necessarily in the other two industries. In addition, the cumulative nature of telecommunications technology demanded cross-licensing; in the other two industries, licenses were mainly used as a source of income.

Also of importance was the firm's placement along the value chain. All of the biotechnology firms studied functioned as suppliers to the large pharmaceutical firms, whereas the respondents in telecommunications and software typically both created and commercially developed their inventions.

A third reason concerns market structure. Entry barriers are higher in biotechnology and telecommunications than in software, where an individual or small group of individuals can start up an enterprise, with only a computer and Internet access.

Fourth, we found that ownership structure might influence patent choices. Some of the firms in our sample were owned by larger firms, some were not. Those in the former category stated that they had to follow the patent policies laid down by their owners, whereas others were more independent. They also felt less vulnerable in the use of patents, since their owner could back them up if necessary.

A fifth reason has to do with the degree of internationalization of the firm's activities. Both our biotech firms and our telecom firms took a global approach to business strategy. Their business partners could be located anywhere around the world. Our software firms typically confined their operations to the Danish market.

Finally, previous experience with patents mattered. Many employees in the biotech firms had previous worked in larger pharmaceutical firms, where patents have traditionally been seen as critical. Thus their patent experiences extended further back in time, and were not necessarily dependent on their current job. In software, by contrast, our respondents typically had no prior experience with patenting.

By understanding what patterns tend to prevail in the three industries with regard to small high-tech firms' use of patents, managers and patent experts can gain new insights into how best to leverage their own patents strategically, and how patents can contribute to the firm's larger competitive strategy. Despite their resource constraints, we found, many small firms were able to leverage their patents effectively, and had developed context-specific strategies that worked for them (for further details, see Davis, 2005). Our findings may also be useful to policy-makers. Even though the criteria for patentability are the same for every invention, the economic impact of the individual patent can vary greatly, both for the firm that owns the patent rights, and the industry in which the firm operates. Any contemplated changes in patent legislation could be informed by a closer understanding of these differences.

Acknowledgements

This chapter is based on a paper that was presented at the Research Workshop, 'Management of Innovation – Are We Looking at the Right

Things?', Vedbaek, Denmark, 7–8 June 2004. I would like to thank Birgitte Andersen, Benjamin Coriat, and Naubahar Sharif for useful feedback on an earlier draft of this work. Special thanks are extended to my research assistant, Kirsten Kjaer MSc in Economics and Business Administration, Copenhagen Business School, for her extensive help as my research assistant in gathering the data, carrying out the interviews, and helping with the initial analysis of the data.

Notes

1 Hall and Ham (1999), for example, discuss the 'patent paradox' in the semiconductor industry – the striking gap between the relative ineffectiveness of patents as demonstrated by the surveys by Cohen *et al.* (2000) and Levin *et al.* (1987), and their widespread use. Both the number of patents in the semiconductor industry, and the propensity to patent, they note, has risen sharply in the past few decades. This does not reflect increased interest in securing exclusive rights, but to enable the firms strengthen their position in 'patent and portfolio' races to reduce the possibility of being held up by external patent owners, to facilitate better terms of access to external technologies. Firms founded after 1982 patent more extensively than pre-1982 entrants. Patent rights were especially critical to these firms in attracting venture capital and securing proprietary rights in niche markets.
2 The source code consists of a series of instructions telling the computer how to operate to carry out the objective of the program. In order to operate a computer, a program must be converted (the source code is translated into machine code using a compiler). This process generates a version of the program in binary code, which is very difficult for programmers to read and interpret. Thus to keep others from understanding and modifying their code, programmers or firms release only binary versions of the software. See von Krogh and von Hippel (2003, p. 1150).

Bibliography

Andersen, B. (ed.) (2005), *Intellectual Property Rights: Innovation, Governance and the Institutional Environment* (Cheltenham: Edward Elgar).
Arora, A. (1997), 'Patents, licensing, and market structure in the chemical industry', *Research Policy*, 26, pp. 391–403.
Arrow, K.A. (1962), 'Economic welfare and the allocation of resources for invention', *The Rate and Direction of Inventive Activity: Economic and Social Factors*, Conference no. 13 (Princeton, NJ: NBER/Princeton University Press).
Arundel, A. (2001), 'The relative effectiveness of patents and secrecy for appropriation', *Research Policy*, 30, pp. 611–24.
Audretsch, D.B. (2002), 'The dynamic role of small firms: evidence from the US', *Small Business Economics*, Feb.–May, 18(1–3), pp. 13–40.
Bekkers, R., Buysters, G. & Verspagen, B. (2002), 'Intellectual property rights, strategic technology agreements and market structure: The case of GSM', *Research Policy*, 31, pp. 1141–61.

Bertin, G.Y. & Wyatt, S. (1988), *Multinationals and Industrial Property: The Control of the World's Technology* (Hemel Hempstead: Harvester Wheatsheaf).

Besen, S.M. & Raskind, L.J. (1991), 'An introduction to the law and economics of intellectual property'. *Journal of Economic Perspectives*, winter, 5(1), pp. 3–27.

Bessen, J. & Hunt, R.M. (2003), 'An Empirical Look at Software Patents', *Working Paper*, no. 03–17, Federal Reserve Bank of Philadelphia, at <www.researchoninnovation.org/swpat.pdf>.

Burgelman, R.A. & Chesbrough, H. (eds) (2001), *Comparative Studies of Technological Evolution* (Amsterdam: JAI Elsevier Science).

Cohen, W.M., Nelson, R.R. & Walsh, J.P. (2000), *Protecting Their Intellectual Assets: Appropriability Conditions and Why US Manufacturing Firms Patent (or Not)* (Cambridge, MA: NBER Working Paper).

Conner, K.R. & Rumelt, R.P. (1991), 'Software piracy: An analysis of protection strategies', *Management Science*, Feb., pp. 125–39.

Dam, K.W. (1995), 'Some economic considerations in the intellectual property protection of software', *Journal of Legal Studies*, 24(2), pp. 321–77.

Davis, L. (2002), 'Is Appropriability a 'Problem' for Innovations in Digital Information Goods' (Copenhagen: LEFIC, Center for Law, Economics and Financial Institutions, Working Paper vol. 1).

Davis, L. (2005), 'Why do small high-tech firms apply for patents, and why not?' (in Andersen).

Glazier, S. (1995), 'Inventing around your competitors' patents', *Managing Intellectual Property*, 51, July–Aug., pp. 10–14.

Granstrand, O. (1999), *The Economics and Management of Intellectual Property* (Cheltenham: Edward Elgar).

Grindley, P.C. & Teece, D.J. (1997), 'Managing intellectual capital: licensing and cross-licensing in semiconductors and electronics', *California Management Review*, 39(2), pp. 8–41.

Hall, B. and Ham, R.M. (1999), 'The Patent Paradox Revisited: Determinants of Patenting in the U.S. Semiconductor Industry', *NBER Working Papers, No 7062* (Cambridge Massachusetts: NBER Inc).

Hall, B. & Ziedonis, R.H. (2001), 'The Patent Paradox Revisited: An Empirical Study of Patenting in the US Semiconductor Industry, 1979–1995', *Rand Journal of Economics*, 32(2), spring, pp. 101–28.

Harabi, N. (1995), 'Appropriability of Technical Innovations – An Empirical Analysis', *Research Policy*, 24, pp. 981–92.

Kaiser, U. & Roende, T. (2004), 'A Danish View on Software Related Patents' (Discussion Paper 2004–05, Centre for Economic & Business Research).

Kingston, W. (2001), 'Innovation needs patent reform', *Research Policy*, 30, pp. 403–23.

Kitch, E.W. (1977), 'The nature and function of the patent system', *Journal of Law and Economics*, Oct. (20), pp. 265–90.

Lefebvre, L.A. & Lefebvre, E. (1993), 'Competitive positioning and innovative efforts in SMEs', *Small Business Economics*, 5(4), pp. 297–306.

Levin, T.C., Klevorick, A.K., Nelson, R.R. & Winter, S.G. (1987), 'Appropriating the returns from industrial research and development', *Brookings Papers on Economic Activity*, 3, pp. 783–820.

Liebeskind, J.P., Lumerman, A., Zucker, L. & Brewer, M. (1996), 'Social Networks, Learning, and Flexibility: Sourcing Scientific Knowledge in New Biotechnology Firms', *Organization Science*, 7(4), July–Aug., pp. 428–43.

Lindman, M.T. (2002), 'Open or closed strategy in developing new products? A case study of industrial NPD in SMEs', *European Journal of Innovation Management*, 5(4), pp. 224–36.

Mansfield, E., Schwartz, M. & Wagner, S. (1981), 'Imitation Costs and Patents: An Empirical Study', *Economic Journal*, 91, Dec., pp. 907–18.

Merges, R.P. & Nelson, R.R. (1994), 'On Limiting or Encouraging Rivalry in Technical Progress: The Effect of Patent Scope Decisions', *Journal of Economic Behavior and Organization*, 25, pp. 1–24.

Nelson, R.R. (1959), 'The simple economics of basic research', *Journal of Political Economy*, 67, June, pp. 297–306.

Oppenlaender, K.H. (1977), 'Patent policies and technical progress in the Federal Republic of Germany', *International Review of Industrial Property and Copyright Law*, 8(2), pp. 97–122.

Pooley, J. & Bratic, W. (1999), 'The value of trade secrets', *Managing Intellectual Property*, (93), Oct., pp. 66–9.

Rivette, K.G. & Kline, D. (2000a), 'Discovering new value in intellectual property', *Harvard Business Review*, Jan–Feb., pp. 54–66.

Rivette, K.G. & Kline, D. (2000b), *Rembrandts in the Attic: Unlocking the Hidden Value of Patents* (Boston, MA: Harvard University Press).

Sakakibara, M. (2001), 'US–Japan patent systems' (in Burgelman & Chesbrough).

Scotchmer, S. (1991), 'Standing on the shoulders of giants: cumulative research and the patent law', *Journal of Economic Perspectives*, 5(1), winter, pp. 29–41.

Shapiro, C. & Varian, H.R. (1999), *Information Rules* (Cambridge, MA: Harvard University Press).

von Krogh, G. & von Hippel, E. (2003), 'Editorial: Special issue on open source software development', *Research Policy*, 32(7), pp. 1149–57.

Index